NotFox
Headline History

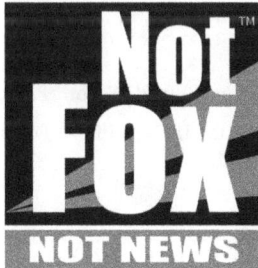

NotFox
FOX
NOT NEWS ™

The Covid Years: 2020-2023

Joseph D Lyman

ISBN: 978-1-7363739-4-1

Typefaces: URW Bookman, by URW Font Foundary, SIL Open Font License v1.1; URW Gothic, by URW Font Foundary, SIL Open Font License v1.1.

Cover: City Globe photo by Joshua Rawson-Harris, Unsplash Open Commercial License, used by permission; Covid Spike Protein photo by the CDC, Unsplash Open Commercial License, used by permission. All other elements are original copyright works of the author.

Headlines: All article titles (headlines) used in the making of this book were collected from U.S. mainstream news sources, and are considered "short phrases," de minimis in nature and outside the scope of U.S. copyright. They have been used in accordance with standard practice and fair use law. The "novel" style portion of this book is presented as a parody and a transformative work of social commentary.

Pinpoint Management, LLC. Fulton, Missouri

This book is dedicated to the idea that we're better off when we understand what the news is and what it is not; and, to the hope that we can eventually find better ways to broadly share the human experience.

Introduction

What is Notfox?

The website NotFox.com was launched in 2015 as a tool to track the confluence of news headlines across the major news providers: ABC, CBS, CNN, Fox, NBC, Newsmax (more recently) and NPR. The site quietly and consistently gathers headlines based on keyword overlap, presents them for real-time evaluation to any site visitors, and logs them away for further study and use.

One of the primary features of NotFox.com is the way it sorts and presents the news of the day. Rather than just providing a list of headlines, it looks at subjects (keywords) that are being talked about across multiple outlets, and prioritizes the ones that are getting the most attention, in real time. The result is an instant, overarching view of the ideas that media outlets are promoting. As anyone who has examined the news knows, the industry players always act in tandem, and are entirely centered around agenda setting theory and cognitive accessibility of agendas. NotFox.com is a way to watch that activity unfold.

For the most part, modern news is highly perishable, and the primarily usage of NotFox.com reflects that reality. With the much-hyped, "twenty-four hour news cycle," and the endless advents of ever-more-impressive distribution technologies, most subjects flit in and out of societal consciousness for only moments at a time. If we still had presses, they'd be yet hot while we moved on to the next new and shiny subject. But thanks to the database storage of headlines going back for years, NotFox.com also has the ability to let us peer into the past of the news media—ground that we're really not meant to tread on—through reports on the site itself, and through books like this one.

What are Headline Histories?

Internet news headlines are the most perishable of all public thoughts, even more so than the articles they entitle. By and large, we consume headlines and articles in a moment, and then move on to the next ones that are always overflowing in the queue.

Headline Histories from NotFox.com give us an opportunity to look back. They leverage the vast database of collected headlines, and organize them into a consumable format. They offer headlines as a history in and of themselves, a frozen snapshot in time. Because they are available in print form only, they offer a durable memory that we can learn from and keep.

Why "The Covid Years"?

The years 2020-2023 provided one of the most spectacular displays of global interaction the earth has ever known, accompanied by the most outlandish barrage of media messaging imaginable. The headlines alone were frustrating, destabilizing, and even traumatic at times. They are a shadow of the articles they announced, and summary of what we all went through (seen through a glass, darkly).

I chose to piece together The Covid Years as a tribute to an unique period in the modern social history of Earth, so that we could, from our comfortable vantage point, examine what we put ourselves through. For many, the wounds and psychological damage of that time period are still fresh; but, it's never too soon to preserve what was, and what might be of value to those who come after us.

The Format of This Book

This book was curated, formatted, and assembled by hand, without the use of Artificial Intelligence which is so prevalent today. The NotFox database has millions of headline entries, which could not possibly all fit in a reasonable volume. So, I selected headlines that were applicable, and formatted them as if they were the text of a novel using the statistical analysis language R. Additional modifications, including highlights and dates of some notable events, were then added.

Some might argue that a list format would have made more sense, lending itself to better sorting and organization. Headlines are, after all, usually presented as a list. However, as a history, it made more sense in my mind to present these headlines in the form of a disjointed story. The novel format gives the headlines an absurd quality when read through, and owing to the fact that they are in chronological order, the continuity and readability are tolerable.

Each chapter represents a span of time, and begins with a related relevant headline. The "paragraphs" are primarily collections of headlines tacked together like an irrational train of thought. Headline dates should be largely accurate, but remember that the dates represent the point at which the article was entered into the NotFox.com database, and not the publication date.

Even though I've worked on this book by hand, thousands of headlines and tens of thousands of words mean that some mistakes may have been made. As I had to process some of the data manually, there will certainly be headlines that contain punctuation problems, and headlines that contain grammatical errors (including some that were put there by their original creators). Also, news outlets adopt varying capitalization rules, which have been preserved herein. It is assumed that the reader will treat this collection of headlines with about as much dignity that they treat headlines in general, and take the errors lightly.

A Note on Biases

You can't gather news headlines without gathering associated biases. Various news outlets have claimed, over the years, to have some level of integrity and objectivity, but readers have consistently doubted these claims (in the case of news they don't agree with) or argued their merits (in the case of news they do agree with). I don't pretend to present a book without biases: in fact, I openly acknowledge that this book is chock-full of them. That said, the biases you'll find in this book are largely imported with the headlines themselves. My curation and introductory materials may well have introduced additional biases, because I am human, but I have attempted to present a large collection of information that represents the history of the news, and not my own views.

A Note on Copyrights

I was, at first, hesitant to approach the idea of publishing an entire book based on headlines that were written by thousands of journalists. There was, in point of fact, no reasonable way for me to obtain permission to create such a beast, nor any way for me to credit them individually. The idea gnawed at me enough, and I ended by researching the copyright question as deeply as I could. My findings have led me to believe that U.S. copyright law, to the best of my understanding, does not require me to obtain said permission. My position rests on three points: *De minimis* authorship and creativity in the selected headlines; effect of the use upon the potential market; and, whether or not the created product is transformative in nature.

The U.S. Copyright Office Circular 33, Works Not Protected by Copyright (March 2021), covers theses issue in part. But the topic is covered even more extensively and specifically in the publication titled Copyright Protections for Press Publishers, A Report of the Register of Copyrights (June 2022); and even further in the publication titled Written Additional Comments in Response to U. S. Copyright Office's Publishers' Protection Study: Request for Additional Comments, 86 Fed. Reg. 62,215 (Nov. 9, 2021).

In the latter two above publications, the U.S. Copyright Office was specifically considering whether news publishers needed additional copyright protections against news aggregator websites (such as NotFox.com). Ultimately, the Copyright Office ruled that no additional protections were needful. In the course of that ruling and its associated research, they covered the question of headlines and "short phrases" quite extensively.

Jane C. Ginsburg seems to have led the legal investigation on the protectability of "short phrases" and headlines. Ultimately, the Copyright Office noted that in some cases headlines may be eligible for copyright protections. They noted that there were, "three arguments as to why some headlines and ledes should be protectable: first, that courts applying the short phrases doctrine have focused on originality or functionality rather than brevity as such, leaving open the possibility that a sufficiently original short phrase might be copyrightable; second, that the examples given by the Compendium of non-protectable words and short phrases—names of individuals or organizations, titles, catchwords, or slogans—tend either to lack all originality or be 'considerably more brief than most headlines or ledes'; and third, that a rule based solely on brevity, without any guide as to how short is too short, could be difficult to implement."

This speaks to the *de minimis* argument, primarily, and establishes that shortness alone cannot stand as a reason to deny protection. In other words, headlines aren't free to be copied without permission solely on the basis of their brevity—they must also lack creativity or originality. To answer this concern, my solution has been to individually curate headlines and filter out any that appear to have a scintilla of creativity and originality. Authors of headlines may or may not agree with my determinations and may certainly object to my judgment, but I have made a good faith effort to include only headlines that are primarily factual, short phrases that are in fact not protectable.

As for the effect of my use on the potential market of news publishers, I can only suppose that curating and reshaping old headlines (old being a relative idea, but strongly on my side of the argument as the word relates to news in particular) would have no impact whatsoever on the news industry, as I am presenting nothing new. I'm not aware of anyone having done what I am attempting in this book, and so I have no metrics to measure against. Even so, I am confident that I am not competing with any news publisher or journalist whatsoever. In fact, as with NotFox.com, these headlines may very well serve as an invitation for readers to utilize online search tools to look up the articles that they refer to, driving business toward news publishers. Therefore, I feel that this second point is addressed.

To the last point—whether this work is transformative in nature—I simply assert that creating a novel out of headlines is absolutely transformative in every sense. I have taken headlines, which have real value only in the very short-term, and turned them into a sort of durable and fascinating history. This provides the public with a benefit that didn't exist when the headlines were created, and salvages those same headlines from almost certain extinction in the public eye, preserving what would otherwise become largely lost to view.

Though I am nothing akin to a lawyer, it is my opinion that I have satisfied the legal tests that might have stood in the way of the publication of a work based on headlines, and have made a good faith effort to avoid infringing on the rights of other authors or publishers.

As for the copyrights that I myself claim, they of course exclude the non-copyrightable headlines themselves, and rest solely on my particular organization and presentation of the same.

Credit

NotFox.com, which was the source for this book, tracks keyword confluence in headlines from the following news outlets:

- ABC (abcnews.go.com)
- CBS (cbsnews.com)
- CNN (cnn.com)
- Fox News (foxnews.com)
- NBC (nbcnews.com)
- Newsmax (newsmax.com)
- NPR (npr.org)

Without these news outlets, the NotFox.com project would be impossible, and this book would be impossible. Without the contributions of countless journalists, none of this would be possible. Just as the NotFox.com aggregator cannot credit each individual author due to technical limitations, I cannot credit every author of the headlines that this book is built on. Their contributions are nevertheless appreciated and meaningful.

The First Year of Covid

You'll notice that the pacing of this book is unbalanced; the number of chapters per-year is not even. This is because the density of news articles relating to Covid was higher toward the beginning of the pandemic, and much lower toward the end. Consequently, the number of headlines and therefore chapters for each year are weighted toward the year 2020, as they should be.

Because the first year of the pandemic was so notable, I've decided to include a brief timeline here in the introduction, to remind (or inform) readers of some of the salient topics and when they were introduced to the public mind. The table that follows is based on news headlines only, and is not a definitive representation of exactly when events occurred but rather when they were first recorded by NotFox.com:

- 1/11 - New coronavirus found
- 1/11 - First mention of US travel ban, deemed "racism" by democrat party leaders
- 1/22 - First mention of Chinese quarantine, first use of the term "lockdown" in the pandemic context
- 1/22 - First mention of vaccine development
- 1/23 - First mention of coronavirus test development
- 1/23 - First link to a map of cases
- 1/24 - Debate on surgical masks begins (starting with "they will not prevent infection")
- 1/24 - First mention of the quarantine of infected individuals in USA (Texas)
- 1/27 - First mention of coronovirus "misinformation"
- 1/30 - WHO declares global health emergency
- 2/1 - Public health emergency declared in the U.S.
- 2/2 - First mention of portable PCR tests
- 2/3 - First mention of pandemic designation possibility
- 2/3 - China introduces "virus tracker" apps
- 2/5 - First testing for asymptomatic infection

- 2/5 - First mention of scarcity of hospital beds, China
- 2/6 - First use of the word "mandate" in relation to virus, in China
- 2/8 - First headline with words "global pandemic," deemed unlikely
- 2/16 - Fauci speaks on the virus
- 2/17 - First mention of surface transmission
- 2/25 - First "front lines" wartime comparison
- 2/27 - First use of the phrase "new normal"
- 2/28 - Disbelief in science used as an attack
- 3/1 - Focus on nursing homes for viral outbreaks
- 3/5 - First mention of mutated virus strains
- 3/6 - First mention of Ivermectin, headline states that FDA warns against its use
- 3/9 - Term "social distancing" coined
- 3/10 - First temperature checks in California restaurant
- 3/10 - First mention of "contact tracing"
- 3/11 - WHO declares "global pandemic"
- 3/13 - First mention of "flattening the curve"
- 3/13 - First instance of Toilet Paper panic in U.S.
- 3/14 - First headline about ventilators
- 2/5 - Scarcity of hospital beds, New York
- 3/19 - CDC approves homemade masks for hospitals etc, including scarves/bandannas
- 3/19 - Passport services restricted, U.S.
- 3/19 - First headline about Hydroxychloroquine
- 3/20 - First U.S. pandemic-related mandate, New York
- 3/29 - First headline with "lab leak"
- 3/30 - First compulsory use of masks, Austria
- 3/31 - Mainstream arguments about mask messaging

- 3/31 - Fauci says, "masks for all being considered"
- 4/1 - Democractic party leaders determine that travel bans are reasonable
- 4/1 - Trump declares that people should wear masks
- 4/1 - European countries start to recommend masks
- 4/3 - CDC recommends face masking in public
- 4/5 - First mandate that workers wear masks, Pentagon
- 4/10 - Apple and Google create virus tracker apps
- 4/16 - First headline about "mask mandates"
- 4/21 - Chile introduces "immunity passport"
- 5/1 - First headline to mention Operation Warp Speed
- 5/20 - CDC says surface transmission not likely
- 6/19 - Focus on ICU bed shortages outside NY starts
- 8/13 - First coronavirus found on frozen food
- 10/16 - First headline mentioning vaccine mandates
- 10/21 - First mention of "Long Covid"
- 11/6 - Use of the word "variant" instead of mutation
- 11/17 - First headline to mention mRNA
- 12/3 - Vaccine cards introduced
- 12/8 - Brazil makes vaccines mandatory

More certainly happened in the first year than is covered in this table, and more happened in the years following, but what I've given gets the reader primed for the book I now present. I sincerely hope it proves fascinating and perhaps even useful, for those who experienced the pandemic and those who are learning about it merely as a point in history.

Chapter 1

First Case of New Mystery Virus Identified Outside of China

January 11ᵗʰ, 2020 – March 16ᵗʰ, 2020

Unlike the rest of the chapters in this book, I chose to begin this one with a notice. Some readers have a tendency to bypass the introductory material of an average book, and dive right in at Chapter One. While this is not normally a grave concern, in the case of this book I fear such an action would lead to abject befuddlement, confusion, frustration, or even irritation. This is not a book in which you can skip the introduction, as it is not an average book.

If you haven't read the introduction, I encourage you to do so. If you're unwilling, I'll give you the summary: This book is a curated collection of headlines from the period of 2020 to 2023, related to the Covid pandemic. It is formatted to read like a novel, but the words are in fact actual headlines that passed through the website NotFox.com over the course of that period. It will not read like a regular novel, it will read like headlines broken into paragraphs and chapters. It is bizarre by design. Enjoy!

New virus prompts U.S. to screen passengers from Wuhan, China. China tries to stop the spread of a deadly new virus at the worst possible time of year. Spread of coronavirus prompts CDC to expand 'enhanced health screenings' to 2 more US airports. **Coronavirus vaccine in 'early stages' [1/22/20]** as focus turns to China's transparency. New Jersey Mandates Severance Pay For Workers Facing Mass Layoffs. Dr. Amesh Adalja: Why Americans should pay attention to the coronavirus outbreak. MAP: Confirmed Cases Of Wuhan Coronavirus. China Hurriedly Building Quarantine Center In Effort To Contain Wuhan Virus. Coronavirus fears close Shanghai Disney Resort.

Coronavirus FAQs: **Do Masks Help? [1/25/20]** Is The Disease Really So Mysterious? Health officials confirm case of new virus in California. Coronavirus outbreak in China shuts Hong Kong Disneyland. China extends Lunar New Year holiday to contain coronavirus as death toll rises. Dr. Amesh Adalja: Coronavirus - addressing the potential of pre-symptomatic spread. Dr. Marc Siegel sounds alarm over China's 'reckless' and 'really scary' response to coronavirus. CDC issues strongest coronavirus warning yet.

Coronavirus in the U.S.: Map of where the virus has been confirmed across the country. Plane carrying US evacuees from China amid coronavirus outbreak diverted to California air base. American Airlines suspends some flights to China amid coronavirus. Racing against a deadly blueprint: Scientists push for vaccine as coronavirus spreads. 5 cases of coronavirus confirmed in US, risk of spreading remains low, CDC says. Americans evacuated out of Wuhan amid coronavirus scare. Coronavirus Has Now Spread To All Regions Of Mainland China. China coronavirus causing chaos for U.S. companies. UC Berkeley deletes post saying xenophobia is "common reaction" to coronavirus. U.S. To Americans: 'Do Not Travel To China,' As Coronavirus Infections Surpass SARS. As Coronavirus Spreads, U.S. Students In China Scramble To Leave. Coronavirus has infected nearly 12,000 people worldwide.

Boston student confirmed as 8th U.S. coronavirus case. China drafts hundreds of doctors to treat coronavirus, state media says. Experts worry about pandemic as coronavirus numbers increase: report. Wuhan coronavirus deaths overtake SARS in China. Chinese turn to virus tracker apps to avoid infected neighborhoods.

China admits "shortcomings" as deadly virus spreads. Chinese doctor who sounded alarm on coronavirus says he was detained -- then got sick. Planes carrying American coronavirus evacuees from China land at California military base. Baby tests positive for coronavirus 30 hours after birth. Coronavirus dents movie box offices in China. What we don't know about the coronavirus. US coronavirus evacuees headed to Texas, Nebraska, may be on last chartered flights: State Department. Global death toll from coronavirus rises. Liz Claman: Coronavirus outbreak already impacting companies, could affect China trade deal. Plane carrying American coronavirus evacuees lands in California, another en route to Texas. Coronavirus leads Royal Caribbean to bar Chinese, Hong Kong and Macau passport holders.

Sen. Tom Cotton: Eliminating coronavirus requires Chinese Communist Party to make big changes. Former CDC director: New study is an eye-opener on how coronavirus is spreading and how little we know. Coronavirus Death Toll Surpasses 800 In Mainland China. Coronavirus testing will keep a Royal Caribbean cruise ship's passengers in NJ until Monday, company says. Spain, UK report new virus cases as they hunt down carriers. LPGA Tour cancels 2 more Asia tournaments due to coronavirus. Dr. Oz on how to protect against coronavirus: Why paper surgical masks are not effective.

Cruise denied entry 'at every port' due to coronavirus rumors, finds place to disembark passengers. China's daily coronavirus death toll tops 100 for 1st time; total deaths top 1,000. China reports its deadliest day yet with more than 100 people killed from the virus, while over 42,000 are infected globally. Coronavirus death toll passes new milestone. Nearly 200 complete coronavirus quarantine in California. Timetable

For A Vaccine Against The New Coronavirus Maybe This Fall. Coronavirus cases top 60,000 as death toll sharply rises. A Change In How 1 Chinese Province Reports Coronavirus Adds Thousands Of Cases. Coronavirus patient took Uber to London emergency room. Coronavirus updates: COVID-19 deaths near 1,500 in China as 15th case confirmed in U.S. COVID-19 updates: 1,700 heath workers infected, first fatality in Japan. What do you need to know about coronavirus?

Coronavirus updates: U.S. to evacuate Americans from quarantined cruise ship. Coronavirus panic could be the endangered pangolin's new threat. Death toll from virus rises to 1,666 globally. Xi's early involvement in virus outbreak raises questions. **Coronavirus cases top 71,000 worldwide [2/16/20]**. Marathon restricted to elite athletes over coronavirus fears. Chartered flights bring 14 coronavirus patients back to U.S.. China says 80 percent of coronavirus cases have been mild, as death toll rises again.

Americans set to be released after coronavirus quarantine. How to avoid falling victim to a coronavirus email scam. More cruise passengers test positive for virus as deaths top 2,000. Coronavirus Update: Diamond Princess Passengers Leave Ship As Expert Slams Quarantine. Coronavirus updates: 2 passengers die after leaving 'chaotic' cruise ship. South Korea reports first coronavirus death as infections linked to church rise. Officials letting last virus-free passengers leave cruise ship. After the Diamond Princess' coronavirus quarantine, travelers left with a tough choice. The 'window of opportunity is narrowing' to contain the spread of the novel coronavirus, the World Health Organization warns.

Amid Coronavirus Outbreak, Hong Kong Tries To Cope. Immunologist: We are clearly at the brink of a pandemic. Coronavirus updates: 5 dead and 200 infected in Italy as Europe braces for COVID-19. As coronavirus cases surge worldwide, Dow plummets 700 points. This drug may help treat coronavirus.

Dr. Peter Hotez: As coronavirus spreads, the US is not fully prepared, but here is how we can be. Tucker Carlson says coronavirus response shows how 'identity politics trumped public health'. Fears that the coronavirus outbreak could turn into a pandemic and reach the US are challenging Trump's sunny assurances that everything is under control. Spanish resort on partial lockdown as Italian man tests positive. **Coronavirus disruption to everyday life in US might be severe, CDC official says [2/25/20].** Bipartisan outrage over coronavirus spills over on Capitol Hill. Stocks plunge after CDC warns of coronavirus spread in U.S. Karl Rove slams Chuck Schumer for 'trying to politicize' coronavirus: 'This is shameful'. Congress prepares for inevitable U.S. coronavirus outbreak. Cruise ship MSC Meraviglia turned away from two Caribbean ports amid coronavirus concerns. **Iran is on the front line of coronavirus outbreak [2/25/20]**.

Trump on coronavirus: Everything is fine. Trump's health officials: It's not. Facebook cracking down on ads that guarantee coronavirus cure. Stocks extend slide as Trump downplays coronavirus fears. CDC says to prepare for the coronavirus. How? Rush Limbaugh: 'Bernie Sanders poses a far greater threat to this country... than the coronavirus'.

Global death toll from coronavirus rises to 2,800. Coronavirus infects woman in Japan for the second time, a first in the country. **U.S. may have first community-transmitted coronavirus case [2/27/20].** Coronavirus gets political: Trump, Dems exchange barbs as U.S. prepares for potential crisis. Preparing for a pandemic: Your questions, answered. Congress Nears Bipartisan Funding Plan To Address Growing Coronavirus Threat. 1st coronavirus case of unknown origin in US was hospitalized for days before being tested: officials. US companies say the coronavirus outbreak could cut China revenues by 50%. After mystery coronavirus case, health officials go into detective mode.

Sean Hannity accuses Democrats of 'weaponizing' coronavirus 'to score cheap, repulsive political points'. 'Fear versus dreams': Coronavirus spread sparks fears for American travelers. Switzerland bans all events over 1,000 people due to coronavirus, 15 confirmed cases in country. Eye Opener: Global markets dive amid coronavirus panic. UC Davis student tested for coronavirus, 2 others isolated. Trump Jr. says Dems, left-wing media have reached a 'new level of sickness' by politicizing coronavirus. Coronavirus risk upgraded to 'very high' as death toll mounts.

Coronavirus quarantines in U.S. appear inevitable, doctor says [2/28/20]. There are at least 62 coronavirus cases in the US. Opinion: How to prepare for the spread of coronavirus. Mexico confirms first 2 coronavirus cases, health official says. Google Employee Tests Positive For Coronavirus; Company Expands Travel Restrictions. Coronavirus Updates: CDC Announces '4 New Presumptive Cases' In The U.S. COVID-19 Latest: Global Markets React, More Cases Reported. Iran prepares to test 'tens of thousands' for coronavirus as number of confirmed cases spikes.

Trump says additional coronavirus cases in US are 'likely'. As first U.S. patient dies, more coronavirus cases in Washington. Possible coronavirus outbreak at Washington state nursing facility. Wash. Investigates More Possible Coronavirus Cases Amid Fears Of A Regional Outbreak. Hong Kong Has Contained Coronavirus So Far -- But At A Significant Cost. 8th person tests positive for coronavirus in Washington state. A possible nursing home outbreak is investigated. Global coronavirus death toll tops 3,000. Liz Peek: Coronavirus concerns aren't only fears jolting the markets; rise of socialist Sanders is, too. Masks may actually increase your risk, surgeon general warns.

New York coronavirus patient is health care worker who traveled to Iran, isolated at home. Dr. Marc Siegel: Why coronavirus death rate is probably not as high as reported. Stephanie Grisham: Coronavirus risk to Americans 'very low' due to Trump administration's 'unprecedented' steps. Illinois sees 4th coronavirus case in woman in her 70s. Coronavirus-inspired 'Wuhan Shake' replaces handshakes in social media footage. Trump considers new travel restrictions to prevent spread of coronavirus. **Coronavirus misinformation spreads rapidly on social media [3/2/20].**

Could homelessness be to blame for rapid coronavirus spread in Washington state?: Seattle radio host. Hannity: This Trump decision likely saved 'thousands and thousands of Americans' from contracting coronavirus. Coronavirus situation in North Korea remains unclear, could be especially deadly, expert says. We're in 'uncharted territory,' health expert says, as coronavirus cases total more than 90,000 people. Coronavirus quarantines more than 2 dozen Washington State firefighters. Coronavirus leads to drop in advertising sales. Personal Essay: Coronavirus Lockdown Is A 'Living Hell'. Coronavirus death toll rises to 9 in Washington state. Scientist corrects Trump seconds after he said this about coronavirus. Anyone can be tested for COVID-19, subject to a doctor's orders: Pence. Coronavirus test kit delay pushes hospitals to make their own. **Coronavirus Fears Lead To Canceled Flights And Concerns Within The Travel Industry [3/4/20].**

More virus cases linked to UAE Tour as riders face isolation. Coronavirus: Los Angeles Declares Emergency; U.S. Reports 80 Cases In 13 States. California records its first coronavirus death. There are six new coronavirus cases in Los Angeles county. Clorox, Netflix and Zoom see stocks rise alongside coronavirus fears. Top hospital braces for coronavirus pandemic with secret warehouse full of emergency supplies. How to live with a coronavirus outbreak. California governor declares state of emergency over coronavirus. **Coronavirus has mutated at least once, second strain detected: study [3/5/20].** Stocks renew slide on concerns of severe coronavirus hit. ER doctor: Americans must live their lives, **98 to 99% of people who get coronavirus will 'do just fine' [3/5/20]**.

As Schools Close Due To Coronavirus, Nearly 300 Million Kids Aren't In Class [3/5/20]. Coronavirus Concerns Stymie Live Music Performances And SXSW. Premier League prohibits handshakes over coronavirus fears. When Coronavirus Struck Seattle, This Lab Was Ready To Start Testing. Trump Says He Still Has To Shake Hands, Despite Coronavirus Concerns. Bodies 'pile up' in morgue as Iran feels strain of coronavirus. First coronavirus case confirmed at Vatican: report. Trump signs $8.3B coronavirus spending bill. Seattle stadium worker tests positive for coronavirus. Retailers accused of price gouging amid coronavirus outbreak. Trump Visit To CDC On Again After Suspect Coronovirus Case Cleared.

Coronavirus panic sparks racist incidents against Asian Americans. Trump signs emergency coronavirus spending package. Coronavirus: Everything you need to know. In Facebook groups, coronavirus misinformation thrives despite broader crackdown. At least 21 coronavirus cases aboard cruise ship off California coast, Pence says. House prepares for telework scenarios amid coronavirus threat.

Coronavirus spreads as outbreak clusters grow in a ship stuck at sea, a nursing home and a New York suburb. US coronavirus cases top 300. Doctor shares CDC's latest coronavirus warnings. New York declares state of emergency as Cuomo announces 21 new coronavirus cases. ACU says CPAC attendee tested positive for coronavirus. Coronavirus: Florida Reports 1st Deaths On East Coast; Cases In D.C. Area, New York. Venice, Milan on lockdown as Italy announces sweeping quarantine. US Army suspends travel for soldiers, families to and from South Korea amid coronavirus outbreak.

Behind the scenes, scientists prep for COVID-19 vaccine test [3/8/20]. Inslee on Trump coronavirus feud: 'I dont care what Donald Trump thinks of me'. Coronavirus: Italy Orders Massive Shutdown; Cruise Ship Gets OK To Dock In California. Connecticut governor announces state's first coronavirus case. Ted Cruz will self-quarantine after interacting with individual with coronavirus. Coronavirus and Congress' likely response in coming months. Coronavirus cases in Massachusetts double in overnight hours, report says. Why CNN is calling the novel coronavirus outbreak a pandemic.

Steve Hilton: We need to be practical and not panic on coronavirus. If not, the poorest Americans may suffer. Coronavirus: U.S. Has 566 Cases; Stricken Cruise Ship To Dock In California. Coronavirus in the US: State-by-state breakdown. **Can "social distancing" help stop the spread of coronavirus? [3/9/20]** Passengers held on Grand Princess cruise ship over coronavirus concerns to receive full refund. Dow falls 2,000 points as investors run from coronavirus. Grand Princess cruise ship docks at Oakland port, passengers set to disembark for coronavirus quarantine. Coronavirus hits travel industry with biggest crisis since 9/11. Reps. Matt Gaetz, Doug Collins Self-Quarantine After CPAC Coronavirus Exposure. Trump and Pence address coronavirus fallout, as cases expected to rise. Trump administration's mixed coronavirus messages.

Xi makes 1st visit since outbreak to Wuhan epicenter. Officials issue stern warning to family that broke coronavirus quarantine. Trump scare shows no American is immune from coronavirus risk. Trump has not been tested for coronavirus. Dow opens up about 850 points after coronavirus and oil fears caused the biggest drop in history. Coronavirus at the airport: How the TSA is fighting outbreak.

Hospital offers drive-thru coronavirus testing for employees. Seven questions about coronavirus, answered. Trump huddles on Hill amid coronavirus concerns, says 'be calm'. Rep. Jeffries blasts Trump for escaping to golf resort during coronavirus crisis. Missouri AG sues Jim Bakker over misleading coronavirus cure claims. In coronavirus wake, Apple says iPhone users can use disinfecting wipes and isopropyl alcohol on their devices. American in Rome describes Italy's coronavirus lockdown: 'The message here is, "Everyone stays at home"'. US nears 1,000 confirmed coronavirus cases, new cases in Michigan, state of emergency declared. Virus impact on US sports grows; more restrictions in Europe.

Lawmakers scramble to create economic plan for coronavirus. Coronavirus fears have prompted China to close Everest access via Tibet, climbers say. Iran blames coronavirus spread on U.S. sanctions. Hundreds of Chinese migrants detained at U.S. border amid coronavirus-tied travel ban. **WHO declares coronavirus global 'pandemic' [3/11/20].** US to hold major international diplomatic meeting 'virtually' due to virus concerns. Coronavirus forces Golden State Warriors to play next home game without fans. Sen. Rick Scott: Coronovirus is on the move -- US must take these 9 crucial steps to contain it. McCarthy knocks Dems after they claim saying 'Chinese coronavirus' is racist.

Watch live: Trump makes statement on coronavirus at 9 p.m. ET. Opinion: Refugees Are Especially Vulnerable To COVID-19. Don't Ignore Their Needs. NBA Suspends Season After Player Tests Positive For Coronavirus. Andy Puzder: Trump coronavirus response will protect America's economy, workers and businesses. China says coronavirus cases falling, it is past peak of disease: report. AOC urges universal income, Medicare-for-all as part of coronavirus response. Markets drop, Europe balks at Trump's new coronavirus travel ban. E.U. blasts Trump's coronavirus travel ban as it unleashes chaos and confusion. Capitol closes to public over coronavirus as lawmakers shutter offices.

Republicans oppose Pelosi's coronavirus legislation, flagging 'major' problems. Opinion: Trump's coronavirus speech was a disaster. DNC moves Biden-Sanders debate to Washington studio with no audience, amid coronavirus concerns. House Democrats' virus bill: Free testing, paid sick leave. Coronavirus expert says US is 'failing' on testing. Supreme Court closes to the public amid coronavirus fears. Liz Peek: Democrats attacking Trump coronavirus response hurt economy -- they shouldn't politicize crisis. Broadway shuts its doors amid coronavirus concerns. Coronavirus pandemic forces shutdown of professional and college sports in the U.S.. Coronavirus-relief bill aims to expand free school lunch program.

Fauci says wider coronavirus testing system will be up and running soon. Opinion: A prison pandemic Steps to avoid the worst. Staying in due to the coronavirus Here's what to stock in your fridge and pantry. Teen sent home for charging classmates for 'squirts' of hand sanitizer amid coronavirus. Wife Of Canada's Trudeau Tests Positive For Coronavirus. How Chinese-language media in U.S. are debunking WeChat coronavirus misinformation. Italy's coronavirus ground zero sees slowdown in new cases after lockdown.

Latest news as coronavirus claims lives and disrupts life for millions. **Houston Mayor on coronavirus panic-buying of water bottles, toilet paper: 'World is not coming to an end' [3/13/20]** Coronavirus leads to 'Wendy Williams Show' suspending production indefinitely. Trump grows more irate as his attempts fail to contain coronavirus fallout. Trump Administration Announces Measures To Speed Coronavirus Testing. Trump condemns CDC for lack of coronavirus testing, blames Obama. **Trump to announce national emergency on coronavirus: Here's what that means [3/13/20].** Watch live: Pelosi speaks about coronavirus response bill. Pelosi says the most important parts of coronavirus bill are "testing, testing,

testing." FDA worried about shortage as blood drives are canceled amid coronavirus concerns.

Spying on coronavirus: A little-known U.S. intel outfit has its most important mission yet. **"Flattening the curve": What it means for fighting coronavirus [3/13/20]**. Delta slashes flights by 40% as virus cripples global travel. Federal government estimates about 38 million Americans will need medicare care amid coronavirus concern. 'Blood of the immune': Doctors want to try an antiquated treatment on coronavirus. Washington state coronavirus survivor's advice: Don't panic, take proper precautions. House passes coronavirus aid package, sending bill to the Senate. The New Coronavirus Can Live On Surfaces For 2-3 Days -- Here's How To Clean Them. House passes coronavirus aid package after national emergency declared. Coronavirus fears could lead to US blood supply shortage. The US is waking up under a national emergency. **Mass cancellations at schools, events and travel are the new normal [3/14/20].**

New York confirms first coronavirus death as cases in state surpass 500. Trump says he has taken coronavirus test. 'We have not reached our peak' on coronavirus, top US infectious disease doctor says. Families, businesses and governments across the country prepare for weeks of closure due to coronavirus. Rick Scott speaks from self-quarantine, reports 'no symptoms' after meeting with Brazil's president.

Life changes drastically for Americans as coronavirus continues to spread. The President said he took the coronavirus test on Friday. Suspected fake COVID-19 test kits seized at LAX. A third NBA player tests positive for coronavirus. Analysis: This pandemic risks bringing out the worst in humanity. ISIS advises terrorists on coronavirus to avoid Europe for jihad.

Mixed messages mar White House response to coronavirus. Bank of America CEO Brian Moynihan on coronavirus: **"This is a war" [3/15/20]**. Academy of Country Music Awards postponed amid coronavirus outbreak. Maine marks 200th borthday, but coronavirus zaps party. Oklahoma governor faces backlash over 'packed' restaurant tweet amid coronavirus pandemic. All public schools in New York City will close and the Federal Reserve is slashing rates as America reels from the coronavirus. Norwegian university bashes US in coronavirus travel guidance. Democratic debate: Biden bristles as Sanders uses coronavirus to push Medicare-for-all?

At debate, Biden says he'd enlist military to confront coronavirus. As coronavirus spreads, is it safe to go to the gym? Australian TV editor suspects Hanks' wife gave him virus. CDC's coronavirus guidelines could dampen sports world's hopes of returning quickly. Sanders hints Tuesday's primaries should be postponed over coronavirus. Store shelves will be restocked amid coronavirus panic, expert says. As Coronavirus Spreads, States Scramble To Reassure Public That Voting Is Safe. States that have postponed primaries due to coronavirus outbreak. France says ibuprofen may aggravate virus. Experts say more evidence is needed.

Starbucks closes some stores and ditches chairs due to virus. Spanish soccer coach, 21, dies from coronavirus after leukemia diagnosis: report. Coronavirus: U.S. Enters 'Quarantine Life' And The WHO Urges: 'Test, Test, Test'.

Chapter 2

Ex-passenger Tested Positive for Coronavirus, but 'Thousands' Left Cruise Ship Without Screening

March 16th, 2020 – March 28th, 2020

Dr. Oz: This is the weak link in pandemics. UberEats waives delivery fees for restaurants as coronavirus forces shutdowns. As coronavirus spreads, immunocompromised young people ask peers to keep them in mind. Real estate brokers switch to virtual open houses amid coronavirus outbreak. Instagram cracks down on coronavirus-related filters purporting to treat or make light of the disease. Tom Hanks, in coronavirus isolation, posts subtle nod to Mr. Rogers. 2020 Daily Trail Markers: Primaries in the time of coronavirus.

Surgeon General warns U.S. to take coronavirus crisis seriously [3/16/20]. Ohio delays primary in late night decision amid coronavirus outbreak. Poll: As Coronavirus Spreads, Fewer Americans See Pandemic As A Real Threat. Coronavirus response: NASCAR'S Wood Brothers Racing team raising money to buy seniors tablets for remote visits. Brit Hume: Trump's coronavirus response a 'mixed bag,' not a 10 out of 10. Trump says coronavirus pandemic could last through summer. Nevada reports first coronavirus death.

Idris Elba, Sophie Trudeau posed for a photo together days before coronavirus diagnosis. Tuesday's pandemic primaries: Everything you need to know. UK residents advised to avoid all foreign travel for 30 days amid coronavirus pandemic. Pence asks construction companies to donate N95 industrial masks to local hospitals. GM, Ford report first US coronavirus cases. **First patient gets potential coronavirus vaccine [3/17/20]**. Guatemala suspends U.S. deportation flights over coronavirus. Italy reports one-third of deaths in global coronavirus pandemic. COVID-19 can't kill live music, determined artists prove.

Andrew Yang responds to White House's goal of sending Americans money for coronavirus relief. West Virginia reports its first confirmed case of coronavirus as the nationwide total surpasses 5,000. White House, Senate turn focus to $1 trillion coronavirus aid package. Madrid nursing home sees at least 17 dead in 5 days amid coronavirus, officials say. Sarah Hyland talks being high risk amid coronavirus outbreak: 'It's really dangerous'. Coronavirus cases top 197,000 globally.

Can you catch coronavirus from surfaces? [3/18/20] Los Angeles votes to let homeless keep tents stay up during day amid coronavirus outbreak. Well-known inmates citing coronoavirus seeking early releases. 'A Socio-Economic Tsunami': How The World Is Dealing With Pandemic. Pence Warns Coronavirus Disruptions Could Last 'Well Into July'. Sheryl Sandberg on Facebook initiative to boost global economy amid coronavirus. Cleaner air, clearer water: Coronavirus shutdowns have unintended climate benefits. China's Xi Jinping meets with Pakistan president -- promptly shakes his hand despite coronavirus warnings.

Trump says U.S.-Canada border closed to "non-essential traffic" [3/18/20]. Coronavirus live blog: National environmental health expert Dr. Linda Lee answers your questions. Typically partisan social media accounts become source of coronavirus info as pandemic transcends partisanship. **Schumer says US almost certainly will see recession over coronavirus havoc [3/18/20]**. Dow Drops 7% As Trump Outlines New Coronavirus Measures. People are putting up Christmas lights during coronavirus pandemic: 'Need some happiness right now'. 5.7 magnitude earthquake strikes Salt Lake City, knocking out coronavirus hotline. Advice from coronavirus quarantine patients: 'We all have a choice with whatever is handed to us'. Coronavirus: U.S. Navy Hospital Ships To Deploy To New York, West Coast. Stocks dive as investors survey mounting coronavirus risks. Fox News offers free access to help educate and protect amid coronavirus pandemic. Senate approves House coronavirus aid bill for Trump's signature.

Amid Coronavirus, San Francisco, New York, Deem Marijuana Businesses 'Essential' [3/18/20]. The House-passed bill, which includes free coronavirus testing and paid emergency leave, now heads to Trump. Gutfeld on plastic bags and the coronavirus. Americans battle economic impact as closures continue across the country amid coronavirus spread. Coronavirus leads some overseas prisons to release inmates; Rikers, other US prisons consider the same. Trump signs coronavirus relief measure ensuring paid sick, emergency leave. Pompeo rips China; says Beijing put 'countless lives at risk', pandemic 'repeatable' without transparency. 'American Idol' suspends filming amid coronavirus pandemic. Trump signs coronavirus relief measure into law.

Rep. Michael Cloud: China's coronavirus blunder the last straw -- move past reliance on them. Coronavirus outbreak could force NBA to permanently change schedule, Adam Silver suggests. **Chloroquine, an old malaria drug, may help treat coronavirus, doctors say [3/19/20]**. Coronavirus patient traveled on Delta flight, passed through New York airports, officials say. Coronavirus live blog: Primary care physician Dr. Nate Favini answers your questions. McConnell set to unveil massive "phase 3" coronavirus stimulus bill. Australia, New Zealand Closing Borders To Foreigners In Bid To Contain Coronavirus.

US is preparing for the possibility of a coronavirus pandemic that could last up to 18 months,' report says. Prince Albert of Monaco tests positive for coronavirus. Trump announces FDA making anti-malaria drug available 'almost immediately' to tackle coronavirus. India may be about to discover "tens of thousands" more COVID-19 cases. Young adults make up nearly a third of U.S. coronavirus cases. Pastor Robert Jeffress on importance of faith amid coronavirus: 'People need hope'. Coronavirus pandemic leads rural school districts to develop new methods to keep curriculum learning going. NBA teams criticized over access to coronavirus tests. Asian countries face new wave of coronavirus cases imported from overseas. Brooklyn Nets defend testing players for coronavirus, used 'private company' to avoid using 'public resources'. Photo of Trump remarks shows 'corona' crossed out and replaced with 'Chinese' virus.

Stars get coronavirus tests, raising concerns of inequality. Coronavirus: These politicians, public officials have tested positive. Coronavirus: What to do if you think you were exposed. Iconic statue lit up with flags of countries afflicted by coronavirus. Dr. Fauci: There is no 'magic drug' for coronavirus. 'There have been a lot of tears': Coronavirus threatens to shut schools until the fall. Sen. Kelly Loeffler reportedly 'dumped millions' in stock before coronavirus tanked markets. **Sens. Richard Burr, Kelly Loeffler sold millions in stock before coronavirus crippled markets, reports find [3/20/20]**. California under coronavirus 'stay-at-home' order; Feinstein, 3 senators accused of coronavirus stock selloff.

Amid shortage, Pence says millions of masks available 'now' for hospitals to buy. Amazon executive Jay Carney talks retail giant's coronavirus precautions. Online videos 'predicted' outbreak, but Trump called coronavirus 'unforeseen problem'. The scramble to help 1st-generation, low-income Harvard students amid coronavirus. Coronavirus response is now "under one roof," FEMA head says. Nikki Haley Resigns From Boeing's Board Over Coronavirus Bailout Bid. Coronavirus symptoms: A list and when to seek help. White House coronavirus task force holds a news briefing. Britain asking 65,000 retired nurses and doctors to return to work to help fight coronavirus.

Doctor names two drugs that could help treat coronavirus. Trends suggest virus in Italy more deadly for males. US-Mexico border closing to non-essential travel. Sean Spicer faces backlash for attending coronavirus briefing, asking Trump a question. Google's coronavirus screening website leads to 130 tests in first 4 days. Amid coronavirus pandemic, N95 mask listings on Amazon flooded with fake reviews. How to volunteer during the coronavirus pandemic. Biden trashes Trump over coronavirus response: 'Step up and do your job, Mr. President'. Doctors made a tool to help decide what to do if you have coronavirus-like symptoms. 'This system is doomed': Doctors, nurses sound off in NBC News coronavirus survey.

Pence Aide Tests Positive For Coronavirus; Contact Tracing Ongoing [3/20/20]. Trump's tone veers wildly under pressure from coronavirus. Pilot spells out 'Stay Home' over Austrian airspace after coronavirus restrictions put in place. Deroy Murdock: Trump fights coronavirus effectively -- political attacks on his response should stop. Local book store offers readers unique access amid coronavirus pandemic.

COVID-19 mortality twice as high for men in Italy as women. Mariano Rivera slams 'foolish' spring breakers amid coronavirus pandemic: 'There's no time to be partying'. Hannah Brown blasted for 'irresponsible' Instagram post amid coronavirus pandemic. Mike Pence says he will be tested for coronavirus after staffer tested positive. Tribes take measures to slow spread of new coronavirus. **Coronavirus prompts 2 Pennsylvania churches to move services to outdoor drive-in [3/21/20]**. Italy reports record-high single-day death toll from coronavirus. Coronavirus questions answered: 'Should you go to an urgent care facility if sick'. **Pandemic: 300,000 cases worldwide, Johns Hopkins reports [3/21/20]**. Dr. Oz offers coronavirus advice: 'Close the borders of your house'. Why 'pandemic bangs' are trending during coronavirus outbreak. 38 NYC inmates, including at Rikers, test positive for coronavirus. Coronavirus updates: Global death toll tops 13,000. Mnuchin confident that stimulus package will keep economy afloat until coronavirus passes.

Coronavirus questions answered: Does the virus stick to clothing? Coronavirus pandemic leads to crisis for travel industry. Coronavirus pandemic emerges as monumental moment in global history. Sen. Rand Paul Has Tested Positive For The Coronavirus. Pennsylvania death row inmate hospitalized with coronavirus symptoms before exoneration trial. Fact check: Trump made 33 false claims about coronavirus in the first weeks of March. Neil Diamond updates 'Sweet Caroline' into coronavirus PSA: 'Hands... washing hands'.

Hannity to Biden: Stop fundraising off and politicizing the coronavirus. **Cuomo calls for more NYC streets to be closed off to cars amid coronavirus [3/22/20]**. Pandemic takes 400 lives in US. Canada, Australia will not send athletes to Olympics because of coronavirus. Analysis: Coronavirus rages as DC struggles to catch up. Prisons And Jails Change Policies To Address Coronavirus Threat Behind Bars.

Iran leader refuses U.S. help, citing virus conspiracy theory. 'This week, it's going to get bad': Surgeon General says people need to take coronavirus seriously. Coronavirus scams claim to offer vaccines, treatment and testing. South Korea sees lowest coronavirus case increase to date, tightens border over fears of imported infections. Manny Pacquiao says 'he's not afraid to die' helping to fight coronavirus in Philippines. **Fed vows "unlimited" stimulus to fight coronavirus recession [3/23/20]**. Germany's Angela Merkel tests negative for coronavirus, continues quarantine.

Tokyo Olympics could be postponed as several countries pull out amid coronavirus. Canadian woman's family doesn't let coronavirus spoil 85th birthday, give social distance surprise. Partisan tensions erupt in the Senate as coronavirus stimulus bill fails for a second time. Trump retweets messages supporting rollback of steps to mitigate coronavirus spread. Sen. Rand Paul kept working for six days after virus test. Lawyers for Julian Assange to apply for bail, citing risk of coronavirus. Let's Not Call It A Bailout; Businesses Didn't Cause The Coronavirus. Man dies after ingesting chloroquine in an attempt to prevent coronavirus. Americans brace for predicted rise in coronavirus cases. People improvise ways to keep celebrations going during coronavirus pandemic. George Takei said he's 'chilled' by Trump's use of phrase 'Chinese virus'. Lights out in Sin City: Thousands lose jobs in Las Vegas as coronavirus shutters city.

House Dems' emergency coronavirus stimulus bill includes $35M for JFK Performing Arts Center. New York Gov. Andrew Cuomo Takes The Spotlight In Coronavirus Response. James Carafano: The coronavirus game plan -- how we got here and where it ends. Mnuchin, Schumer optimistic on coronavirus stimulus package, say deal is close. **Tokyo Summer Olympics Will Be Postponed Due To Coronavirus, Japan Says [3/24/20]**. Bella Hadid shares coronavirus do's and don'ts while eating burrito topless: 'Don't be selfish!'.

Trump blasts nonsense in coronavirus bill, calls on Congress to approve aid. Watch live: Mass. governor speaks as non-essential businesses close. This is how South Korea flattened its coronavirus curve. Cubs' Anthony Rizzo provides nearly 700 hot meals to health care **workers on coronavirus front lines [3/24/20]**. New Hampshire sees first coronavirus death. Trail Blazers' CJ McCollum cautions fans to take coronavirus outbreak 'seriously'. During coronavirus, Costco designates special hours for shoppers 60 and older. Pence says White House not considering a nationwide coronavirus lockdown.

Korean Basketball League cancels season due to coronavirus concerns: report. Pence says 2000 ventilators en route to New York amid coronavirus crisis. Cuomo takes national spotlight amid coronavirus pandemic. 3 US Navy sailors aboard Theodore Roosevelt test positive for coronavirus, defense officials say. Health Checks Await Travelers Entering China, As It Tries To Block COVID-19 Rebound.

Sweden takes softer approach on coronavirus lockdown than European neighbors [3/24/20]. FACT CHECK: Trump Compares Coronavirus To The Flu, But It Could Be 10 Times Deadlier. Dems fume at Trump over resistance to using economic freeze to fight coronavirus. State Department has repatriated more than 9,000 Americans amid coronavirus crisis. Dana Perino calls proposed $35M for Kennedy Center in House coronavirus bill 'the new bridge to nowhere'. Terrence McNally, Tony-winning playwright, dead at 81 from COVID-19 complications. Meghan Markle, Prince Harry pay tribute to health care workers amid coronavirus pandemic. The U.S military can do a lot to fight COVID-19. But Trump's holding it back.

5 members of Missouri family test positive for coronavirus. **No longer neutral: Tech companies embrace moderation [censorship] on coronavirus [3/25/20]**. Coronavirus updates: Senate, White House reach $2 trillion aid deal. UK deploys 500 transit police to prevent unnecessary travel amid coronavirus outbreak. Red Sox minor leaguer tests positive for virus, complex shut. NBA star Karl-Anthony Towns reveals mom is in medically induced coma, believes she has coronavirus. Eye Opener at 8: Senate reaches $2 trillion coronavirus stimulus deal. Clemson's Trevor Lawrence, girlfriend allowed to revive coronavirus victims fundraiser after confusion.

Pelosi indicates potential support for Senate's new coronavirus bill, as details emerge. WATCH: New York City details statistics of 15K cases of coronavirus. United Kingdom detains nearly 100 migrants trying to enter country during coronavirus outbreak. **White House, Senate agree on $2 trillion coronavirus relief bill [3/25/20]**. Coronavirus relief bill coming as Trump hopes for Easter reopening. Biden tempers attacks on Trump as coronavirus crisis builds. New York City to close some streets during coronavirus outbreak, Cuomo says. Cuomo: 40,000 volunteer for surge health care force to fight coronavirus.

Recovered coronavirus patient's message to ICU staff goes viral: 'You are all rockstars'. Medical school seeks to graduate students early to fight coronavirus. Coronavirus leads to huge increase in demand for cleaning supplies. California police get groceries, food for man, 95, staying home during coronavirus. Rep. Seth Moulton in self-quarantine after experiencing coronavirus symptoms. Game Zero: Spread of virus linked to Champions League match. Senate standoff threatens to delay coronavirus stimulus bill. Miller Lite to donate $1M to unemployed bartenders amid coronavirus outbreak. Larry Kudlow: 'We're trying to do the best we can to cushion the economic consequences of the virus'. Coronavirus government response updates: 'Large sections' of US could reopen: Trump.

Kellyanne Conway blasts 'feckless' NYC Mayor de Blasio, says he was 'totally irresponsible' about coronavirus. Arkansas pastor, wife, 'dozens' in church infected with COVID-19, he says. Judge denies Tekashi 6ix9ine's request to serve out sentence at home amid coronavirus fears. Coronavirus live updates: U.S. death toll crosses 1,000. Trump's New Chief Of Staff Not Yet Fully On The Job Amid Coronavirus Crisis.

New York mayor Bill de Blasio warns half of all New Yorkers will get coronavirus. Celebs who have adopted dogs amid coronavirus pandemic. Trump under fire over arbitrary coronavirus deadline. Karl-Anthony Towns' father 'recovering well' after coronavirus diagnosis, agent says. Tim Scott on why he and other GOP senators objected to coronavirus relief payments. Coronavirus relief bill moves to the House for Friday vote. Pregnant women face birth alone during coronavirus. **New Orleans: For Katrina-ravaged city, coronavirus is 'the disaster that's going to define our generation,' official says [3/26/20]**. Missouri man plotting coronavirus hospital bombing killed in shooting, FBI says. South Korea adopts 'no-tolerance' coronavirus quarantine policy, violators risk deportation, jail. IOC declines to blame Olympic boxing event for virus cases.

3D-printing technology battles coronavirus outbreak. 2020 Indy 500 postponed from May to August due to coronavirus crisis. Trump campaign offices to stay closed through April because of coronavirus. Coronavirus Cases Spike In Navajo Nation, Where Water Service Is Often Scarce. Georgia's worst-hit hospital fills 3 ICU units with 'critically ill' coronavirus patients. Drew Brees, wife to donate $5M to Louisiana for meals amid surge in COVID-19 cases. AOC blasts coronavirus stimulus, blames GOP for not granting checks to all immigrants.

National Cathedral canon missioner credits 'blessings and miracles' for discovery of 5,000 respirator masks. Fox News Poll: Recession fears mount as coronavirus jolts US economy. U.S. Surpasses China In Cases Of Coronavirus. Show Me the Relief Money -- No Promises On When Coronavirus Checks Are Coming. Jame Comey says he's 'unsure how to use Twitter now' amid virus outbreak, shares 'social distance selfie'.

Tucker Carlson slams NYC leaders for 'endangering' public in early stages of coronavirus pandemic. Coronavirus updates: U.S. now has most cases in world. CPAP Machines Were Seen As Ventilator Alternatives, But Could Spread COVID-19. Coronavirus updates: States seek help for COVID-19-strained hospitals. GOP rep plans to introduce bill allowing Bureau of Prisons to stop inmate movement amid coronavirus. The President downplayed the impact of coronavirus. Now his assessments conflict with the deadly reality.. Barr tells federal prisons to send inmates home amid coronavirus outbreak.

Coronavirus 'hot spots' like Detroit, Chicago and New Orleans will face worse outbreaks next week. Opioid Addiction Is 'A Disease Of Isolation,' So Pandemic Puts Recovery At Risk. U.S. epidemiologist: 'I do not know what the national plan is' on coronavirus. What to do if you think you have coronavirus symptoms. Mayor predicts over half of NYC will get coronavirus. Congressional leaders scramble to derail Massie bid to drag out vote on $2T coronavirus bill. Coronavirus government response updates: Drama as House passes $2T relief package. The $2 trillion deal to combat the economic woes of coronavirus includes sending checks directly to individuals. It now goes to Trump to sign.. Inside Iceland's unique response to combating coronavirus. Coronavirus live updates: Italy's death toll reaches record 969 deaths in 1 day.

Trump is expected to sign a $2 trillion package to address the economic crisis caused by coronavirus. Here's what that means for you. Kristen Bell to host Nickelodeon special for kids worried about coronavirus. Instacart workers slam pandemic working conditions, call for work stoppage. Abbott says Texas is prepared for uptick in coronavirus cases. NYPD commissioner on coronavirus' impact on the force: 'They are in the middle of a fight'. Jon Bon Jovi says he believes his son contracted 'mild version' of coronavirus. Cameras that detect people with coronavirus fevers? Experts are skeptical.

As Louisiana braces for surge of coronavirus cases, state pleads for federal help. World Health Organization under the microscope: what went wrong with coronavirus? Opinion: Remembering Some Of Those We've Already Lost To The Pandemic. $2 Trillion Coronavirus Relief Bill Presents A Reckoning For Libertarians. Why some COVID-19 patients may face problems even after recovery. First NYPD detective dies from coronavirus. NYPD detective becomes first NYC office to die from coronavirus.

Chapter 3

Italy's Coronavirus Death Toll Passes 10,000. Many Are Asking Why the Fatality Rate Is So High

March 28th, 2020 – April 10th, 2020

New Jersey golfers collect supplies to donate to local hospital amid coronavirus outbreak. Italy remains Europe's epicenter of coronavirus. Florida man cautions about fake coronavirus stimulus check scam. Rabbi Sam Bregman: Coronavirus is like a biblical plague -- But hardship brings vision, clarity and growth. Animal Shelters Urge Humans Confined To Home By Coronavirus Outbreak To Adopt. More sailors aboard USS Theodore Roosevelt test positive for coronavirus, officials say. As the number of US coronavirus deaths doubled in just two days, the House speaker criticized the President's response to the pandemic. **Sweden remains open as other countries lock down over coronavirus [3/29/20]**. Canadian PM Justin Trudeau's wife, Sophie, recovers from coronavirus, says 'feeling so much better'. Catching up on TV during lockdown.

Coronavirus measures in Africa escalate to violence as police, military enforce lockdowns [3/29/20]. Billie Eilish, Mariah Carey and more live stream from their homes for coronavirus benefit. Jeannie Cunnion: Coronavirus -- Lessons from a mom of 5 about parenting in a pandemic. Popular NYPD officer shares #ClapBecauseWeCare video dedicated to coronavirus first responders. Coronavirus live updates: Trump extends social distancing guidelines to April 30. Coronavirus outbreak hits Maryland nursing home. FDA OKs emergency authorization of drugs touted by Trump to fight coronavirus. Mnuchin lays out when Americans can expect their coronavirus rescue package checks.

Coronavirus updates: Trump extends shutdown, Fauci warns 200k could die. How bad could the coronavirus outbreak get? New dates announced for Tokyo 2020 Olympics postponed over coronavirus concerns. Antibodies from recovered COVID-19 patients could be key to fighting virus. Former Utah House Speaker Bob Garff dies from coronavirus. **USNS Comfort hospital ship arrives in New York harbor amid coronavirus outbreak [3/30/20]**. Heather Locklear thanks workers during the coronavirus, makes fun of her 'Melrose Place' character. Coronavirus prompts Colombia's left-wing ELN rebel group to announce humanitarian ceasefire. Coronavirus patient zero in New York is out of hospital, Gov. Cuomo says. Texas governor mandates 14-day coronavirus quarantine for travelers from 7 more states, cities.

NYC bar operator the 1st person arrested for violating COVID-19 executive order. Coronavirus government response updates: Trump changes timeline after dire warning. Coronavirus updates: NY governor to health care workers: "Please come help us". Coronavirus aid questions answered: Am I eligible for $500 per-child payment? US is split on the federal handling of the pandemic, but an increasing number say they feel prepared to manage an infection in their family. Trump shows off new rapid coronavirus test kit in Rose Garden, as HHS says 1 million Americans tested. Watch: Acosta quotes Trump's past coronavirus claims to him. Lessons to learn from South Korea's successful coronavirus fight. 'COVID on my face,' colleagues fall ill: NYC doctors, nurses plead for help. Brit Hume says media covering coronavirus press briefings 'missing something'.

'So many patients dying': Doctors say NYC public hospitals reeling from coronavirus. U.S. spies having trouble assessing coronavirus spread in China, Russia: report. Massie calls for Congress to hold virtual public hearings on coronavirus. NYC paramedics stretched thin on front lines of coronavirus outbreak. 'Essential' Child Care Workers Struggle To Balance Family Needs, Safety. Belgium woman, 90, with coronavirus dies after telling doctors to save ventilator for younger patients. NYPD to hand out fines for violating social-distancing rules amid coronavirus, de Blasio says. Taco Bell offering free tacos on Tuesday as a 'thank you' during coronavirus pandemic. 'Das Coronavirus' Podcast Captivates Germany With Scientific Info On The Pandemic. Psychoanalyst: Con men prey on 'primitive' fear during coronavirus crisis. IRS releases more info on how to get coronavirus stimulus checks ASAP.

Ryan Reynolds, Blake Lively donate $400,000 to New York hospitals fighting the coronavirus. New York governor: Virus is "more dangerous than we expected". USA Rugby files for bankruptcy, cites coronavirus as main factor. Governor Cuomo on brother Chris Cuomo's coronavirus diagnosis and protecting their mother. **COVID-19 vaccine candidates: 6 front-runners [3/31/20]**. Airbnb apologizes to hosts for coronavirus cancellation policies, will pay out $250 million. New York, 'Still In Search Of The Apex,' Sees Another Spike In Coronavirus Cases.

Jerusalem sanitizes stones of Western Wall amid pandemic. To Stop The Pandemic, Seema Verma Is 'Getting Rid Of A Lot Of Regulations'. Alec Baldwin suggests Trump is the 'virus in the U.S.': 'Vaccine arrives in November'. **Trump discusses the potential need for Americans to wear masks [3/31/20]**. Coronavirus live updates: New York City death toll over 1,000. Texas Marine vet, middle school principal dead from coronavirus, officials say.

Empire State Building lights up to honor coronavirus fighters [4/1/20]. Von Spakovsky, Adams & Mitchell: Coronavirus and elections -- changes increase risk of voter fraud. Elephants in Thailand face starvation as coronavirus severely impacts tourism. Don't Nag Your Husband During Lockdown, Malaysia's Government Advises Women. Fact-checking Trump's attempt to erase his previous coronavirus response. Dr. Oz: President Trump presented the country with a 'somber' truth about coronavirus deaths. Coronavirus economic updates: Dow plunges as Trump warns of 'painful' weeks to come. Biden casts doubts on Democrats' July convention amid coronavirus crisis.

Difference between coronavirus and seasonal allergies: Your questions answered by an expert. Trump admin will not reopen Obamacare exchanges during coronavirus pandemic. Dodgers, Angels stadium workers calling for financial help amid coronavirus pandemic. **New estimates show 25% to 50% of virus carriers can infect others blindly [4/1/20]** It's prompting US officials to rethink who should wear masks. 5 things to know about the military's coronavirus response. Authoritarians see opportunity to crack down in coronavirus pandemic. **U.S. surpasses 200,000 cases of coronavirus [4/1/20]**.

Boston Globe editorial board blames coronavirus' spread on Trump: He has 'blood on his hands'. State Department ramps up efforts to repatriate thousands of Americans stranded due to coronavirus measures. Loeffler defends trades after reportedly buying stock in company that makes coronavirus protective garments. Moscow To Launch New Surveillance App To Track Residents In Coronavirus Lockdown. CNN analyst mocked for claiming it's a 'GOP campaign message' to blame China for virus outbreak. Daniel Turner: Defeating coronavirus would be impossible without energy workers who power the fight. Fountains Of Wayne's Adam Schlesinger Dies At 52 After

Contracting COVID-19. New York City paramedic documents "battlefield triage" during coronavirus outbreak. Oversight Committee urges FDA to ban e-cigarettes, vaping over coronavirus risks. CNN avoids majority of White House virus presser, trashes Trump for 'shameless' focus on 'political' anti-cartel efforts.

Tekashi 6ix9ine should be considered for early release because of coronavirus, judge says. FACT CHECK: Defense Chief Claims Some Are Calling For Military Shutdown Due To Virus. Australia begins testing 2 potential coronavirus vaccines, including one from U.S. Deroy Murdock: Pelosi attack on Trump coronavirus response is false and ignores all he's done. L.A. mayor urges residents to wear masks when they're not home. WHO concerned by 'rapid escalation' of virus, as U.S. death toll nears 5,000. Gravity Payments employees offer to take pay cut amid pandemic. After more than 3 weeks of coronavirus related layoffs, there's been a 3,000% increase in unemployment claims. Feds distribute thousands of masks, other supplies seized from hoarders during coronavirus pandemic.

Beyond fever and cough: Coronavirus symptoms take new shape. Police in India raise coronavirus awareness with virus costumes while directing traffic, on patrol. Bella Hadid ditches bra in series of quarantine snaps amid coronavirus crisis. Coronavirus sees demand for telemedicine rise as experts weigh the pros and cons. Trump considers next steps in dealing with coronavirus pandemic. "Shoot them dead": Duterte orders police to kill Filipinos who defy coronavirus lockdown. **Can you catch coronavirus by breathing near an infected person? [4/2/20]**

Disney's annual passholders complain about still being charged amid coronavirus closure. Stolen SUV in California found hauling 192 rolls of toilet paper amid coronavirus outbreak, police say. FDA Loosens Restrictions On Gay Blood Donors Amid 'Urgent Need' Caused By Coronavirus. Judge won't delay Wisconsin's April 7 primary election over coronavirus concerns. Wisconsin won't move next week's primary, despite COVID-19 threat. How has coronavirus changed the U.S.-Mexico border situation?

Guidance on face masks: Trump releasing new recommendations. Funeral directors overwhelmed by COVID-19 death toll. Dan Crenshaw slams Biden, ex-Obama aide for criticizing U.S. coronavirus response. Former NFL great talks about battle with coronavirus, 'I don't want to die here'. Democrats shelve national convention until mid-August over coronavirus concerns. The Coronavirus Small Business Loan Program: What You Need To Know.

Ari Fleischer: Trump's coronavirus communications challenge -- Why these two things are critical. Meek Mill, Jay-Z charity sends masks to prisons to protect prisoners from coronavirus. Watch live: Coronavirus Task Force gives update on COVID-19 response. Trump says administration "hit 3M hard" over face masks. Country duo 'Big & Rich' to perform their coronavirus PSA 'Stay Home' live. No work: Pandemic has been catastrophic for house cleaners and nannies. Trump denies a major recession is on the horizon as coronavirus hits economy. **New York ER doctor: Smart to recommend public use masks because of asymptomatic spread of coronavirus [4/3/20]**. Nick Cordero 'stable,' 'responding well' to medication after two negative coronavirus tests, wife says.

Chris Cuomo shares Covid-19 experience: 'The beast comes at night'. Coronavirus response at Washington state nursing home leads to $611,000 in fines. Coronavirus could worsen the US childhood obesity crisis. Spain Briefly Passes Italy In COVID-19 Cases But Officials See Growth Rate Slowing. **Coronavirus cases top 1 million globally [4/3/20]** . Supreme Court postpones April oral arguments over coronavirus concerns.

Pet adoptions, fostering spike amid coronavirus restrictions. Watch live: Trump says CDC recommends "voluntary" cloth masks in public. **Immunologist says he has a possible cure for the coronavirus [4/3/20]**. Coronavirus deaths pass 59,000 globally. Steve Forbes says coronavirus hit US economy like 'a sledgehammer'. Non-COVID emergencies take a back seat, putting patients at risk. Keir Starmer elected leader of Britain's Labour Party amid coronavirus crisis. Couple in India names newborn twins Corona and Covid. Heads Bow And Sirens Wail As China Observes Day Of Mourning Amid Pandemic. **Walmart and Target limit number of shoppers amid coronavirus pandemic [4/4/20]**. Spain now second highest number of coronavirus cases, deaths in the world.

Making your own face mask Some fabrics work better than others, study finds. UN chief calls for 'large-scale' coronavirus response of 10 percent of global GDP. Campaigning during coronavirus: Candidates look for new ways to connect. Thousands of Americans stuck abroad during pandemic. Alabama joins states under coronavirus stay-at-home order. Queen to call for 'good-humoured resolve' as coronavirus deaths rise in U.K.. Scientists dispute Chinese herbal traditions to treat COVID-19. Coronavirus updates: U.S. deaths top 8,500 as Trump warns of "toughest week" ahead. Gig Workers Struggle To Get Financial Help During Pandemic. Coronavirus cases surge inside Chicago jail.

Queen Elizabeth II To Address U.K. In Rare Televised Speech About The Coronavirus. "A backlog of funerals" in coronavirus' epicenter. Gottlieb says "very aggressive surveillance" needed to track future coronavirus spread. Nebraska docs urge statewide coronavirus stay-at-home order, predict thousands of cases have gone undetected. Giuliani says doctors, not 'national bureaucracy,' should decide whether to use hydroxychloroquine for coronavirus. Queen calls for 'good-humored resolve' as coronavirus deaths rise in U.K.. Trump says 1.6 million Americans tested for coronavirus. Coronavirus updates: Trump says 1.6. million Americans have been tested for coronavirus.

Woody Harrelson latest star sharing coronavirus conspiracy theories tied to 5G. What does it take to convert a hotel bedroom into a COVID-19 care room? Liz Peek: Pelosi's partisan coronavirus investigation -- expect this reaction from crisis-weary voters. Justin Verlander donating MLB paychecks to coronavirus relief efforts during season's shutdown. Japan's Abe Says He Will Declare State Of Emergency As Coronavirus Cases Surge. Tiger at Bronx Zoo tests positive for coronavirus. Thousands of coronavirus-infected New Yorkers treated with anti-malarial drug.

Photos from the 1918 Spanish flu pandemic. **Pastors describe spreading the gospel online during pandemic [4/6/20]**. Hospitals Are Sourcing Masks from Auto Body Shops, HHS Inspector General Finds. California retirement community angry at plan to move homeless with coronavirus to nearby hotels. Arizona pot dispensary ordered to stop advertising coronavirus treatment. Doctor explains how and when to wear a face mask. Coronavirus government response updates: White House warns of dire two weeks ahead.

Queen Elizabeth: Monarch addresses UK amid pandemic. Coronavirus economic updates: Dow spikes more than 1,600 points. Trump, Biden speak by phone about coronavirus. Arkansas Gov. Hutchinson Says State Has A 'Targeted Response' To Coronavirus. Voting during a pandemic Here's what happened in 1918. Answering Your Coronavirus Questions: Masks, Ventilators And Making Choices. A Tiger Has Coronavirus. Should You Worry About Your Pets? Opinion: Religious gatherings around the globe inflame the virus.

Essential workers show why they're essential. Before the White House, Trump called NIH 'terrible,' questioned vaccines. Prince Andrew accuser says she's being tested for coronavirus. California inmates make face masks to distribute in hopes to curb coronavirus spread. Roseanne Barr says coronavirus is a ploy to 'get rid' of her generation, is planning lawsuit over TV show cancellation. Coronavirus relief: Wisconsin TSA officers buy lunch for airport workers whose hours were cut during pandemic.

As Americans are urged to wear masks, choosing to use one is a 'lose-lose situation' for people of color. African Americans may be dying from COVID-19 at a higher rate. New York governor says hospital ship will now take coronavirus patients. Gov. Cuomo says Navy hospital ship will now take coronavirus patients. Women and children at higher risk of violence and sexual abuse during coronavirus lockdown. Labor Secretary Scalia: Getting virus under control is first step to reopening economy. Trump removes watchdog tapped for virus rescue oversight. Etsy CEO on sellers making face masks during COVID-19 pandemic: Americans helping Americans.

Mayo Clinic launches trials of blood test to detect who has recovered and might have immunity to coronavirus. Prince William sends tweet wishing Boris Johnson a 'speedy recovery' as PM battles coronavirus. Queen Elizabeth has been updated hourly on Boris Johnson's coronavirus battle, source says. Coronavirus unknowns ignite concerns for pregnant women, newborns. Coronavirus lockdowns have sent pollution plummeting. Environmentalists worry about what comes next.. New York suffers single deadliest day of coronavirus fatalities. Wisconsin voters face long waits, lines amid coronavirus outbreak.

Texas AG expects coronavirus abortion ban will reach Supreme Court. L.A. mandates masks for essential trips. Fear of coronavirus reaching Mississippi prisons worries advocates. 'Where Is This Going To Lead': Roma People In Europe Face Coronavirus Disaster. Health departments are sending police the addresses of people who have coronavirus. "Think about all the blessings": Passover amid the pandemic.

End of Wuhan lockdown could trigger "resurgence in infections". UN health agency on defensive after Trump slams it on virus. Library workers fight for safer working conditions amid coronavirus pandemic. Boston grocery store workers stand 6 feet apart to protest lack of masks, wages amid coronavirus outbreak. Carol Burnett talks toughest adjustment amid coronavirus quarantine. Coronavirus prompts changes to funeral industry amid concerns of 'unprecedented' situation. For Counties, The Coronavirus Brings Major Budget Problems. Refugees in Germany give back by sewing coronavirus face masks for the retired. Polls suggest public approval of Trump's job combating coronavirus fading. Teachers caravan California community to inspire students during pandemic. Hawley: 'Phase four' coronavirus aid bill should 'protect every single job in this country' until crisis ends.

New York-area coronavirus outbreak originated primarily in Europe, not China: report. CDC releases new data as debate grows over racial disparities in coronavirus deaths. New Zealand is winning the war on coronavirus: here's why. Here's the latest on the coronavirus pandemic. California fast-tracks plans to house homeless residents amid COVID-19 outbreak. Workers continue to suffer from devastating job losses and reduced hours during coronavirus pandemic. 'Boulangeries Are Helping Us Make It Through': In France, Bakeries Remain Essential. National Guard deployed to NJ veterans home as coronavirus outbreak leaves 37 dead in two weeks. **Coronavirus pandemic forces funeral homes, morgues into the frontline fight [4/9/20]**. Chicago businesses facing up to $120,000 in fines after violating coronavirus prevention measures: report.

New York governor says coronavirus has killed 4,000 more people than 9/11. Princeton historian: America can beat coronavirus if we don't 'defeat ourselves'. Recovered coronavirus patient on donating plasma to help others: 'A great feeling'. Florida teacher goes out of her way to help struggling student during coronavirus lockdown. FEMA Predicted Pandemic Effects Last Summer. National Guard deployed to New Jersey veterans home with at least 10 coronavirus deaths. Rose Namajunas pulls out of UFC 249 after two deaths in family due to coronavirus, manager says. Bret Baier says China stepping up international 'propaganda game' to look 'benevolent' amid pandemic.

Can you get coronavirus twice? Obama to mayors on coronavirus: The biggest mistake leaders can make is to misinform. Coronavirus 5G conspiracy theory debunked: Experts say there's no connection. EU Finance Ministers Reach $590 Billion Coronavirus Rescue Deal. Coronavirus May Reshape Who Votes And How In The 2020 Election. Coronavirus updates: COVID-19 hospital admissions drop in 2 hard-hit states. 'Fight of a generation': Coronavirus could trigger violent unrest, Security Council warned. Experiencing coronavirus-related nightmares Expert explains pandemic dreams?

Tyler Perry on coronavirus in African-American communities. Hit hardest by coronavirus deaths, NY Latinos now mourn together. Yemen, Already Facing A Health Crisis, Confirms 1st Coronavirus Case. Families grieve loss of loved ones as pandemic grips entire world. New York Times op-ed: Coronavirus dispelling the 'myth' that America is 'best country on earth'. Hobbies offer Americans a respite from social isolation amid pandemic. **Apple And Google Build Smartphone Tool To Track COVID-19 [4/10/20]**.

Chapter 4

How to Make China's Communist Party Pay for the COVID-19 Pandemic

April 10ᵗʰ, 2020 – April 29ᵗʰ, 2020

Demographics: Surgeon general explains how coronavirus disproportionately affects people of color. 15-year-old boy from Amazon tribe dies of coronavirus. Coronavirus questions answered: Do we have a plan for the second wave of the coronavirus? How is coronavirus affecting immigration into the U.S.? A plan to save coronavirus patients from dying at home. NYC midtown hotel hands out food to homeless population during coronavirus. Coronavirus updates: **U.S. COVID-19 cases top 500,000 [4/10/20]**. Governors Call For $500 Billion Bailout Amid Standoff Over Coronavirus Relief Funds. The U.S.'s struggle to gain control of the coronavirus crisis is rooted in these two traits. US has the most virus-related deaths in the world.

The United States is now reporting more coronavirus deaths than any other country. Retired Illinois fire department captain dies from coronavirus complications: report. Dr. Manny Alvarez: Coronavirus and Easter 2020 -- Why I have hope. Tulane University doctor on the coronavirus' impact on African-Americans. **U.S. surpasses 20,000 coronavirus deaths [4/12/20]**, the highest national death toll. U.S. Has Most Coronavirus Deaths In The World. Nurses treating coronavirus patients find tires slashed at New York hospital. Woman accidentally tans company logo onto her leg during coronavirus lockdown. Michigan man and son, 20, laid to rest after losing battle to coronavirus within 3-day span. New York Coronavirus Deaths Pass 9,000.

Police visit Cowboys QB Dak Prescott's home after report of 'party' during coronavirus pandemic. Matthew McConaughey, wife Camila donate 80K face masks to coronavirus first-responders in Texas, Louisiana. Russian border new battleground as China's COVID-19 cases sharply rise: report. Trump campaign, RNC raise $212 million in first quarter amid impeachment, coronavirus. Tim Scott on disparities in coronavirus death rates. Sailor aboard USS Theodore Roosevelt dies of coronavirus. Rapper Gucci Mane slammed for insensitive coronavirus tweet. Trump administration weighing WHO funding options amid coronavirus outbreak. Coronavirus economic updates: 'Historic' deal to cut oil production reached by OPEC.

Mariah Carey dedicates emotional Easter performance to coronavirus medical workers. Cuomo, northeastern governors announce 'coordinated' regional effort to reopen amid coronavirus. Coronavirus antibody testing must be covered free, feds say. Coastal states are working together to to determine how to reopen from stay-at-home orders issued to limit the spread of Covid-19. How Runners Can Keep Themselves And Others Safe During The Pandemic.

Trump administration 'hastily' moves to delay census operations because of coronavirus, frustrating Dems. Outside coronavirus hot spots, medical practices suffering from lack of patients. Taiwan releases December email to WHO showing unheeded warning about coronavirus. Los Angeles Unified students will not receive 'F' grade amid coronavirus. Trump uses coronavirus briefing to air his grievances. Nonprofits providing essential services warn of impending funding crisis. Fact check: False claims from Trump's bitter pandemic briefing. WWE deemed an "essential" business during pandemic. Florida police, veterans group send off fallen vet as coronavirus puts military honors on hold. Cuomo says "no time for politics" as virus death toll jumps. Global pandemic takes staggering toll on NYC Transit workers. Italy records fewest new coronavirus cases in a month. These medical workers are tackling the coronavirus. They're also saddled with student debt.

Dems call for breakdown of coronavirus cases by race, ethnicity. Coronavirus updates: **U.S. death toll tops 25,000 [4/14/20]**. Trump announces US will halt funding to World Health Organization over coronavirus response. India extends world's largest coronavirus lockdown. Major League Baseball to have 27 teams participate in coronavirus antibody test, report says. 'I got a little cocky:' Chris Cuomo on his fight against Covid. Guatemala health minister compares U.S. to Wuhan, claims deportations causing spike in coronavirus cases. People With Disabilities Fear Pandemic Will Worsen Medical Biases. South Dakota governor shuns stay-at-home order as virus cases climb.

'As Dangerous As It Sounds': Reactions To U.S. Plan To Defund WHO During A Pandemic. VP Pence's daughter Charlotte launches new show for kids to understand coronavirus. IRS launches online form to get coronavirus stimulus checks faster. Carnival CEO says bookings for 2021 'are strong' despite coronavirus outbreak. Coronavirus has infected more than 9,000 US health care workers, CDC says. Gov. **Cuomo will require residents wear a mask or mouth and nose covering wherever they are unable to maintain social distancing [4/15/20]**. White House doubles down on WHO funding cutoff, details coronavirus mismanagement. Coronavirus hits workers at big poultry processor. When ventilators come off, delirium sets in for many former coronavirus patients. Sources believe coronavirus originated in Wuhan lab as part of China's efforts to compete with US. WHO suggests access to alcohol 'should be restricted' in Europe during coronavirus lockdown. **Coronavirus cases top 2 million globally [4/16/20]**.

Theory: US explores possibility Covid-19 started in Chinese lab [4/16/20]. What's It Going To Take To End The Shutdown? 5 Keys To Containing Coronavirus. UN hamstrung and reluctant to take on China, coronavirus cover-up. Tracing the ripple effects of coronavirus' economic impact. 5.2 million more Americans file for unemployment amid COVID-19 crisis. Bezos Hopes To Start Amazon Workers Coronavirus Testing 'Soon'. "A Perfect Storm:" Extremists Look For Ways To Exploit Coronavirus Pandemic.

ICE Releases Hundreds Of Immigrants As Coronavirus Spreads in Detention Centers. **US, Canada have funded Chinese lab eyed as likely source of coronavirus outbreak [4/16/20]**. Treasury Dept. working to iron out 'glitches' in direct deposit, as millions await coronavirus stimulus payment. Coronavirus might have killed 33-year-old Florida nurse, family claims. Washington state island seen as one of the places 'safest' from coronavirus. Florida coronavirus patient emerges from coma on Easter after plasma treatment, report says. 'My So-Called Life' cast reunites after 26 years via Zoom during coronavirus quarantine. Japan expanding state of emergency as number of coronavirus cases soar. Trump unveils three-phase plan for states to reopen amid coronavirus pandemic.

Michael Cohen, Trump's ex-lawyer, to be released from prison due to coronavirus: source. Coronavirus updates: Blacks make up as many as 30% of cases, per early CDC figures. CRISPR And Spit Might Be Keys To Faster, Cheaper, Easier Tests For The Coronavirus. Chefs accuse insurance companies of denying claims amid coronavirus pandemic. China raises Wuhan virus death toll 50%. Sophie, Countess of Wessex, helps cook meals for NHS emergency room workers battling coronavirus. The primary fiasco in Wisconsin was a wake-up call. **Coronavirus could cripple voting in November [4/17/20]**.

Impact of coronavirus on SAT and other standardized tests. Trump and Cuomo spar over coronavirus response. Analysis: Kelly Loeffler just blamed socialism for her coronavirus stock sell-off. Protesters gather at Minnesota governor's mansion over lockdown, chant 'open up'. Coronavirus FAQs: Can Sunlight Kill The Virus? How Risky Is An Elevator Ride? COVID-19 Is Cutting Into Vital Money U.S. Migrant Workers Send Back Home. West Virginia Aims To Test All Nursing Home Residents, Workers for COVID-19. Pence says states have enough COVID-19 tests to start phase one of White House recovery plan. Federal prison worker who died tests positive for coronavirus. Vernon Brewer: Coronavirus isolation -- I was quarantined while battling cancer and learned 4 important lessons. South African gang rivals work together to help people amid pandemic. Who's Hit Hardest By COVID-19? Why Obesity, Stress And Race All Matter. 540 people died in New York over the past 24 hours from coronavirus.

Coronavirus test troubles cloud Trump's efforts to reopen country. Pandemic costing youth sports millions, creating uncertainty. NJ governor says coronavirus is a "different enemy" than the flu. Prescriptions for anti-anxiety meds spike amid coronavirus outbreak, new report finds. Trump's Saturday coronavirus briefing was littered with false claims, old and new. Andy Puzder: Trump coronavirus guidelines will get us back to normal and safeguard public health victories. Pandemic: A snapshot of life in New Orleans.

Pope Francis: Amid coronavirus trials, 'we must not let hope abandon us'. Bangladesh funeral attracts 100,000 people, shattering coronavirus social distancing rules. Japanese hospitals overwhelmed as nation tops 10,000 coronavirus cases. Nick Cordero has leg amputated due to coronavirus complications. COVID-19 hits global drug trade, experts say.

Shake Shack makes big donation to help feed NYC coronavirus health workers. Coronavirus questions answered: Are vapers more vulnerable?

Michigan girl, 5, daughter of first responders, dies from coronavirus: report. Families recreate classic paintings amid coronavirus quarantine. US coronavirus deaths top 40,000. Texas Gov. Abbott on reopening state during fight against coronavirus: God's hand is working? Dogs could sniff out coronavirus cases at rate of 750 per hour, experts believe.

Bosnians start hunger strike to protest coronavirus quarantine. Florida woman charged with violating coronavirus order after party at Airbnb rental led to shooting: police. Coronavirus leads New York ICUs to see shortages in dialysis equipment: report. WHO head warns worst of virus is still ahead. White House: Data On COVID-19 And Race Still Weeks Away. **The coronavirus crisis has producers running out of places to store excess barrels of crude, driving prices below zero [4/20/20]**. WHO chief warns the worst of the coronavirus is still ahead.

Rachael Bovard: Coronavirus reveals scary truth about big tech's unchecked power over our lives [4/20/20]. Army Resuming Basic Training With Measures Against Coronavirus Exposure. CNN's April Ryan asks if protesters of stay-at-home guidelines should decline medical care if they get coronavirus. Phoenix protesters target coronavirus restrictions with rally inside state capitol. Negotiations over interim coronavirus aid bill hit snag on state, local government funding. Coronavirus: Hospital accused of delivering bodies to Pennsylvania medical examiner by pickup truck. Coronavirus updates from April 20, 2020. Cemetery races to keep up as New York virus deaths mount. Missouri files suit against China for 'enormous' consequences of coronavirus 'deceit'. The Senate minority leader says details need to be ironed out on the $450 billion coronavirus deal, but it could be passed as soon as today.

House members asked to come back to DC to vote on new coronavirus relief package.

Herd of sheep flocks to McDonald's in Wales amid coronavirus closures. Cal Thomas: Amid coronavirus, arbitrary executive orders by some governors naturally cause problems. **The coronavirus dilemma: Are we using ventilators too much? [4/21/20]** READ: Text of the $484B coronavirus phase 3.5 bill. Director of Trump admin vaccine agency suddenly departs. Coronavirus checks aren't coming for many minority Americans. Here's why. Will coronavirus antibody tests tell you when to go back to work Maybe not.. NY, NJ airports have highest number of TSA employees testing positive for coronavirus. "Friends" cast joins All In Challenge to raise money for coronavirus relief.

Coronavirus could have a deadlier second wave later this year, CDC director warns [4/22/20]. N.Y. Gov. Andrew Cuomo Says President Trump Promised Help With Coronavirus Testing. Connecticut police to test 'pandemic drone' that monitors health of residents. A leading model has upped its projected coronavirus death toll in August to 66,000, a 10% increase from its previous prediction. Ai Weiwei on the coronavirus pandemic: 'China will never learn'.

Even With COVID-19 Cases, Suing Cruise Lines Is 'Extraordinarily Difficult'. Chilling new book about pandemic draws similarities to coronavirus. Tim Allen on 'Last Man Standing' season being cut short due to coronavirus: 'It was real peculiar'. GOP Rep. Stefanik introduces coronavirus student loan relief bill. 1st U.S. coronavirus death was weeks earlier than initially believed. Testing "critical" amid concern of virus second wave, FDA head says. Coronavirus updates: World sees growing toll amid warnings of second wave. Courteney Cox calls for an end to illegal wildlife trade: It 'caused' coronavirus. Fox News Executive Tries To Rein In Stars As They Cheer On Anti-Lockdown Rallies.

Russian space official tests positive for coronavirus after attending Soyuz crew launch to International Space Station. Dem overseeing $2T in coronavirus funds accused of violating federal law requiring disclosure of stock sales. Dr. Nicole Saphier explains why getting a flu shot can help fight coronavirus pandemic. Be careful how you clean in the fight against coronavirus: CDC. Who is Dr. Rick Bright: Official ousted after Covid-19 treatment clash has long history of working on vaccine preparedness. Great economy, health care system prepared Europe's powerhouse: How Germany has tackled coronavirus outbreak. Trump cheers America's production of ventilators, sending them to other countries hit hard by coronavirus.

A study of patients treated at Northwell Health, New York's largest health system, shows how dire the outlook is for patients with severe coronavirus disease. **Potential coronavirus vaccine enters human testing trial [4/23/20]**. Poison control sees spike in calls for cleaner, disinfectant accidents amid COVID-19 pandemic. Florida man put COVID-19 warning sign on his door to avoid arrest, police say. U.S. blames China for delayed virus response, but pulls funding from WHO. Iowa woman sets up 'giving tree' of face masks on family farm amid pandemic.

'Anyone but Trump': Swing state hit hard by coronavirus could flip on Trump in 2020. Spain wants refund for faulty coronavirus tests Chinese company sent as replacement for first defective batch. US astronaut returns to world changed by COVID-19 after 9 months in space. Iran Hopes Slowing Rise Of COVID-19 Cases Means The Worst Is Over. Some argue the benefits of reopening the US economy outweigh the human toll of the coronavirus pandemic. Ethicists say that's immoral. LA to track, publicly share up-to-date list of restaurants with positive coronavirus cases. New York mom with coronavirus spread it to 17 of her children: report. In a series of now-deleted tweets, Michael Caputo made derogatory racial comments and said

Democrats wanted the coronavirus to kill millions of people. Flight attendant shares eerie photos of life on planes during the coronavirus outbreak. Ohio police department asks crooks to follow 'freeze tag' rules amid coronavirus: No 'tag backs'. USS Theodore Roosevelt's entire crew has been tested for coronavirus; over 800 positive, officials say.

Preliminary study results suggest the drug Trump touted doesn't work for very sick coronavirus patients. Washington state's Green River Killer, other inmates denied coronavirus release in 5-4 vote. China's diplomats show teeth in defending virus response. COVID-19 hackers targeting medical providers, FBI says. Kaley Cuoco jokes she'll kick husband Karl Cook out of their new house after coronavirus quarantine. Jimmy Failla: Coronavirus and the NFL Draft -- The surprising things we learned on Thursday night. Coronavirus package falls short for lenders to Latino, minority businesses.

U.S. Coronavirus Death Toll Passes 50,000 [4/24/20]. Nursing home emerges from coronavirus crisis with anguished lessons learned. Coronavirus updates: Virus spreading fast in states that may reopen, study says. Michael Avenatti released from prison over virus concerns. Georgia reopens for business amid pandemic. Thousands hit Southern California beaches to cool off amid coronavirus stay-at-home order. Robert Hutchinson: Coronavirus gives online education a big boost, shows high-priced colleges are a scam. **Global coronavirus death toll nears 200,000, as world leaders commit to finding vaccine [4/25/20]**.

Connecticut town grounds drone program to fight coronavirus amid outcry. There's "no evidence" coronavirus survivors can't be reinfected, WHO says. Worldwide coronavirus death toll passes 200,000. Andrew McCarthy: On coronavirus restrictions, burden of proof is on government to show justification. Mississippi medical center hit by coronavirus and tornado gets masks donated from nonprofit.

Nancy Pelosi 'owes America an apology' for coronavirus relief delays, McCarthy says. Christen Limbaugh Bloom: God using coronavirus crisis to touch hearts of individuals, create revival in church. Dressing down: Fashion sense during lockdown. Michigan lawmaker apologizes for wearing mask that appears to resemble Confederate flag. Coronavirus cancels summer baseball in Cape Cod for future major leaguers. **Science Becomes A Dividing Issue In Year Of Election And Pandemic [4/26/20]**. Gowdy: Trump should be 'comforter in chief,' leave medical advice to health professionals during coronavirus. Rapper DMX hosts Bible study on Instagram Live during coronavirus.

Expert advice on how to enter the workforce altered by coronavirus. Idaho mother apologizes after playground arrest amid coronavirus outbreak. **New Zealand Says It Has Won 'Battle' Against COVID-19 [4/27/20]**. CDC Adds 6 Symptoms To Its COVID-19 List. Automakers adjust to 'new normal' as they prepare to reopen plants.

In Detroit, grief runs deep as city grapples with COVID-19. Russia says predicting the end of the lockdown is a 'shot in the dark'. **Religious freedom attorneys pick their battles amid pandemic [4/27/20].** 'The pandemic is far from over,' WHO says. Coronavirus lingers in the air of crowded spaces, study finds. Bill Gates predicts when we'll get a coronavirus vaccine. S. Korea is leading the pack in its coronavirus response. The price? A new way of life. States see coronavirus tension as some start lifting stay-at-home orders, others stay put. Calif. Governor Warns That Packed Beaches Put Coronavirus Pandemic Progress At Risk. Analysis: This is what coronavirus capitalism looks like. 'Silent hypoxia' may be killing COVID-19 patients, but there's hope.

This is what coronavirus capitalism looks like. Trump campaign, RNC ramp up virtual outreach amid coronavirus crisis. Kentucky reopens some health care operations as virus cases top 4,000. There may be more than 15,000 'excess deaths' linked to coronavirus in the US, study suggests. Nick Cordero suffers infection in his lungs, blood amid ongoing coronavirus fight. Pentagon agency working on cloning antibodies to fight COVID-19. Sean Penn's nonprofit to expand free virus testing sites.

Telecom masts in continental Europe attacked in wake of bizarre 5G coronavirus conspiracy theory. At least 317 immigrants in ICE custody test positive for COVID-19. There has been nearly 12,000 confirmed coronavirus deaths in New York City. Minneapolis tightens coronavirus restrictions with move to close fields, playgrounds, other public areas. Trump again says virus is "going to go away". Leaving Off Mask At Mayo Clinic, Pence Said He Wanted To Look Workers 'In The Eye'. Mnuchin: Large companies should apologize for seeking coronavirus small-business loans. **Tucker rips YouTube for pulling 'problematic' coronavirus video: 'Censorship never is about science' [4/29/20]**. As lockdowns drag on, is it OK to ease up on social distancing? Poll: Half Of Americans Financially Affected By Coronavirus.

Eye Opener: U.S. exceeds a million coronavirus cases [4/29/20]. Eye Opener at 8: Pence forgoes mask during Mayo Clinic visit. Coronavirus in New York: Subway worker demands hazard pay after sharing video showing homeless filling train cars. Large coronavirus trial of drug remdesivir shows promise. Dutch teens sail home across the Atlantic due to coronavirus travel restrictions. Navy holds off on reinstating captain fired after raising coronavirus concerns, wants deeper probe. Navy Seeks 'Deeper Review' In Probe Of Pandemic-Struck Warship Captain's Firing. Coronavirus in New York: Gov. Cuomo unveils mask artwork, but raises some eyebrows. 'Clear-cut' evidence coronavirus drug remdesivir works, Fauci says. Spain official apologizes for spraying beach with bleach to protect children from coronavirus.

Why The U.S. Government Stopped Funding A Research Project On Bats And Coronaviruses. 2 guards at ICE jail die after contracting coronavirus. Opinion: Pence unmasked shows his obedience to Trump. Costco will start requiring customers to wear masks Monday.

Chapter 5

'Dangerous & disrespectful': Doctors Tear Into Pence's Maskless Hospital Visit

April 29th, 2020 – May 22nd, 2020

Experimental drug shows potential in treating COVID-19. Navy opens full investigation into coronavirus-stricken USS Theodore Roosevelt. FDA reportedly will approve Covid-19 treatment remdesivir, which US-funded trial shows has 'positive effect' on recovery. Newsom to close all California beaches, state parks over coronavirus: memo.

Coronavirus and food: Does cooking kill it? South Korea Reports No New Domestic Coronavirus Cases. FDA working to make remdesivir available to coronavirus patients 'as quickly as possible'. Coronavirus has infected 500 TSA employees, agency says. Virus patient in drug trial left hospital "improving drastically". Report details poor conditions at ICE jails with coronavirus cases.

Broadway star Nick Cordero suffers virus setback, but wife is hopeful. African Americans Hit Hardest By COVID-19 But Most Likely To Say Faith Has Grown. Boris Johnson: U.K. Is 'Past The Peak' Of Its Coronavirus Outbreak. Michigan protesters storm state Capitol in fight over coronavirus rules: 'Men with rifles yelling at us'. Trump pushes fast vaccine development despite concerns. Answering Your Coronavirus Questions: COVID-19 And Kidneys, Masks And Pets. NYPD promotions move forward despite coronavirus, with pared-down ceremony. McCarthy fumes after Pelosi names Maxine Waters, 6 other Dems to oversee coronavirus funds. Murray's cursing, muttering highlight virus video tennis. Rep. Ted Budd: Coronavirus lockdowns -- ensure safety but don't infringe on our civil liberties. Jordan Spieth's hole-in-one nixed over coronavirus precautions on golf course. Michigan expands coronavirus testing but grapples with PPE shortages.

Bangladesh factories resume work, risking new virus cases. Mike Pence: Much of the coronavirus epidemic could be 'behind us by early June'. Mark Levin blasts Cuomo for coronavirus response: Nursing homes 'begged' him not to do this. Trump administration investigating origins of the coronavirus. Even after coronavirus pandemic ends, 40 percent of Americans plan to avoid public spaces, report says. Coronavirus sparks increased interest in home births but expert advises against it. FDA allows emergency use of remdesivir to treat coronavirus patients after promising study. Tennessee pushes forward with reopening businesses despite the rise of COVID-19 cases. Comparing Covid-19 to the flu is not fair. Tom Homan: Liberal judges use coronavirus as excuse to free detained illegal immigrants, endangering public. Tucker Carlson on coronavirus lockdowns: 'That's not how our system works'. **The governor invoked the state's Riot Control act to authorize drastic lockdown measures because coronavirus 'is running amok' [5/2/20]**. Brazil's President Bolsonaro continues to downplay coronavirus threat. What will Hollywood look like after the coronavirus pandemic?

Another round of coronavirus will likely coincide with flu season in the fall. Here's what we can do to stop it. Dressing up and staying in: Coronavirus' effect on fashion is more than skin deep. GOP rep unveils bill to probe WHO's coronavirus response, past actions. Pelosi And McConnell Decline White House Offer Of Coronavirus Tests For Capitol Hill. Dr. Birx: As US reopens, protecting those at high risk for coronavirus remains 'very critical'. California's Coronavirus Testing Still A Frustrating Patchwork Of Haves And Have-Nots. Boris Johnson opens up about coronavirus fight, says it was 50-50 on whether he would be intubated. Mississippi governor reconsiders reopening state after new spike in coronavirus cases, deaths. The pandemic drove many people across the nation outside, some for recreation and others in protest. Rome seagulls hunt rats, pigeons as coronavirus lockdown deprives them of human scraps.

DeSantis is ready to declare victory but the coronavirus picture in Florida is still unclear. U.S.-Canada border closure leaves families separated amid coronavirus pandemic. News outlets have reported Trump's daily intel briefing mentioned the virus as early as January 3. It's unclear whether the President read those reports. Procession held for Colorado paramedic who died from coronavirus while volunteering in NYC. COVID-19 vaccine hunt heats up globally, still no guarantee. Senate's return sets stage for showdown over coronavirus relief package.

Photographers bring their talents together to provide aid in the fight against the coronavirus. J.Crew Bankruptcy Filing May Not Be The Last For Retailers Slammed By Pandemic. Millions Return To Work In Italy After Weeks Of Lockdown. Trump takes shot at California for wanting tighter border during coronavirus pandemic. Coronavirus 'cancel the rent' movement should be about finding solutions for all sides, advocates say. World leaders pledge billions for virus vaccine research. FDA Cracks Down On Antibody Tests For Coronavirus.

Romney proposes hazard pay plan for essential workers. Security guard shot and killed after enforcing face mask policy: officials. White House Official Delivers Speech In Mandarin To Send Coronavirus Message. Answering Your Coronavirus Questions: The Economy, Vaccines And COVID-19 Survivors. Analysis: Skin-hunger and coronajerks. The Dutch are inventing new words to describe the impact of the virus. Newsom's office refuses records request on 'murky' $1B mask deal with Chinese company. Eye Opener: New projection predicts spike in coronavirus deaths.

Destruction of Amazon rainforest accelerates amid coronavirus. Transit systems face plunging ridership amid virus fears. Coronavirus outbreak at Massachusetts nursing home kills 54 residents. Amid pandemic, Alaska man supplies groceries for entire town during 7-hour Costco runs. **Another 1,700 virus deaths reported at New York nursing homes [5/5/20]**. Despite Delays Caused By Coronavirus, Regular Season Baseball Starts In Korea. Trust in government hits record high globally during pandemic. White House coronavirus task force to be wound down around Memorial Day.

Government gone too far? States rebuked for coronavirus lockdown measures [5/5/20]. Feds bring first fraud charges stemming from coronavirus loans. Trump's spy chief pick grilled over claims intel shows coronavirus originated in Chinese lab. Indiana man paints enormous US flag on field to honor coronavirus health workers. Coronavirus creates eerie scene on Capitol Hill with Senate back in session. Whistleblower complaint alleges virus warnings were ignored. Chicago medical examiner to probe deaths as far back as November for evidence of Covid-19.

Broncos' Kareem Jackson says 'it doesn't make sense to play any games' amid coronavirus pandemic. Coronavirus and heat waves pose new risks, experts say. Here's why some people are not wearing masks during the coronavirus crisis. Model forecasts 134,000 US deaths from Covid-19. Trump to phase out White House coronavirus task force. Coronavirus relief: USDA to buy $470 million in surplus food for donation. In change of plans, Trump now says coronavirus task force will continue 'indefinitely'. Portland changes World Naked Bike Ride event due to coronavirus, still encourages people to bike naked.

Uber to cut up 15% of staff as coronavirus takes toll. Cuomo: Most new virus patients in N.Y are at home, not working. Tyson will reopen its biggest pork plant after a Covid-19 outbreak. The people in power don't look like the people hit hardest by Covid-19. WATCH: Coronavirus daily update: May 06, 2020. In Muir interview, Trump walks back talk of vaccine by year's end. Maryland readies for 'stage one' of coronavirus reopening plan, Gov. Hogan says. Coronavirus job losses have hit people of color the hardest. UK's Boris Johnson to face reckoning over coronavirus response. Judge Andrew Napolitano: Coronavirus crisis -- Does America still have a Constitution? Precision public health may be the answer to COVID-19: Opinion.

More kids hospitalized with possible COVID-19 complication. Former CDC Director Frieden on potential increase in virus deaths, when the U.S. could restart the economy. Neiman Marcus declares bankruptcy after coronavirus hit. Trump's personal valet tests positive for Covid-19. Why are viruses hard to kill? Virologists explain why these tiny parasites are so tough to treat. **Dozens more children hospitalized in New York with rare symptoms that could be linked to coronavirus [5/6/20]**.

How will COVID-19 impact the 2020 elections? Amtrak To Require Masks Starting Monday To Avoid Spread Of Coronavirus. Coronavirus found in semen of male coronavirus patients, Chinese researchers say. Gilead may have a breakout coronavirus drug in remdesivir, but how do you market a pandemic treatment? Ted Cruz slams San Antonio plan declaring 'Chinese virus' to be hate speech: 'This is NUTS'. **Alabama cop appears to body-slam Walmart shopper for not wearing face mask: video [5/8/20]**. Analysis: It took 4 months for a virus to do this to the US. Putting A Price On COVID-19 Treatment Remdesivir.

The coronavirus jobs crisis is historically deep, but here's why economists say it won't be as bad as the downturn in the 1930s. Kim Jong Un praises China's handling of coronavirus. Trump participates in WWII memorial ceremony commemorating VE Day amid coronavirus. As FTC issues fresh warning, here are 5 COVID-19 scams to be aware of. Your Boss May Soon Track You At Work For Coronavirus Safety. President Trump confirmed that Katie Miller tested positive for the virus and noted she has been in contact with the Vice President. Coronavirus FAQs: Do Temperature Screenings Help? Can Mosquitoes Spread It?

The President hoped this would be the week he emerged into a nation recovering from pandemic. Instead the virus came to him. **Report says cellphone data suggests October shutdown at Wuhan lab, but experts are skeptical [5/8/20]**. Triple combination therapy shows promise for COVID-19 patients. Women Bear The Brunt Of Coronavirus Job Losses. Obama says White House response to coronavirus has been 'absolute chaotic disaster'. Canada to give essential workers a pay raise. Rep. Jeff Van Drew: Dems won't help Republicans hold China accountable on coronavirus because of politics. WWII Marine vet, 99, wins battle with coronavirus: 'I've gone through hell more than once and this came almost as close'. In Northern Virginia, A Grassroots Push To Help Latinos Combat Coronavirus. Dr. Scott Atlas on states reopening amid coronavirus pandemic: 'There should be no fear and panic anymore'. Top Health Officials Enter Self-Quarantine After Exposure To Coronavirus. **Global coronavirus infections top 4 million, US death toll passes 78,000 [5/10/20]**. McCarthy blasts Pelosi for keeping House out of session during pandemic: 'Our founders would be ashamed'. Analysis: Trump stokes fears about voter fraud as virus draws closer to him.

Rural Minnesota business owner calls on governor to fully reopen the state amid coronavirus outbreak. Key coronavirus model projects 137k deaths in U.S. by August. South Korea Records Spike In New Coronavirus Cases After Nightclub Outbreak. UK's road map for phased-in easing of lockdown envisions schools opening June 1st. On Mother's Day, world leaders try optimistic tone as coronavirus spreads. Pediatric doctor on front lines of coronavirus pandemic gets special Mother's Day surprise on air. Why it matters that the NIH canceled a coronavirus research grant.

Analysis: As virus draws closer to him, Trump turns to 2020 and stokes fears about voter fraud. 'A breaking point': Anti-lockdown efforts during Spanish flu offer a cautionary tale for coronavirus. Football in the fall? Fauci: 'The virus will make the decision for us'. Does warmer weather slow coronavirus? 'Cluster' of coronavirus cases in California linked to coughing birthday party attendee, officials say. Drug trio shortens duration and alleviates coronavirus symptoms, study says. Disney reopens its Shanghai theme park with masks and limits. Florida city closes beaches a week after reopening due to visitors defying coronavirus social distancing.

Video shows food executives removing masks ahead of Pence event. New COVID-19 infections in China, South Korea raise alarm over second wave. White House directs West Wing staffers to wear masks. NYC coronavirus death toll worse than official tally, CDC study says. Biden, DNC haul in more than $60 million in April despite coronavirus fundraising challenges. Concerts, tours could become virtual experiences following coronavirus pandemic, expert says. Schumer tells Fauci before Senate coronavirus testimony: 'Let it rip'. Bryan Adams goes on expletive-laced tirade about China and the coronavirus. CDC says NYC coronavirus death toll may be much higher. Grenell declassifies names of Obama officials who unmasked Flynn, report says. Inside the race to find a coronavirus vaccine: A look at human trials and revolutionary approaches. How high schoolers are reclaiming prom during coronavirus pandemic.

Fauci, other top health officials testify before Senate on reopening country amid coronavirus [5/10/20]. N.Y. doctor on coronavirus testing and what's needed to reopen U.S. economy. Man who wore KKK hood as mask won't be charged. MGM Resorts International reveals safety plan for reopening, asks guests to wear masks on casino floor. Graham introduces bill to sanction China if it refuses to cooperate on coronavirus investigation. Biden blasts McConnell claim about Obama pandemic prep as a 'Bunch of malarkey'. **Spanish woman, 113, beats coronavirus, got 'bored' in isolation, report says [5/12/20]**.

Tucker warns against deifying Fauci over virus response: 'He is not the one person that should be in charge'. NY Times says reporter 'went too far' during TV appearance blasting Trump admin's virus response. Analysis: Trump, right-wing media distract from bad virus news. Cotton calls CDC's botched testing rollout 'probably the worst mistake' of US coronavirus response. No NYC pedestrian deaths reported amid coronavirus lockdown. Powell warns of a possible sustained recession from pandemic. 4 cruise ship workers die of non-coronavirus causes within 2 weeks aboard liners stranded at sea. A pastor says coronavirus has killed 44 people in his parish. He warns the death toll reveals a troubling truth..

Twitter takes new steps to fight misleading misinformation on coronavirus [5/13/20]. Dr. Agus addresses concerns about U.S. reopening too soon amid coronavirus crisis. Democrats accuse Republicans of 'bad faith' as they invoke national debt to pause pandemic aid. **New Mexico man, 108, survives coronavirus a century after living through Spanish flu, report says [5/13/20]**. Laura Ingraham torches liberal 'frauds and tyrants' for actions during coronavirus shutdowns. Polar bears, snowstorms and isolation: Women endure Arctic Circle lockdown. Crowded flights leave passengers scared amid pandemic. EU: Possible virus drug approval 'before the summer'. De Blasio calls for NYC health commissioner to 'apologize' after rejecting NYPD coronavirus mask plea. Chris Wallace: Joe Biden's role in Flynn unmasking is 'fair game' for questions. Some countries are seeing a spike in known coronavirus deaths. Others are struggling to find a path to normalcy.

Trump vows to resupply national stockpile, saying 'cupboards were bare' amid coronavirus pandemic. New coronavirus case counts are going down in almost half of US states. But it's too soon to celebrate. Nursing home workers say they were told to wear coffee filters and garbage bags and that a flu shot would protect them from the coronavirus. TikTok cereal stunt on NYC subway amid pandemic is 'despicable,' transit authority says. MSNBC host fails to ask Biden about Flynn unmasking request after he denied any involvement in case. Analysis: Trump's betting his 2016 instincts will get him through the pandemic. It's grilling season: How to have a safe cookout and create new traditions in the time of coronavirus. While new cases are generally slowing down, experts say the virus will likely spread for at least 18 months. California biopharmaceutical company claims coronavirus antibody breakthrough. Biden botches unemployment, fatality figures related to coronavirus.

Germany, Europe's Largest Economy, Enters Recession Due To Coronavirus [5/15/20]. The President repeats his goal of developing a virus vaccine before the end of the year, a timeline experts call highly ambitious. New York bishop angry about this after 2 churches lose more than 100 people to coronavirus. The President unveiled a crash plan to develop a coronavirus vaccine by the end of the year. Experts say 12-18 months is more realistic. Coronavirus inspires Chinese dissident artist's new work in support of Hong Kong protests.

Wolf calls out China for trying to steal US coronavirus vaccine research: 'We need to stay on it'. With Historic Vote, House Will Allow Proxy Voting, Remote Hearings During Pandemic. House passes Democrats' $3T coronavirus 'HEROES' aid: Stimulus checks, money for states, rent assistance. Japanese spirit Amabie, a mythical mermaid monster, revived to ward off coronavirus. VA nurse whose special teddy bears soothed coronavirus patients to be recognized at NASCAR's 'The Real Heroes 400'. Where coronavirus cases are falling and rising the most in the US.

Deroy Murdock: Stark difference between Cuomo and DeSantis' handling of nursing homes during coronavirus pandemic. The former Prersident criticizes leadership on coronavirus response in a virtual commencement address to historically black colleges and universities. Obama to HBCU grads: Pandemic spotlights inequalities. 'She Wasn't Alone,' A Doctor Reflects On New York City's Coronavirus Peak. Snapshot: The Jersey Shore under lockdown. Gottlieb alarmed by "deeply concerning" coronavirus symptoms among some children. 'Pharma Bro' Martin Shkreli Denied Release From Prison To Research Coronavirus Cure. A person received a positive Covid-19 diagnosis the day after attending a Mother's Day service, officials say. Nigeria impounds British plane, claims it violated rules designed to stop spread of coronavirus. Canadian aerobatic jet crashes amid pandemic show; 1 dead. Medicaid Clinics And Doctors Have Been Last In Line For COVID-19 Relief Funding. EU calls for independent probe of WHO's pandemic response. **China says it will back probe into virus origin, but not yet [5/18/20]**.

NASCAR holds first race after delaying season over COVID-19. There are positive early results from coronavirus vaccine trial. Europe reopens widely; China gives $2 billion to virus fight. Dow soars on vaccine and bailout optimism. Charleston engineer teams up with boat builder to develop new safety device to protect coronavirus workers. Dave Rubin considering leaving California over coronavirus restrictions: 'I've built my career and family here'.

US surpasses 90,000 coronavirus deaths [5/18/20]. Trump reveals he's taking hydroxychloroquine; CDC criticized over early virus response. **Coronavirus vaccine showing**

promise in early human trials [5/18/20]. Trump takes hydroxychloroquine, but does it help against COVID-19? Coronavirus had infected hundreds in Michigan as Biden, Sanders campaigned there, report finds. Cultural chasm: Why the election hinges on financial victims of the virus. UK unemployment claims surge 69% as pandemic takes hold. Trump says he's taking hydroxychloroquine to prevent COVID-19, despite risks of unproven drug. Pelosi slams Trump for taking hydroxychloroquine, calls him 'morbidly obese'. Annie Glenn, wife of late U.S. Sen. John Glenn, dies of coronavirus. Larry Elder: Coronavirus lockdown casualties -- 'despair' may cause more damage than COVID-19.

Maryland Reports Largest Rise Yet In Coronavirus Cases, 4 Days After Reopening. Illinois governor's family firm owns stake in companies involved in coronavirus testing. Florida Ousts Top COVID-19 Data Scientist. What expert studying hydroxychloroquine told White House. Coronavirus survivor, 43, shares shocking photo showing 50-lb weight loss. The states were among the first to reopen. Now they face questions over their coronavirus cases reporting. Michigan flooding hits record levels, Whitmer says floods 'historic event' playing out in middle of coronavirus pandemic. Florida under scrutiny for Covid-19 data. Survey shows effect of virus on food scarcity, rent payments. **WHO reports most coronavirus cases in one day as total number nears 5 million [5/20/20]**. Ex-CDC director Tom Frieden: Coronavirus outbreak at Arkansas church shows 'what you do affects others'.

Jennifer Lopez's workout selfie with 'masked' man in background sent fans into frenzy -- explanation revealed. Coronavirus testing is 'a mess' in the US, report says. Cancer Treatment Centers of America CEO warns of 'shadow curve' of undiagnosed illnesses amid coronavirus. Illinois House votes to remove Republican rep from session for refusing to wear mask. LA company must stop marketing radish paste as coronavirus preventative, judge says. 'Enough is enough': Judge Napolitano reacts to calls for NYC lockdown to end. If Trump doesn't wear mask at Michigan auto plant, he'll be asked not to return, state official says.

North Dakota coronavirus survivor credits plasma donation for recovery. Macy's Sees A $1.1 Billion Loss, While Pandemic Lifts 'Essential' Stores Like Walmart. Tyson publicly reveals COVID-19 test results after plant-wide testing at North Carolina facility. Pandemic Makes Evident 'Grotesque' Gender Inequality In Household Work. At least 4 states combined numbers from two tests, possibly providing a misleading picture of coronavirus spread. Fox News Poll: Biden more trusted on coronavirus, Trump on economy. MSNBC's Nicolle Wallace: What right does Trump have to 'spread lies' about the pandemic on social media? Ukrainian tennis player shows how she stays in shape during coronavirus outbreak: Pushing cars. South Korea's Foreign Minister: 'Were not going back to life pre-COVID'. Coronavirus testing shortfall in crisis-affected areas risks undetected outbreaks.

Singles listing coronavirus antibody test results on dating apps. Nation adds more than 25,000 Covid-19 cases. Kelly Ripa reveals she's secretly been taping 'Live' from the Caribbean after coronavirus left her stranded. **Coronavirus 'does not spread easily' from surfaces, revised CDC website says [5/20/20]**. Analysis: Trump's reelection plan is unmasked in Michigan. Official COVID-19 Death Tally In Russia's Dagestan Masks 'Catastrophe,' Residents Say. **Trump says houses of worship will be deemed "essential services" [5/22/20]**. 77 Nobel Laureates Denounce Trump Officials For Pulling Coronavirus Research Grant.

Chapter 6

Preliminary Results From Two Leading Vaccine Trials Show Promise

April 29th, 2020 – July 7th, 2020

New York Knicks legend Patrick Ewing tests positive for coronavirus. New recording of John Prine's Angel From Montgomery released by Recording Academy for COVID-19 relief. Betty White, 98, says she's 'blessed with incredibly good health' amid the coronavirus pandemic. Racist incidents against Africans amid China's virus crackdown spark outcry. WHO calls South America new coronavirus epicenter. New York's one-day coronavirus death toll drops below 100. Drone footage reveals mass graves in new virus hot spot. The horrifying reality of Brazil's Covid-19 outbreak. **North Dakota governor makes emotional plea to avoid other states divide over face masks [5/23/20]**. NC veterans make video for those who can't receive military funeral honor guard during coronavirus. Former U.K. Prime Minister Tony Blair questions Trump's coronavirus strategy.

Dr. Birx: 'Critically important' that people wear masks as states reopen amid higher than expected death tolls. Second Missouri stylist who worked with coronavirus symptoms tests positive; 147 clients, co-workers exposed. Fine dining chefs stick a fork in fancy to stay afloat amid pandemic. Opinion: The coronavirus has made me anxious. Just not in the way I thought. Hundreds flock to Florida beach amid pandemic. WWII veteran beats COVID-19, honored on 100th birthday. Too Little

Or Too Much Time With The Kids? Grandparenting Is Tough In A Pandemic.

White House bans most travel from Brazil to U.S. as coronavirus cases surge. Steve Hilton: There won't be a coronavirus recovery unless we reopen schools now. **N.Y. public workers killed by virus to get line-of-duty death benefits [5/25/20]**. Right now, we are 'right in the middle of the first wave, globally,' and still in a phase where Covid-19 is actually on the way up, health officials say. Several grads test positive for coronavirus after prep school's drive-thru ceremony. Pandemic takes toll on Trump properties while President golfs at one. Photos show plenty of people flocked to beaches, but not a lot of social distancing or masks.

'Maskne': Suffering from acne or breakouts under your mask Here's what to do. VIDEO: Virus Hunters Seek To Solve The Mystery Of Coronavirus Origins. Coronavirus outbreaks at meat processing plants force North Carolina farmers to euthanize 1.5 million chickens. Video shows mob berating woman without coronavirus mask at Staten Island supermarket. Trump-Biden sparring escalates for a summer shadowed by the coronavirus. ER Visit For A COVID-Like Cough Stuck Man With A $3,278 Bill. Coronavirus fatalities in Italy largely among elderly, underlying conditions. Rep. Tlaib blames hospitals' pandemic struggles on 'broken health care system'. ER Visit For COVID-19 Symptoms Stuck Man With A $3,278 Bill.

House Republicans plan to sue Pelosi in bid to stop proxy voting amid coronavirus concerns. Answering Your Coronavirus Questions: Global Health, Small Businesses, Silver Linings. **Nobel Prize winner: Coronavirus lockdowns cost lives instead of saving them [5/27/20]**. Coronavirus vaccine developed in China shows promise after early study in 100 people. Majority of US small businesses optimistic in face of coronavirus pandemic, study says. France's virus tracing app ready to go, parliament to vote. **France bans all use of drug**

touted by Trump [hydroxychloroquine] in COVID-19 patients [5/27/20]. Military sees third coronavirus-related death after Army reservist in Wisconsin dies: Pentagon. Coronavirus government response: Cuomo wears mask as he arrives to meet Trump.

Asymptomatic COVID-19 cases may be more common than suspected [5/27/20]. Understanding the massive scale of coronavirus in the US. My dad died from coronavirus. I'm not just grieving -- I'm angry. 6 feet likely not far enough to stop COVID-19 transmission: experts. COVID-19 Has Killed Close To 300 U.S. Health Care Workers, New Data From CDC Shows. Amazon Is Offering To Keep 125,000 Workers It Hired For The Pandemic. Barr taps top prosecutor to probe "unmasking" by Obama officials. Why the coronavirus crash is hurting women more than men. To Lure Back Tourists, Cyprus Says It Will Cover Costs If They Contract Coronavirus. Boston Marathon Canceled, Will Be A Virtual Event Because Of Coronavirus. Veteran who died reveals pandemic's effect on mental health. How Americans can help stop another 100,000 Covid-19 deaths. As US deaths top 100,000, Trump's coronavirus task force is curtailed.

New Zealand Now Has Just 1 Active COVID-19 Case. Possible coronavirus-linked MIS-C inflammatory condition reported in children at Texas pediatric hospitals. How offices, trains and hotels may change post-lockdown. Coronavirus FAQs: Is It Safer To Fly Or Drive? Is Air Conditioning A Threat? Key West high school follows coronavirus social distancing measures with Jet Ski graduation. Should I Get Tested For Coronavirus Just For The Heck Of It? Pandemic: Life on L.A.'s Skid Row. NHL plans to test players for COVID-19 daily if games resume. Wuhan tested millions of people for COVID-19 in just days: Could US cities do the same? Gilead says drug helped moderately ill coronavirus patients.

George Floyd protests could spread coronavirus, New York Gov. Andrew Cuomo warns. Some scientists fear 'superspreaders may prompt new COVID-19 outbreaks as states reopen. Nearly 26,000 Nursing Home Residents Have Died From COVID-19, Federal Data Show. 'Mission Impossible 7' set to begin production again in September after shutting down due to COVID-19. N.C. Governor: 'Very Unlikely' RNC Can Proceed Without Social Distancing, Masks. Trump says GOP forced to find new state to host convention as North Carolina stands by coronavirus measures. **Fauci says U.S. could have "couple of hundred million" vaccine doses by new year [6/3/20]**.

No Evidence Hydroxychloroquine Is Helpful In Preventing COVID-19, Study Finds. NIH Director Hopes For At Least 1 Safe And Effective Vaccine By Year's End. Travel technology company develops social distance middle seat designs for plane travel during pandemic. In UK, man caught driving over 130 mph to get his first McDonald's burger since lockdown.

First came a pandemic. Then, looting. Small businesses pick up the pieces as their debt mounts. Unemployment rate falls to 13.3 percent as economy gains surprise 2.5 million jobs despite coronavirus. Here's a luxury hotel during coronavirus. Key Republicans say May jobs report suggests new coronavirus spending unnecessary. Trump touts racial equality while referring to COVID-19 as 'China plague'. Martha MacCallum: Jobs report is 'vindication' for coronavirus 'lockdown rebellion'. Thousands defy coronavirus bans to take a knee at George Floyd protests around the world. 'We know what we have to lose now': Pandemic, protests has Michigan tilting Biden's way. **Worldwide coronavirus death toll reaches 400,000 [6/7/20]**.

'We know what we have to lose now': Pandemic, protests have Michigan tilting Biden's way. Coronavirus cases on the rise in California, several other states: report. Kansas resident tests positive for COVID-19, attended protest without mask, health officials say. BP to cut 10,000 jobs worldwide amid virus pandemic. Cuomo urges protesters to get COVID-19 tests as NYC reopening. China demands proof from Rick Scott on coronavirus accusations. Florida lawyer who dressed as coronavirus 'Grim Reaper' seen at crowded George Floyd protests.

Anger, activism grow over police abuse amid French lockdown. Spike in coronavirus cases in Napa County, Calif. linked to Memorial Day gatherings. Brazil Must Be Open With Its Coronavirus Data, Supreme Court Justice Rules. Groceries were already hard to find for millions. Covid-19 is making it worse. Judge Blocks Deportation Of Honduran Teenager Due To Pandemic. Patti LuPone says 'this country is doomed' amid coronavirus crisis, reveals plans if Trump wins second term. **Fauci says asymptomatic coronavirus transmission is possible following WHO confusion [6/10/20].** Coronavirus travel restrictions have upended the cocaine trade, report says. United Airlines Adds A Step To Check-In: Stating You Don't Have COVID-19 Symptoms. Hispanics at disproportionate risk from Covid-19, experts say. Amid COVID-19, Moscow recorded almost 60% more deaths in May than usual.

Moderna's enormous coronavirus vaccine Phase III trial will start next month [6/11/20]. New data suggest Russia may have a lot more COVID deaths than it says. Stocks Tumble As Coronavirus Cases Spike In The Sunbelt. Dr. Saphier predicts impact of protests on coronavirus spread will be known in 'next two weeks'. Rev. Dr. William Barber on Trump photo-op, impact of pandemic on voting rights. Florida, South Carolina coronavirus figures are the states' highest yet for a single day. Stocks Rebound After Dramatic Plunge Spurred By A Spike In Coronavirus Cases. L.A. County's homeless population rose nearly 13% before pandemic. CDC posts tips for minimizing everyday coronavirus risk. Coronavirus FAQs: Convertibles, Dishwashing, Dog's Paws, Bowling, Travel With Kids.

Mutation could make coronavirus more infectious, study suggests [6/13/20]. Coronavirus cases are rising in many states, but the infectious disease expert says to watch how many people are hospitalized. Margo Price on husband's coronavirus recovery, life under lockdown. Cuomo warns New Yorkers to stay 'smart on coronavirus, before warning revelers: Dont make me come down there? Newt Gingrich: Testing wont help fight coronavirus unless we do this. Cuomo threatens to shut down Manhattan, Hamptons again if coronavirus social-distancing rules broken.

Health Experts Link Rise In Arizona Coronavirus Cases To End Of Stay-At-Home Order. Ohio State requiring returning players to sign COVID-19 waivers. Stocks down as coronavirus outbreaks flare in U.S., China. Supreme Court refuses to hear cases on 'qualified immunity' for police. Charles Barkley: 'Catastrophic mistake' if NBA cancels rest of season over coronavirus. Ex-eBay employees charged with mailing spiders, cockroaches and pig mask to critics. The Great Pandemic Bake-Off May Be Over. The Cost Of Thailand's Coronavirus Success: Despair... And Suicide. **First drug [dexamethasone] proves able to improve survival from COVID-19 [6/16/20]**. Early Results Show Benefit Of Steroid For Very Sick COVID-19 Patients. Travelers mark New Zealand's first new COVID cases in 24 days. Navy Calls 1,629 Reservists To Shipyards Left Shorthanded By COVID-19 Pandemic.

Improving ventilation in buildings could help reduce spread of virus. Senate Judiciary Committee held hearing on police use of force, qualified immunity. Friends had a night out in Florida. Now, they all have Covid-19. 'Pandemic pricing' is here. Rents are dropping across US. Every GOP senator who attended a news conference today wore a mask. Whitmer to extend Michigan's state of emergency amid coronavirus. Amid Confusion About Reopening, An Expert Explains How To Assess

COVID-19 Risk. Trump tells 'Hannity' coronavirus is 'fading away' ahead of controversial Tulsa rally.

Coronavirus' return to Beijing disrupts life and rattles nerves. Roche's Acetmra arthritis drug falls short in coronavirus trial. COVID-19 spreading among young people, Alabama hot spots and more to know. 16 friends had a night out in Florida. Now they have Covid-19. 'So You Think You Can Dance' upcoming season not 'moving forward' due to coronavirus pandemic. **Fauci: Americans ignoring science during pandemic is "frustrating" [6/19/20]**. Dont expect a cure-all COVID-19 vaccine, scientists say. Babies with COVID-19 tend to have mild illness, study finds. Half Of States Where Pentagon Lifts Travel Ban Have Rising Coronavirus Infections. Rise in coronavirus cases in L.A. puts Latinos at even greater risk, doctors say.

Patriots allow at-risk season ticket holders to pass on 2020 without losing seats next year amid pandemic fears. Trump holds first campaign rally since coronavirus pandemic began. Actor-comedian D.L. Hughley tests positive for coronavirus after collapsing onstage. The Latest Pandemic Shortage: Coins Are The New Toilet Paper. In his return to the campaign trail, the President said he told officials to slow down coronavirus testing and used a racist term to describe Covid-19. More than 7,000 Brazilians died of coronavirus in one week. The President is mocking measures that may mitigate infections, which is counterproductive as fewer Covid-19 cases would likely promote a fast economic recovery. Top Trump fundraiser sought to cash in on valuable 3M masks. Some states see an increase in young people getting coronavirus.

Ousted US attorney refused to sign Justice Department letter criticizing New York's Covid restrictions. 2 more Trump campaign members in Tulsa test positive for coronavirus. Meghan Markle, Prince Harry send charity a thank-you letter for distributing meals amid coronavirus pandemic. Wall Street

Journal Editorial Board: Dems pushing strict lockdowns run most states with highest jobless rates. Kelley Parker: After coronavirus lockdown -- This mom wants leaders to step up with a plan keep us safe, open. A surge in cases shows the coronavirus won't go away soon. Eye Opener: Texas governor urges people to wear masks. Tennis Star Novak Djokovic Tests Positive For Coronavirus. The European Union is considering the recommendation due to the surge of coronavirus cases in the US, according to two EU diplomats. Massive Saharan dust cloud makes its way to Southern states still battling coronavirus.

Baseball Is Coming Back For A Pandemic-Shortened 2020 Season. Coronavirus hospitalizations surge in Arizona, Texas. Analysis: Trump is using the pandemic as a racist punchline. NYC Could See 22,000 Public Employee Lay-offs Because Of COVID-19. Texas' governor is urging people to stay home as states report surges of new Covid-19 cases. Cowboys Ezekiel Elliott gives coronavirus health update, issues warning about season. Johnny Damon on MLB's coronavirus-impacted 60-game season: 'I just hope everything stays on track'. Record-breaking spike in new COVID-19 cases causes several states to consider pausing reopenings.

First volunteer receives experimental COVID-19 vaccine developed by Imperial College in UK trial. Texas Governor Hits 'Pause' On Further Reopening, Amid COVID-19 Surge. Airlines losing billions of dollars as coronavirus curtails travel. **Doctor says states should consider going into lockdown again as COVID cases rise [6/25/20]**. DeVos issues rule steering more virus aid to private schools. GOP Sens. Cornyn and Cruz say they don't understand why federal funds are being pulled from coronavirus testing sites. The 37,077 new coronavirus diagnoses on Thursday passes the previous record set on April 24. Release of 'Tenet' pushed back again as coronavirus numbers grow.

White House virus task force to hold first public meeting in nearly two months. Virus testing, tracking still plagued by reporting delays. **Mandatory masks? Biden says as president he would require wearing face coverings in public [6/26/20].** Florida reports nearly 9,000 more coronavirus cases. Pence to hold coronavirus task force briefing. Wallets Are Already On Lockdown: People Pare Spending As Sunbelt Cases Surge. Texas city balks at county's coronavirus mandates, says it won't enforce it. Liz Cheney posts photo of former VP in face mask and says 'real men wear masks'.

Christopher Nolan's 'Tenet' delays release again amid reported coronavirus spikes. Coronavirus threatens war-torn Yemen amid humanitarian catastrophe. The President, concerned how it would look if he got sick, insists on stronger protections even as he seeks to move past the pandemic. Essential Vocab For COVID-19: From Asymptomatic To Zoonotic. Measures to protect Trump from coronavirus scale up even as he seeks to move on. Some 85 people contracted Covid-19 after visiting a restaurant, Michigan health official says. Pence postpones Florida, Arizona campaign events amid increase in coronavirus cases there. 12 states pause reopening as coronavirus cases surge in US.

Global coronavirus cases surpass 10 million [6/28/20]. The race for a coronavirus vaccine. Gottlieb expects COVID deaths to rise again amid "major epidemics" across the South. **Coronavirus death toll surpasses 500,000 worldwide [6/28/20].** CBS News poll: Majority of Americans say coronavirus fight going badly. Voting During the Pandemic, The Wild West of Testing, Probiotics. Dr. Nicole Saphier: Correct coronavirus mistakes -- as first wave continues, we can learn from these lessons. Gilead prices coronavirus drug at $2,340 for rich countries. Britain's COVID-19 app: The game changer that wasn't. Dr. Oz: 'Draconian' lockdowns will return if Americans are not 'meticulous' about social distancing.

More than 200 people are advised to quarantine after possible Covid-19 exposure at gym in West Virginia. McConnell makes appeal for wearing masks: It is about protecting everyone we encounter? New York Announces Lowest Number Of Hospitalizations During The Pandemic. At least 143 people at the University of Georgia test positive for Covid-19. Experts say spread of coronavirus in the US is now hard to control. Twins coaches to have new roles in pandemic-shortened 2020 season, team says.

Toronto mayor wants masks mandatory, citing U.S. problems. Dr. Peter Hotez: Case numbers don't look good in Texas, need new strategies against COVID-19. New York restaurant opens for the first time as state loosens lockdown restrictions. Biden says he won't hold rallies due to coronavirus. Stocks notch best quarter since 1998 despite virus surge. Southern hospitals inundated by surge of COVID-19 cases. Green, Yellow, Orange or Red This New Tool Shows COVID-19 Risk In Your County. Doctor on the importance of face coverings as coronavirus cases surge.

Trump's allies desert him over masks. California and Florida chart different coronavirus paths. Almost 40% of Asian and Black Americans say they're facing more discrimination during the pandemic. Americans are exhausted from poor sleep during the lockdown. Nationwide surge in coronavirus cases prompts states to reimpose restrictions. A healthy 30-year-old man went out for an evening to catch up with friends. A week later, he was in the hospital thanks to Covid-19.

Drive-Through Naturalizations Make New U.S. Citizens In The COVID-19 Era. COVID-19 Exploits Cracks In Chilean Society. Paul McCartney, other stars urge U.K. government to support the live music industry impacted by COVID-19. US hits another bleak coronavirus milestone. Herman Cain is receiving treatment for coronavirus. Some young people are running disturbing Covid-19 competitions.

Biden blasts Trump over coronavirus response. COVID-19 spike in Ohio due to people not wearing masks, expert says. Chicago issues emergency coronavirus travel order on people from these states. Pence's Arizona trip was delayed by Secret Service agents getting COVID-19. Coronavirus infections going up in 36 states. Opinion: Seven reasons to wear a mask this July 4 weekend. Opinion: One surefire way to stop Covid-19. Business As Usual During The Pandemic, This Time Through Plexiglass. As Americans prepare for July 4, Covid-19 patients are rapidly filling hospitals across the South and West. Kimberly Guilfoyle -- Donald Trump Jr.'s girlfriend and top Trump campaign official -- tests positive for coronavirus. Kimberly Guilfoyle, Trump campaign official and girlfriend of president's son, tests positive for coronavirus. "Unnecessary situation": Surging virus cases frustrate experts. Trump steps back, done with being 'daily voice' of coronavirus response. Americans adjust to muted July 4 celebrations amid coronavirus pandemic.

Penn State is tracking those in contact with a 21-year-old student who died of Covid-19 complications. MLB vets David Price, Felix Hernandez opt out of 2020 season over coronavirus fears. Dr. Mark Goldfelder: Coronavirus nursing home crisis -- 6 things we must do now to protect seniors. Coronavirus forces California winery owner, Maine resort general manager to navigate new travel restrictions. Arizona gym CEO details fight to stay open during coronavirus pandemic. **Coronavirus can linger in air, and experts say WHO and CDC should tell people that [7/5/20]**. The question now is if Republican Party members will continue to be silent as Trump peddles fiction about a deadly virus, and if so, will they pay a price in November. After COVID-19, China moves to kick its exotic meat habit. Covid-19 antibody drug moves into phase 3 trials. Local Matters: Boston faces pandemic-induced eviction crisis. Trump is "enabling the virus," Cuomo says.

Chapter 7

Herd Immunity May Not Be Achievable in Fight Against Coronavirus

July 7ᵗʰ, 2020 – September 5ᵗʰ, 2020

Florida Department of Education orders all its schools to reopen campuses in August after coronavirus closures. Melbourne Resumes Lockdown As COVID-19 Cases Surge. "The Rules of Contagion" and how coronavirus and other outbreaks spread. Brazil's president tests positive for COVID-19. England pubs forced to close days after reopening after customer tests positive for coronavirus. How blood type may affect your coronavirus risk. Texas Sets State Record With More Than 10,000 New Coronavirus Cases Reported Tuesday.

States Sue Education Department Over Allocation Of Pandemic Funds To Schools. It's not just you. The pandemic could actually be making PMS worse. Tourist rescued after being stranded in airport for more than 100 days due to coronavirus travel restrictions. NASCAR's Jimmie Johnson cleared to race after 2 negative COVID-19 tests. Texas struggles with COVID-19 testing demands. Birx touted the importance of masks and says to avoid gatherings in places seeing a Covid-19 spike. International Golf Events Ryder Cup And Presidents Cup Postponed Due To The Pandemic. 2020 Daily Trail Markers: GOP convention city's COVID count rises. Mississippi: 26 legislators have tested positive for Covid-19. Texas Lt. Gov. Patrick calls teachers 'essential workers' who need to be back in the classroom this fall. What experts say Americans must do to prevent Covid-19 from spinning out of control. **California**

security guard charged with murder after shooting customer who didn't wear a mask [7/9/20]. Some People Agree To Disagree Over What's Safe During The Pandemic. Fetal coronavirus infection may be possible, Italian study suggests.

A surge in Covid-19 cases has experts urging states to pause reopening plans. Here's how things went off track. Coronavirus has infected nearly every patient in this California town's hospital, and more keep coming. Workers are exhausted, but the virus is not. Coronavirus has infected almost every patient as this hospital. And medics are overwhelmed. Atlanta Mayor Keisha Lance Bottoms on testing positive for COVID-19 and requiring masks in public. Over the past 13 days, Miami-Dade County has seen a staggering increase in Covid-19 hospitalizations, the use of ICU beds and the use of ventilatiors. 'Pleading' from aides led to Trump agreeing to wear mask. California Will Release Up To 8,000 Prisoners Due To Coronavirus. **World Health Organization acknowledges coronavirus can be airborne [7/10/20]**. Mexico exhuming bodies to make room for recently deceased, as coronavirus cases surge. Trump 2020 spokesman says Roger Stone commutation done to correct the 'partisanship of the past'. Inside the detective-style hunt for missed COVID-19 cases. Parts of U.S. scramble to shut down as country breaks another virus record.

Trump's decision to spare Roger Stone from prison shows the President is focusing on his political fortunes rather than the pandemic. 'Few dozen' US Marines get coronavirus on Japan's Okinawa, official says. Trump wears a mask during visit to wounded service members at Walter Reed. Dr. Dark on Texas' coronavirus spike: More people have died there 'than those who died during the 9/11 attacks'. Love in the time of coronavirus: Strict guidelines reshape U.K. weddings. A family lost their father to COVID-19. The obituary blamed the 'carelessness of politicians.'. White House seeks to discredit Fauci amid coronavirus surge. An inside look at a Texas hospital overwhelmed by coronavirus patients. Hundreds of people gathered at a lake. Now some have Covid-19. Coronavirus cases linked to Michigan sandbar, Fourth of July party. Japanese officials "shocked" by COVID outbreak at U.S. military bases.

Can Congress investigate Trump's commutation of Roger Stone's sentence? Boris Johnson says Britons 'should be wearing face masks in shops amid coronavirus. Washington Post's Jennifer Rubin mocked for calling New York government's COVID response 'competent'. Guy Fieri's restaurant closed 3 days after opening due to COVID scare: report. Private firms that run ICE detention centers promise Congress they'll work to stop COVID-19 spread. Empire State Building sets reopening date, updates safety protocols amid pandemic. Latin America and the Caribbean have reported more coronavirus deaths than North America. What Happens When A Pandemic And An Epidemic Collide. Some shoe and clothing boutiques devastated by COVID. Texas voters go to the polls for runoffs amid coronavirus spikes.

Almost half the country's states have set new daily COVID-19 records this month. The Senate Majority Leader is breaking from the President to deliver a dire analysis about the US battle with the coronavirus. Coronavirus is spreading faster than ever in the U.S. Here are the states breaking records. Covid-19 is a 'pandemic of historic proportions,' expert says, as cases climb in the South and Southwest. Inside the Trump administration's sidelining of experts in the coronavirus pandemic. See what Trump supporters are saying as pandemic worsens. Oklahoma's governor says he has tested positive for COVID-19. Doctor weighs in on Trump administration stripping CDC of control of COVID-19 data.

As Coronavirus Cases Surge In Florida, Can Schools Safely Reopen? 'Bracing for more deaths': COVID-19 spike hits Texas nursing homes. Homeward Bound: Pets' Incredible COVID-19 Journeys To Reunite With Owners. Rush Limbaugh slams

Florida labs that failed to report negative COVID tests: 'Incompetence ... or corruption'. New Mexico records its second-largest single-day Covid-19 case increase. China becomes first economy to grow since virus pandemic. DNC targets Trump's coronavirus response in new drive to court seniors. Georgia governor suspends all local mask mandates, encourages but doesn't requires masks for residents.

U.S., U.K. and Canada say Russian hackers are targeting COVID vaccine research. Laundry's worst cycle: COVID impact on dry cleaners and tailors. **3 churches sue Newsom after California bans singing in places of worship because of coronavirus [7/16/20]**. 'Meaningless' FDA Certificates Are Used To Tout Dubious Face Masks. LA County sees record number of daily new coronavirus cases. Meeting abruptly ends after turning into anti-mask protest. Californians on edge over renewed shutdown over coronavirus fears. Brazil's coronavirus curve may hold the key to a global vaccine. Drive-in concerts provide live music experience during coronavirus pandemic.

Florida coronavirus patient went from diagnosis to dying in her daughter's arms in a matter of days. India Surpasses 1 Million Confirmed Coronavirus Cases. CNN's Harlow clashes with Trump adviser in heated interview on coronavirus response. Bob Marley anthem "reimagined" to help kids impacted by pandemic. Texas ER doctor says some hospitals 'running out of tests' as state grapples with coronavirus surge. A 'viral stun gun': How monoclonal antibodies can help fight COVID-19. Trump says 'I don't agree' with CDC director's mask message. **MAP: Breaking down which states require -- or don't require -- face masks in public [7/18/20]**. Experts say this 'bridge to a vaccine' may be a reason for optimism. Here's how it works. No end in sight, Congress confronts new virus crisis rescue.

Anthony Fauci praises New York's coronavirus response: 'They did it correctly'. 'He's unteachable': Doctor blasts Trump's latest mask remarks. Rep. McCarthy identifies key issues to address in next coronavirus relief bill. Analysis: Donald Trump is sealing his fate as the coronavirus denier-in-chief. **How top health officials changed their minds about face masks [7/19/20]**. Jack Nicklaus and wife had coronavirus. Coronavirus test result delays hobble pandemic response nationwide. Oxford vaccine is safe and induces early immune reaction, early results suggest. FDA commissioner 'cautiously optimistic' about coronavirus vaccine after trial showed 'robust' immune response. China uses Muslim Uighur forced labor to mass produce coronavirus PPE exported globally: report.

Oxford's Covid-19 vaccine appears safe and induces immune response, early results suggest, but more research is needed. White House roundup: Coronavirus response, John Lewis, niece's tell-all book. Trump official says latest coronavirus surge is 'very clear'. **More than 600,000 people worldwide have died from Covid-19 [7/20/20]**. Analysis: Trump's pandemic reversals betray election anxiety. Changing course in a pandemic: How one man, afraid to leave his front porch, turned a panicked moment into a movement. US needs to lower Covid-19 transmission rate to reopen schools, surgeon general says. Jacksonville sheriff warns Republican Convention amid coronavirus could put community at risk.

2 judges in lawsuit over Atlanta mask rule recuse themselves. Biden proposes investment in caregiving community amid pandemic. 1 in 3 NYC small businesses won't survive pandemic. Texas coronavirus deaths rising as hospitals reach ICU capacity. Fact check: At his first coronavirus briefing since April, Trump repeats a handful of classic false claims. How politics could impact a coronavirus vaccine. Hours before the daily US Covid-19 death toll topped 1,000 for the first time in two weeks, Trump warned the crisis may get worse before it got better. Top epidemiologist on continuing challenges of COVID-19. In change of tone, President Trump says pandemic will likely

get worse before it gets better. White House cherry-picking data on US Covid-19 death toll.

United Airlines' mask mandate expands to areas in airports. US government and Pfizer reach $1.95 billion deal to produce millions of Covid-19 vaccine doses. In change of tone, Trump says pandemic will likely get worse before it gets better. California surpasses New York in confirmed coronavirus cases. MSNBC's Chuck Todd blasted by left for saying Trump 'has turned a corner' on masks. 13 nuns at Michigan convent die of COVID-19. US deaths during coronavirus outbreak period were 179K higher than usual: report.

Fauci: 'I don't see us eradicating' virus. McConnell set to unveil new virus aid, despite GOP revolt. Nine-year-old girl is the youngest to die from coronavirus in Florida, health officials say. Watchdog finds flawed virus response at California prison. Delta has banned 120 passengers for refusing to wear masks. On opening day, amid pandemic, Fauci throws 1st pitch for Washington Nationals. Covid-19 "will end up as a Top 10 leading cause of death" in 2020, CDC statisticians tell CNN. Trump cancels Florida portion of RNC as coronavirus cases surge: 'Not the right time'. Trump cancels Jacksonville convention over COVID-19 fears, but still urges schools to reopen. Mounting virus cases spark concern in Florida nursing homes.

Breastfeeding and coronavirus: Mothers with COVID-19 unlikely to pass virus if they use proper hygiene. Thousands of families evicted in Sao Paulo amid pandemic. Coronavirus FAQ: What Does It Mean If I Can Blow Out A Candle While Wearing A Mask? After downplaying the health crisis, the President this week has tried to show Americans he's taking the pandemic seriously. A survey's findings on coronavirus symptoms and Dr. Fauci's comments on a vaccine come as global case numbers set a new high. Isabelle Papadimitriou: Daughter invites governor to funeral after mom's Covid-19 death. Of all the coronavirus decisions the President has made, his back-to-school reopening gamble may be his riskiest. Jobless Americans are anxiously watching as Congress debates the next coronavirus relief bill. Chicago nurse attacked by man on train who ranted about coronavirus, dramatic video shows. North Korea Reports 1st Suspected Case Of Coronavirus.

The US topped 1,000 deaths for 4 days in a row last week and models project that there will be up to 175,000 deaths linked to the virus by August 15. How Covid-19 numbers are looking across the country. Courteney Cox says she hasn't seen boyfriend Johnny McDaid in person in 133 days: 'Covid sucks'. Some police in Arkansas refuse to enforce coronavirus mask orders because they lack the manpower. North Korea's Kim marks war anniversary amid virus concerns. Is new COVID-19 stimulus relief on the way?

Child hospitalizations from Covid-19 surge 23% in Florida. MLB postpones two games as Marlins members test positive for COVID-19. Vietnam Confirms 11 New Coronavirus Cases, Imposes Quarantines And Evacuations. Competing claims over bill to address looming Social Security, Medicare insolvency in GOP coronavirus package. Oregon officer in quarantine after drunk man with coronavirus spits on him in McDonald's drive-thru. Following weeks of sharp increases, new coronavirus cases are flattening or decreasing in hotbeds like Arizona, Texas and Florida.

Girls, Has The Pandemic Made You Think Of Quitting School? Call Your Mentor. Opinion: Covid-19 relief bills show that Trump is a failure at negotiating. Trump's national security adviser tests positive for COVID-19. 49ers' Richard Sherman predicts NFL will forge ahead if team has Marlins-like coronavirus outbreak. Doctor who 'selflessly' cared for 'sickest patients' dies of coronavirus. North Korean who caused coronavirus scare was fleeing sexual assault investigation, report says.

MLB postpones Miami Marlins games over virus outbreak. **Heart damage lingers in COVID-19 patients, even after recovery [7/28/20]**. Trump under fire for promoting false COVID-19 claims on Twitter. Portland business owner on impact of riots, coronavirus: It's terrifying? Tucker Carlson: Big Tech censors COVID-19 video featuring doctors. Rome Opera has COVID-19 friendly opening night at ancient chariot racing site. Jim Jordan explodes at Big Tech hearing, drags Jamie Raskin's wife for unmasking Flynn. Trump push on short-term coronavirus aid draws frosty GOP reception. **FDA could issue emergency use authorization for coronavirus vaccine in a matter of weeks [7/29/20]**. Fauci suggests goggles, eye shield for better protection against coronavirus.

Schools weigh reopening as U.S. COVID-19 deaths top 150,000. Big Tech companies report mixed earnings amid pandemic. Negotiations stalled on next coronavirus relief package as unemployment benefits expire Friday. CDC's Redfield should sound alarm about suicides amid coronavirus outbreak, critic says. 'Living hell': Mismanagement blamed for coronavirus cases, deaths at San Quentin prison. Fauci testifies on coronavirus response as cases in US rise. Florida sets new record for Covid-19 deaths for 4th straight day. **Doctor: Flu may be "nonexistent this fall" due to COVID measures [7/31/20]**.

No deal: Hill coronavirus relief talks falter as benefits expire. Miami-Dade mayor tells residents to prepare for Hurricane Isaias, closes coronavirus testing sites. In Rural Missouri, Latinx Communities Learn To Contain And Cope With The Coronavirus. Cardinals, Brewers game postponed again after several new COVID-19 cases, threatening fragile MLB season: report. Congressman tests positive for Covid-19 and slams Republicans who won't wear masks. South Africa coronavirus cases surge past 500,000.

New CDC forecast projects 20,000 Covid-19 deaths in 21 days. The White House coronavirus task force coordinator says the deadly virus is now more widespread than when it first took hold in the US earlier this year. Depression and anxiety are spiking in America because of COVID. Here's what to do. Why do some people get very sick and even die from Covid-19, while similar people show no symptoms? Dr. Sanjay Gupta explains. Pandemic ushers in a 'new normal' for historically underfunded HBCUs. No one is immune to coronavirus, expert says, with infections rising in both rural and urban communities. Alabama Budget On Stronger Footing Than Other States During COVID-19. Virus outbreak hits cruise ship that stopped at dozens of ports. Maryland Gov. Hogan at odds with state officials over mandate to keep private schools closed amid coronavirus.

White House mandates randomized coronavirus testing for staff. The political landscape has tilted in Joe Biden's favor as the President struggles to manage the coronavirus outbreak and the financial crisis that followed. Behind the Trump administration's mixed messaging on coronavirus. Fact check: Another Trump briefing, more Trump falsehoods on coronavirus and mail-in voting. Norway cruise ship passengers with coronavirus reach 43. Pub in Spain bans popular sing-along song amid coronavirus fears: 'There will be no... touching hands'. While people may be tired of the pandemic, some states have gotten it right by not letting up on restrictions. Coronavirus contact tracing in the U.S. is falling behind. Trump holds news conference as COVID threatens school openings. After 'Severe' Delays, 6 States Band Together To Buy Coronavirus Tests. Alex Berenson proclaims COVID-19 spike in Sun Belt is likely 'behind us,' more evidence against lockdowns. De Blasio announces NYC coronavirus checkpoints to make sure people adhering to quarantine rules. Source: Trump still not grasping the severity of the pandemic. **Why Fauci thinks the US doesn't have to lockdown [8/5/20]**.

Moderna's virus vaccine costs far more than rival treatments. Facebook, Twitter remove Trump video over false COVID-19 claims. For Colorado 4-H Kids The Livestock Show Goes On Despite The Pandemic. 'Endless hurdles': How entrepreneurs are trying to weather the coronavirus pandemic. Cruise company's first trip forced to return to port in Alaska days after launching due to COVID-19 case. NASCAR driver Spencer Davis tests positive for COVID-19. Michelle Obama Says She's Dealing With 'Low-Grade Depression' During Lockdown. Black teen forced to take off Black Lives Matter mask at high school graduation ceremony. How Arizona is turning things around on Covid-19. Coronavirus: 7-year-old youngest to die in Georgia, health officials say.

Swiss ink deal with Moderna for 4.5M doses of COVID vaccine. No deal: Democrats and White House negotiators clash over coronavirus relief bill. India's Coronavirus Cases Top 2 Million -- More Than 62,000 Reported In One Day. Dad who got coronavirus after son went out is released from hospital. Delta CEO: 'Well over 100 people' banned from flying after refusing to wear masks. Bestselling author Lionel Shriver calls coronavirus 'oversold': 'I'd like to sign on with COVID's agent'. Ohio Gov. DeWine tells 'Your World' positive coronavirus test 'certainly scared me'.

My patients ignoring COVID-19 guidelines is bad. Their reasons why are worse. Inside the US federal prison hit hardest by Covid-19. **Free speech experts call on public schools to not penalize students for sharing images of maskless classmates [8/8/20]**. Susan Rice dismisses Republican harping on Benghazi amid pandemic: Fine, let them. What's in President Trump's four coronavirus relief executive orders? Kellyanne Conway says Americans aren't fooled by Biden policies, the former VP has benefited from lockdown. Mid-American Conference postpones fall sports schedule, including football, over coronavirus concerns. With coronavirus aid bill stalled, White House adviser questions Democrats' good will.

US tops 5 million Covid-19 cases [8/9/20]. Five states make up more than 40% of tally. Feeding America CEO on how the COVID-19 pandemic is impacting access to food. Trump signs executive actions on economic impact of coronavirus. Australia's Victoria state sees deadliest day in coronavirus pandemic, but fewer new infections. FDA: We won't 'cut corners' to approve a Covid-19 vaccine. Mets' Marcus Stroman opts out of season over virus concerns. Citing Covid-19, White House considers barring some citizens from entering country. Coronavirus cases linked to overnight Michigan camp increase to 21. Why do we develop lifelong immunity to some diseases, but not others? Iran shuts down newspaper after expert accuses regime of coronavirus cover-up.

March on Washington reconfigured to comply with virus rules. **Coronavirus can spread through air up to 16 feet, study finds [8/11/20]**. NJ gym that defied coronavirus restrictions gets license rescinded: report. Texas coronavirus cases soar past 500,000. Stevie Nicks says the coronavirus pandemic is a real 'American Horror Story'. **Wisconsin state agency tells employees to wear masks during Zoom calls, even if home alone [8/12/20]**. Dems say Mnuchin offered to meet but refused to budge on COVID bill. Andrew Lloyd Webber says he is participating in coronavirus vaccination trial: 'I am excited'. Betsy McCaughey: Cuomo's coronavirus response -- NY Gov should stop bragging, his state fared the worst.

Former Obama finance adviser: We haven't heard how Biden would have handled COVID differently. Landlords could exploit COVID-19 victims to fast-track evictions, housing advocates say. Ben Shapiro: Democrats slammed federal presence in US cities, but they want to 'send the feds to yell at you about masks'. New York City's Annual 9/11 light Installation canceled over coronavirus. Oregon State president says SEC not seeing 'reality' over coronavirus risk.

Any attempt to get herd immunity would lead to massive death tolls, Fauci warns [8/14/20]. Coronavirus-linked heart condition becomes growing concern for NCAA athletes. Here's what CDC says for those who have recovered from Covid-19. Alex Berenson slams mainstream media for 'obscuring what the risks really are' from coronavirus. Need A Laptop Colleges Boost Loaner Programs Amid Pandemic. Reds player tests positive for coronavirus, Pirates series postponed. As students head back to campus, US colleges try to prevent and combat Covid-19 cases.

I didn't get COVID-19. But it still damaged my health. **Why some can't accept reality of Covid-19 [8/16/20].** Pelosi calls members back to Capitol Hill to consider USPS legislation, calls post office 'Election Central' amid coronavirus. Lasting immunity seen after mild COVID-19 infection: report. New Zealand postpones general election due to COVID-19. Doctor on new saliva test for COVID-19 and what we're learning about immunity. WHO reports record global Covid-19 increase over 24 hours. A high school student in Oklahoma knowingly went to school with coronavirus. **U.S. coronavirus death toll surpasses 170,000 [8/18/20].** Strong earthquake in Philippines kills 1, damages coronavirus quarantine center, roads. Two dozen coronavirus cases linked to wedding reception, health officials say.

Coronavirus cases discovered in minks on Utah farms, first in the US. Michigan State And Notre Dame Suspend In-Person Learning Over COVID-19 Concerns. Bill Gates: US fumbled coronavirus response because 'we believe in freedom'. While the vast majority of cities closed their schools during the pandemic killed an estimated 5 million people worldwide, three opted to keep them open. Coronavirus case at Sturgis Motorcycle Rally prompts health department warning. Survivor thought Covid-19 was political. Then he got sick.

Kamala Harris accepts historic VP nomination, says 'there is no vaccine for racism'. Teachers could stay in classroom if exposed to COVID-19. Children could be "major drivers" of COVID spread, doctor says. Daycare, Grandparent, Pod Or Nanny How To Manage The Risks Of Pandemic Child Care. Behind Maduro's 'bioterrorism' accusations amid Venezuelan coronavirus crackdown.

'I didn't know I was in this world' -- the pandemic falls on an East Texas family like a tornado. Coronavirus killed this widowed dad. His three children are left without parents. Biden says he'd shut down country to fight coronavirus if recommended. Nearly 70,000 lives could be saved in the next 3 months if more Americans wore masks, researchers say. At one university, students' steps are tracked to stop the coronavirus. Italy's daily coronavirus cases top 1,000 for first time since May; vacationers contributing to surge. **Trump announces emergency authorization of breakthrough coronavirus treatment [8/23/20]**. NYC residents wait in quarter-mile long line for food, jobs remain scarce during pandemic. Another COVID-19 Medical Mystery: Patients Come Off Ventilator But Linger In A Coma. Camp claims zero coronavirus cases among its 450 campers and staff this summer.

GOP backs Trump despite pandemic performance. GOP glosses over Trump's pandemic failures on Night 1 of RNC. Minnesota farmers hopeful, though losses continue amid coronavirus. The Ohio State University suspends 228 students for violating pandemic precautions even before classes begin. Africa now free of wild poliovirus, but polio threat remains. FDA's Hahn Apologizes For Overselling Plasma's Benefits As A COVID-19 Treatment. Covid-19 superspreading event in Boston may have led to 20,000 cases, researcher says.

'People Are Anxious': Melania Trump Takes On Pandemic, Protests In RNC Speech. COVID-19 daily cases on the decline nationally, experts point to masks, decreased testing as causes.

Homeless essential workers face greater risk of COVID-19. U.K. to require masks for secondary schools in COVID-19 hot spots. Russia launches coronavirus vaccine trials in Moscow. Uncertainty shrouds Tour de France racing against COVID-19. Hurricane Laura collides with coronavirus pandemic.

As Coronavirus Infections Rise, Masks In Paris Become Mandatory In All Public Places [8/27/20]. DHS mulling plan to collect phone numbers from all arriving air travelers for COVID-19 tracing. What A Nasal Spray Vaccine Against COVID-19 Might Do Even Better Than A Shot. RNC in Charlotte tied to 4 cases of Covid-19. California chicken plant told to close after 8 die of COVID-19. His first Covid-19 infection left him with a sore throat, cough, headache, nausea and diarrhea. The second put him in the hospital. Group Whose NIH Grant For Virus Research Was Revoked Just Got A New Grant. 1,200 students have tested positive for Covid-19 at the University of Alabama. Pets boosting morale during coronavirus pandemic, study says.

Gottlieb says "full approval" of coronavirus vaccine for general population unlikely before 2021. Florida reports 2,500 new Covid-19 cases. Brazilian Indigenous leader Raoni Metuktire tests positive for coronavirus, hospitalized. Coronavirus-Hit Brazil Considers Major Public Funds For Poor And Unemployed. Coronavirus missteps from CDC and FDA worry health experts. Russia's virus cases exceed 1 million, globally 4th highest. Uber riders who violate face covering policy must soon take mask selfie for service. Here's how long it took the US to reach 6 million Covid-19 cases. ICE makes 2,000 arrests in largest sweep of the pandemic.

As a newcomer adviser eclipses Dr. Fauci in influence, the President and his aides are resigned to the virus' inevitable spread. New research finds it could take a month for patients to clear the virus. Coronavirus: Face shields offer less protection for others than regular masks, study finds. Making Gyms Safer: Why The Virus Is Less Likely To Spread There Than In A Bar.

Analysis: Trump grows impatient with the pandemic. Steroids confirmed to cut death risk for very ill COVID patients. United Airlines plans to cut 16,000 jobs as coronavirus continues to hammer demand. United Plans 16,000 Furloughs As Airlines Cut Jobs During Pandemic Downturn. As Labor Day approaches, fears of COVID-19 spikes loom.

Hall of Fame pitcher Tom Seaver dies of COVID-19, dementia at 75. COVID crash: Companies that have filed for bankruptcy. Alex Azar says vaccine timeline "has nothing to do with elections". Percentage of Americans reporting depression symptoms triples during coronavirus pandemic, study shows. U.S. opts out of WHO-linked global COVID-19 vaccine effort. **Penn State football team doctor says a third of COVID-positive athletes had heart inflammation [9/3/20]**. 'Tenet' is a breathtaking film worth seeing. It deserved better than a pandemic premiere.. Penn State clarifies comments on coronavirus-related heart condition made by team physician. "The Batman" star Robert Pattinson tests positive for COVID-19. Tokyo Olympic CEO: Vaccine not requirement to hold games. Gov. Cuomo orders NY schools to report coronavirus cases daily. If you plan to be social for Labor Day weekend, here's how to lower your risk of Covid-19 infection. New Global Coronavirus Death Forecast Is Chilling -- And Controversial.

Chapter 8

Protests Over Vaccines and Masks Show They're a Victim of Their Own Success

September 5th, 2020 – November 9th, 2020

'Walking Dead' star Michael Rooker says he's been isolating in airstream during coronavirus fight. **Kamala Harris a COVID-19 vaccine before election: 'I would not trust Donald Trump' [9/5/2020].** Here's how the NFL has handled the coronavirus pandemic. Rep. Waltz, Cathcart: Coronavirus is a battle -- as war vets we know mental health is critical to defeat it. Pandemic turns summer into European tourism's leanest season. Major union says supermarkets should throw out shoppers who refuse to wear masks. Americans push coronavirus regulations to the brink on holiday.

Trump tries and fails to get reporter to remove mask at news conference. Hartford delays first day of school due to ransomware virus. McConnell says Senate will vote on slimmed-down COVID bill this week. School buses in focus as kids return to classes amid coronavirus pandemic. Citing A COVID-19 Shortfall, DHS Increases Visa Fees For Touring Artists. COVID-19 cases among children surpass half a million. **Pfizer-BioNTech vaccine could be ready for approval by mid-October -- but there are still 'unknowns' [9/8/2020].**

New York City begins phase 1 of reopening after three months of coronavirus lockdown. Charlie Kirk: Trump can attack Biden on coronavirus and win votes -- here's how. Oxford vaccine trial on hold because of potential safety issue. Health officials insist coronavirus vaccine will be based on science: 'No shortcuts'. Can A Parade Of Coffins Scare People Into Wearing Masks? Biden slams Trump for concealing pandemic threat. Senate GOP's latest coronavirus legislation includes key school-choice provisions. Trump admits downplaying virus, but told Woodward it was "deadly". Biden blasts Trump over reports he downplayed coronavirus threat: 'It's a disgrace'. Coronavirus-related deaths of young teachers raise alarm.

Vaccine developers hustle to meet FDA data requirements to submit for approval. Senate fails to advance slimmed-down GOP coronavirus relief bill. On the Texas border amid coronavirus, families are seeking medical care in Mexico. Trump says he didn't lie about the coronavirus. Ilhan Omar says Trump should resign for downplaying coronavirus. Five things to know about frequent mass testing for COVID-19. Sean Hannity: Biden 'did everything wrong' in response to coronavirus, is hoping 'you will all forget'. The President is not just downplaying the coronavirus -- he's twisting history to try to disguise his culpability in 190,000 American deaths. Minorities underrepresented in vaccine trials, despite being hit hardest. College students admit in police cam video they tested positive for COVID-19 then had a party. COVID-19 health concerns for 9/11 first responders. Adults With COVID-19 Twice As Likely To Have Eaten At Restaurants, CDC Study.

2 Giants-Padres games postponed after positive SF virus test. COVID-19 and the California fires have a connection. Here's how to fight both. Gottlieb says vaccine unlikely to be widely available until 2021. Pompeo bringing back 'Madison Dinners' mid-pandemic. WHO reports the highest single-day increase in global infections since the pandemic began. Dr. Ashish Jha: "We have not rounded a corner" on virus vaccine.

WHO reports new daily record in COVID-19 cases. **CDC finds kids without symptoms can transmit COVID-19 to adults [9/14/2020]**. Trump in 'Fox & Friends' interview claims coronavirus vaccine coming in a matter of weeks? Petalo, not

Charmin: Virus brings Mexican toilet paper to US. Texas county to pay coronavirus survivors for plasma donations. COVID-19 slams Cleveland's baseball bars, clubs. Pennsylvania Officials Stand By Pandemic Response After Judge Rules Against Orders. Trump claims he "up-played" coronavirus. Latinos Report Financial Strain As Pandemic Erodes Income And Savings.

Nearly 60 coronavirus tests undergo performance checks by FDA. As Campuses Become COVID-19 Hot Spots, Colleges Strain Under Financial Pressures. Antibody drug may cut Covid-19 hospitalizations, company says. ABC's Jonathan Karl says reporting from indoor Trump rally amid pandemic is like 'taking your family with you to Fallujah'. Trump contradicts CDC director on Covid-19 vaccines after Biden slams president's promises. U.S. to ship free Covid-19 vaccines within day of authorization. Trump's interference deepens disastrous pandemic response. WHO Europe chief urges nations to keep up COVID quarantines. Even a third of Americans getting vaccinated against Covid-19 won't be enough, Fauci says.

Officiant of wedding liked to 7 virus deaths remains defiant. How New York City is trying to speed up Covid-19 test results. Dana Perino presses Bob Woodward over decision to sit on Trump coronavirus tapes: 'Do you feel any responsibility'. **Biden: "I trust vaccines, I trust scientists, but I don't trust Donald Trump" [9/16/2020]**. Fauci would bet on effective and safe coronavirus vaccine by November or December. Texas coronavirus patient, 70, undergoes double lung transplant. National Museum of African American History and Culture reopens, six months after pandemic closure.

New York Lt. Gov. Kathy Hochul on state's pandemic response. During coronavirus vaccine development, medical groups urge FDA to 'maintain transparency'. 'Coronavirus Death Scoreboard' display stirs controversy in Illinois town. Virus measures targeted by protesters despite case spikes. Gottlieb "deeply concerned" about uptick in coronavirus cases heading into fall. Israel starts second lockdown as Europe braces for second COVID-19 wave. The US is barreling into the ultimate political stress test, a Supreme Court battle and an election, occurring in the middle of an again-worsening pandemic.

Flu season may be very mild this year, thanks to COVID-19 precautions. Trump's vaccine chief: We'll know about vaccine efficacy between October and January. The pandemic gave the world a second chance to fix the climate crisis. We're about to waste it. Houston doctor dies after battle with Covid-19. Nurses and doctors discuss lingering mental health issues as a result of COVID-19 pandemic. Chinese tycoon who called Xi Jinping a 'clown' and ripped his coronavirus response gets 18-year sentence. Ralph Lauren to lay off 3,600 workers after coronavirus hit.

Analysis: 200,000 Americans dead, but Trump says Covid affects 'virtually nobody'. New Dashboard Tracks Coronavirus Cases In Schools Across 47 States. Single-dose vaccine tested as US experts say no corners cut. 'Most' Americans likely vulnerable to coronavirus infection, CDC director says. Missouri governor, opponent of mandatory masks, has COVID-19. Houston, FAU still waiting after virus disrupts 3 more games.

Thousands on flights may have been exposed to virus in 2020, CDC says. Trump claims the White House can overrule the FDA's attempt to toughen vaccine guidelines. A sign reminding people of the 200,000 US Covid deaths vandalized five times in 6 days. **California just became the first US state to surpass 800,000 confirmed coronavirus infections [9/25/2020]**. US nears 7 million virus cases as 23 states report rising numbers. 'Daily Show' mocks Virginia gov's COVID diagnosis as proof virus 'disproportionately affects Black people'. COVID-19 forces Texas A&M to keep fans out of Midnight Yell. Amid pandemic, confidence in CDC erodes with questions of political interference.

COVID-19 won't stop the longest competitive off-road rally in the US. **Worldwide coronavirus deaths near 1 million [9/27/2020]**. Military suicides up as much as 20% during pandemic. Baseball Made It, So Far, Through A Pandemic. Football Hopes To Follow.

Only 10 states are seeing downward trends in new Covid-19 cases, and NYC now has a surge. Pandemic Threatens Long-Term Job Security After Hospitality Industry Layoffs. Wisconsin conservatives ask judge to block governor's mask order. NYC to fine people who refuse to wear masks. Biden calls out Trump for suggesting 'injecting bleach' to treat coronavirus. "Super healthy" college student dies from COVID-19 complications.

Las Vegas Raiders in hot seat again after several players attend indoor charity event without masks: report. Gruden: Raiders players made 'mistake' not wearing masks. **Things most likely will never be the way they were before the pandemic. The sooner we accept that, the better [10/1/2020]**. Leaders in several states warn residents to be on guard as worrying Covid-19 trends emerge. China encouraging 'revenge travel' following coronavirus lockdowns to help economy. Paris bars face possible closure as virus patients fill ICUs. Lockdown leads to Covid-related dreams -- and nightmares. Trump aide Hope Hicks tests positive for COVID-19. Trump will "begin quarantine process" after Hope Hicks contracts COVID-19. Watch live: President Trump, First Lady test positive for Covid-19.

Markets React Cautiously To News Of Trump Testing Positive For COVID-19. Pompeo tests negative for coronavirus, wishes Trump and first lady a 'speedy recovery'. Where Trump Has Been Over This Past Week Ahead Of Testing Positive For The Coronavirus. Trump tests positive for coronavirus: the timeline. Top Republicans say they are praying for Trump after positive coronavirus test. Pelosi gets tested for coronavirus, raises 'concerns' on accuracy of White House tests as she awaits results. Corey Lewandowski describes White House COVID testing procedure.

Trump's coronavirus diagnosis sets off testing chain: How contact tracing works. Trump's positive COVID test upends presidential race, thrusts spotlight back on coronavirus. Sean Hannity on Trump's positive coronavirus test: 'Sad' but 'predictable' that it will be politicized. Trump joins list of world leaders who have tested positive for virus. Coronavirus test caused brain fluid leak in woman with rare health condition: report. Lawmakers react to President Trump having coronavirus. Trump diagnosis renews calls for Capitol Hill coronavirus testing. Fast food drive-thrus are slower during coronavirus pandemic: Study. 11 positive coronavirus tests traced to presidential debate, Cleveland officials say.

Obama sends Trump 'best wishes' over coronavirus diagnosis: 'Were all Americans'. Trump tweets "Going well" after being flown to Walter Reed for COVID-19 treatment. **How the pandemic and politics gave us a golden age of conspiracy theories [10/3/2020]**. Trump's Doctors Give Update On President's Health After Positive Coronavirus Test. Trump campaign says Pence expected to add more events as president deals with coronavirus. Trump's coronavirus diagnosis shakes up presidential race one month before Election Day. Majority of Americans say the pandemic has made them watch their spending habits more closely. Pelosi says she hopes Trump's 'heart will be opened' and he'll change course on coronavirus. Pope Francis Laments Failures Of Market Capitalism In Blueprint For Post-COVID World. Biden tests negative for COVID-19, continues on campaign trail. Cabrera to Trump adviser: Most Covid-19 victims don't get a joy ride. AG Barr to self-quarantine out of caution amid coronavirus worries.

The President's seconds-long outing underscored his relaxed attitude toward the virus and a willingness to endanger his staff. Alarm and schadenfreude: How Trump's Covid diagnosis was received around the world. Wisconsin's COVID-19 outbreak continues to grow. Coronavirus worsens Arizona's teacher shortage. Republicans press forward with Supreme Court confirmation despite COVID cases. 'Masks matter': Biden criticizes Trump for removing mask when he arrived at the White House. Joe Biden takes shot at Trump over wearing masks with Twitter meme. White House staff, Secret Service eye virus with fear, anger.

Opinion: Biden checkmates Trump on Covid. **Teen arrested at Florida school after refusing to wear mask [10/6/2020]**. Thousands of empty chairs placed outside White House to represent US coronavirus deaths. Twitter, Facebook censor Trump's message comparing coronavirus to flu. Pentagon: Top officials are quarantining after Covid-19 exposure. Minneapolis fire stations lockdowned Monday. In 10 years, Covid might be like the flu. Trump likening them now is 'morally reprehensible' doctors say. Here's how the President's decision to stop negotiations could affect Americans struggling with fallout from the pandemic.

Why is Trump getting a drug to fight Covid-19 that almost no one else can? Debate Forces Pence Into Spotlight As Coronavirus Crisis Engulfs White House. Doctor on FDA's COVID vaccine guidelines and VP debate safety. Ironic Twist: Last Spring Trump Halted Research Key To COVID-19 Drug He's Now Taken. Wisconsin activates field hospital as coronavirus keeps surging. Pence and Harris prepare for a debate clash on coronavirus. Trump returns to Oval Office despite coronavirus infection. Pence, Harris participate in VP debate as Covid cases surge in the White House. **Harris on taking a COVID vaccine: If Trump tells me to take it, I won't [10/7/2020]**.

Pence, Harris spar over federal Covid-19 response as Trump's illness looms. WTA players reveal why they returned to the courts amid coronavirus uncertainty. 'SNL' Nixes Morgan

Wallen Appearance After Singer Violates COVID-19 Safety Protocols. Ousted vaccine director: I was a fly in the ointment. New Scrutiny On Trump's Gold Star Family Event After COVID-19 Outbreak. Smokey Skies Are The New Normal. Are They Making Us Sick?

Is it safe for Trump to return to campaign trail after COVID diagnosis? Titans return zero positive COVID-19 cases in latest round of testing, aim to open training facility Saturday. McConnell: New coronavirus relief 'unlikely in the next 3 weeks' as White House preps biggest offer yet. Public evacuation shelters amid COVID-19 might not be safest option, FEMA warns. Chicago Loses A Beloved Teacher To COVID-19. What the Texas State Fair looks like during the coronavirus pandemic. Why I'm in a Covid vaccine trial, and how it honors my father. Warren vows Biden will 'hold Trump accountable' for pandemic. Doctor says Trump no longer at risk of transmitting virus.

COVID-19 Stalks A Montana Town Already Grappling With Asbestos Disease. Nearly 2 million are grieving Covid dead. That's a pandemic, too. Broncos coach: virus outbreak shows who the 'whiners are'. Dr. David Ho: The AIDS pioneer shifts to COVID-19. Live Updates: Trump coronavirus diagnosis. **Police Arrest Anti-Lockdown Protest Leader In New York's Orthodox Jewish Community [10/12/2020]**. Titans see no new COVID-19 cases as team gears up for Tuesday night game. NYC virus lockdown protest leader ordered away from reporter. Vanderbilt-Missouri is the first SEC game postponed due to Covid. Johnson & Johnson pauses COVID vaccine trial over sick participant. Trump mocks Fauci's pitching arm and his Covid predictions. Doctor on risk of coronavirus reinfection, latest on vaccine trials.

Person with coronavirus who ate at New Hampshire restaurant may have exposed others to virus: officials. Wisconsin restaurant installs virus-killing lights in its dining room, bar area. Pfizer to start testing its vaccine in children as young as 12. Minnesota coronavirus cases traced to Trump, Biden campaign events: reports. Michelin guide to pause awarding stars to California restaurants, citing wildfires and COVID-19. Why "strength" is the wrong metaphor to use against coronavirus. New Covid cases surge in Midwest as weather cools and resistance heats up.

The President, 19 days before the election, is trying to pull the wool over voters' eyes by arguing the pandemic is almost over, so they won't hold him accountable. Kamala Harris' Travel Suspended After 2 People Near Her Test Positive For Coronavirus. COVID spike arrives late, hits hard in rural Kansas county. Jewish leaders call COVID rules blatantly anti-Semitic. Trump and Biden hold competing town halls as Covid cases spike and millions cast their votes early. Colts reveal positive coronavirus tests days before Week 6 game. Healthy young people may wait for coronavirus vaccine until 2022, WHO official says. Pfizer COVID-19 Vaccine Won't Be Ready By Election Day. 2 USS Theodore Roosevelt sailors test positive for COVID 19. 67-year-old survives Covid-19 after 196 days in hospital. Georgia's pandemic primary was a disaster. Experts fear the state is still vulnerable to a repeat..

Coronavirus case increases hit record highs in at least 7 states. For the next several months, new Covid-19 infections, hospitalizations and deaths are expected to keep rising. Here are seven ways to stay healthy and sane.. Wichita mayor threatened over mask mandate, police say. No masks at church service Trump attended. New research sheds light on COVID spread inside airplane cabins. Man loses 8 family members and his business to coronavirus. As global infections pass 40 million, the COVID-19 fight goes local. Top Palestinian Official Receiving COVID-19 Treatment In Israeli Hospital.

Hispanics see highest increase in coronavirus deaths over summer, CDC report finds. **Trump trashes Fauci and makes**

baseless claims that people are tired of hearing about Covid-19 [10/19/2020]. As virus surges, Iran breaks one-day record for deaths again. Democrats and White House still far apart as coronavirus relief bill deadline looms. U.K. Preparing COVID-19 Vaccine Trials That Deliberately Expose Study Subjects. How the pandemic is deepening gender inequality nationwide. Trump calls out Lesley Stahl for not wearing mask at White House following 'extremely hostile' interview. Ireland is first EU country to return to coronavirus lockdown. Early voting begins in Wisconsin as the state sees a surge in new coronavirus cases. Coronavirus uptick leads Illinois Gov. Pritzker to clamp down on bars, restaurants in some areas.

Doctor weighs in on coronavirus vaccine timeline, surge in U.S. cases. Volunteer in AstraZeneca coronavirus clinical trial dies, report says. Cleaning company is more profitable than it was pre-COVID. Live Updates: New COVID-19 cases reported worldwide reach new high. Watch live: N.J. governor speaks amid new COVID-19 surge. Sen. Van Hollen claims 'McConnell's fingerprints areall over the death' of COVID-19 relief package.

Trump and Biden debate coronavirus relief bill for Americans. FDA approves remdesivir as COVID-19 treatment. Wisconsin admits 1st patient to field hospital, reports record COVID-19 deaths. Biden slams Trump on coronavirus, says president's quit on America? AstraZeneca, Johnson & Johnson to resume COVID-19 vaccine trials. Some doctors fighting the pandemic now have another thing to worry about.

Wilco's Jeff Tweedy on staying productive through the pandemic. Governor asks to use El Paso military hospital as COVID-19 surges. Pence's Chief Of Staff Has The Coronavirus. Pence Will Continue To Campaign. King: That was the peak of the Covid-19 surge. We passed it. Gottlieb warns of "dangerous tipping point" as virus spread accelerates. CDC official sounded alarm on Covid-19 months ago. She was silenced. Five Pence aides test positive for Covid-19.

US should consider national mask mandate for the winter, former USDA commissioner writes in op-ed. El Paso imposes curfew as virus cases overwhelm hospitals. Coronavirus outbreak at Massachusetts nursing home leaves 5 dead. White House sends mixed messages about controlling the coronavirus pandemic. El Paso, Texas, Judge Issues 2-Week Curfew To Stem Surge Of COVID-19 Cases. Eli Lilly Ends Coronavirus Antibody Treatment Trial, Other Studies Go On. Facebook's Sheryl Sandberg has career advice for working women during COVID-19. Putin orders national mask mandate as COVID cases spike in Russia. Hospitals across 38 states report increase in coronavirus patients. 'Gold Rush' star Rick Ness talks mining during a pandemic: 'I had one goal in mind and that was redemption'. Live Updates: Wisconsin faces "urgent" COVID crisis as U.S. cases surge. In battleground states, Trump grapples with a surging foe: Covid.

As COVID-19 Cases Surge In Illinois, A Clash Over Safety Guidelines. Trump's coronavirus response takes center stage in final election push. Coronavirus mutation spread across Europe: report. New Jersey coronavirus hospitalizations surpass 1,000.

Dems, Pelosi 'show no evidence of compromising' on key issues in coronavirus relief: Kudlow. Long Island 'Superspreader Events' Threaten To Undo Its Success At Controlling Virus. Thousands flock to Halloween parade in Wuhan, China. Financial lessons from the coronavirus pandemic. U.S. Hits New Coronavirus Record With More Than 88,500 New Cases. Covid-19 antibodies diminish over time, but experts say there's no reason to be alarmed. The President used a Midwestern campaign swing to push a baseless claim that medical workers are inflating the coronavirus death toll for profit.

COVID-19 considered a top issue in GOP ads in just 2 battleground states. England To Return To Lockdown In Coming Days. Australia records zero local coronavirus cases for first time since June. White House blasts Fauci after he says U.S. 'poorly' prepared for Covid-19 winter. The 2020 election comes as Americans deal with the ongoing pandemic, a resulting recession and an unresolved reckoning over race. Nearly 150 COVID cases linked to services in Boston-area church.

What kind of mask should you wear to vote on Election Day? In 2020, Gubernatorial Elections Are All About COVID-19. Doctors warn the worst of the COVID-19 surge is yet to come. Analysis: **It's Election Day, 96 million Americans have already voted and 9.3 million people have been infected with Covid-19 [11/3/2020]**. Denver Broncos president and CEO test positive for COVID-19. U.S. fights COVID-19 surge amid record new cases. Election Shows Stark Partisan Divide On Economy, Coronavirus. San Francisco 49ers player tests positive for coronavirus. U.S. Sets Coronavirus Record With Daily New Cases Pushing Past 100,000.

Cal-Washington game canceled after positive coronavirus test. College Football Week 10 preview: Clemson-Notre Dame highlights the schedule while coronavirus still rampant. General in charge of COVID vaccine distribution worries many won't take it. Northern Denmark In Lockdown Over Coronavirus Variant Outbreak In Minks. Televangelist who blamed COVID-19 on premarital sex dies from virus. Rachel Maddow self-isolating after potential coronavirus exposure amid election coverage.

Doctors fear more death as Dakotas experience virus 'sorrow'. WHO reports coronavirus discovered among mink populations in 6 countries.

Chapter 9

Biden Unveils Transition Covid-19 Advisory Board to 'Help Shape' Approach to Coronavirus Pandemic

November 9th, 2020 – December 22nd, 2020

Pandemic threatens Latin America's next generation: UN. Joe Biden announces his Covid-19 plan. **Pfizer says early analysis shows its vaccine is 90% effective [11/9/2020]**. Expert voices cautious optimism coronavirus vaccine is within reach.

Texas county grapples with surge of coronavirus cases. California seeing biggest jump in virus cases in months. Sen. Rick Scott: COVID changed everything this year -- including voting. Here's how we restore trust. Report: Children lose basic skills under virus restrictions. 'The Vaccine's On Its Way, Folks,' Fauci Says As Brooklyn Names Him A COVID Hero. U.S. sets record for coronavirus hospitalizations with over 60,000. Eye Opener: More than 60,000 Americans hospitalized with COVID-19. **Coronavirus hospitalizations in the US reach record high, data shows [11/11/2020].** Why Poorer Countries Aren't Likely To Get The Pfizer Vaccine Any Time Soon. Ohio State-Maryland game canceled over positive COVID-19 cases.

Navajo Nation Combats A New 'Monster': Coronavirus. Ohio Governor DeWine on COVID-19 surge, Trump's handling of pandemic. 'Trump vaccine'-trashing Cuomo snubbed Azar, skipped 17 White House meetings. Restaurants, gyms, hotels pose highest COVID risk, study says. Local leaders implement drastic changes as COVID-19 cases surge. Amid surge, Covid survivor warns others to take virus seriously. Live updates: Texas court halts county coronavirus order closing non-essential businesses.

Hospitals In Montana Strain Under COVID-19 Spike. Biden to push for new coronavirus stimulus deal as cases spike. Chicago mayor defends appearing at large Biden celebration days before issuing Thanksgiving lockdown. **Coronavirus surge in Mississippi depletes ICU bed availability in state's capital: official [11/13/2020]**. New House member says "masks are oppressive" amid COVID-19 surge. U.S. shatters third consecutive daily coronavirus record. States Announce New Mandates As COVID-19 Cases Rise Sharply In The U.S. NY doctor slams Gov. Cuomo for doubting potential coronavirus vaccine touted by Trump.

The Masters continue to thrill golf fans despite coronavirus shake up. Joe Biden has spent his early days as President-elect pleading with Americans to pay attention to the relentless surge of coronavirus. **Americans don't seem to be responding to the virus as they did in April. Unless that changes, the current skyrocketing numbers won't change [11/15/2020]**. UK's Boris Johnson self-isolates after possible COVID exposure. U.S. Hits 11 Million Coronavirus Cases, Adding 1 Million In A Week.

Boris Johnson self-isolating after lawmaker he met with tested positive for coronavirus. Top Trump pandemic adviser tells Michigan to "rise up" against restrictions. House Returns With 1st Widespread Coronavirus Testing Program, Lame-Duck Agenda. Sweden puts limit on gatherings to curb virus. How many doses of Moderna's coronavirus vaccine will be available? Navajo Nation Enters New Lockdown As Coronavirus Cases Rise. Iowa Doctor Says Money And Staffing Needed To Handle Coronavirus In Nursing Homes. Early data shows Moderna's COVID-19 vaccine is 94.5% effective. A boy lost both parents to Covid-19. His family asks for help celebrating his birthday.

Federal prison left inmates with virus in housing for a week. Ted Cruz calls Democratic senator an 'ass' following Senate floor mask dispute. **PA gov announces new COVID rules, including wearing a mask in your house [11/17/2020]**. She survived the pandemic. Her husband did not. Now she's speaking out. What to know about Pfizer and Moderna's COVID-19 vaccine trials. **State officials tighten COVID-19 restrictions as cases climb to more than 11.3 million nationwide [11/17/2020]**. As Covid-19 cases surge, Congress sounds pessimistic about a new relief package. Pfizer-BioNTech to seek Covid-19 vaccine approval in 'days' after successful trial.

Add to Biden's transition challenges: Imposing Covid-19 precautions on cramped West Wing. How many of his own coronavirus recommendations did Gavin Newsom violate? Delta blocks middle seats as COVID-19 precaution through March 2021. Judge orders Trump administration to stop deporting unaccompanied minors amid coronavirus pandemic. Georgia Democrats grapple over reaching voters in-person amid worsening pandemic. Anthony Edwards taken first in COVID-delayed NBA draft. 'Good Doctor' actor Richard Schiff taken off oxygen amid coronavirus hospitalization: 'Cautiously optimistic'.

Leslie Marshall: Gavin Newsom is my governor and I'm a Dem, but he made a big COVID mistake. ER doctor says closing schools alone won't stop coronavirus from spreading. Over 182,000 prison inmates have tested positive since coronavirus pandemic began. Africa Surpasses 2 Million Coronavirus Cases. Gov. Cuomo faces scrutiny over COVID book deal as residents suffer financial impacts of lockdowns. Minnesota governor announces new COVID restrictions ahead of Thanksgiving. Trump administration cuts off emergency Federal Reserve programs as coronavirus cases spike. Suit alleges Tyson Foods plant manager bet on how many workers would get coronavirus. White House Coronavirus Task Force says pandemic is worsening. California adopts stricter workplace coronavirus safety rules. Barbershop owner helps run restaurant when its staff is exposed to COVID-19. Journalist questions viral CNN interview of nurse who claimed 'deathbed denialism' of coronavirus.

Teen cancer survivor dies after coronavirus diagnosis as Kentucky sees surge in illnesses. Ben Carson Says He Was 'Desperately Ill' With The Coronavirus. Trump takes credit for Pfizer vaccine development, says Americans wouldn't have one yet without his leadership. The US recorded 195,000 new Covid-19 cases in a day. An expert says spread is now 'faster' and 'broader' than ever. Trump calls into virtual G20 summit, talks COVID-19 with world leaders. Canada's largest city goes into 28-day lockdown. States issue new restrictions to contain surge of coronavirus infections.

Dr. Inglesby: People should stay home for holiday, US in 'uncharted territory' with coronavirus pandemic. US has seen staggering virus numbers, but this resurgence has been unprecedented. Bill Gates confident almost all Covid-19 vaccines will work well. Wisconsin congressman says he tested positive for COVID-19. 2 Kansas City fire department members die from COVID-19. During the pandemic, Thanksgiving celebrations are smaller and so are the turkeys.

COVID-19 cases climbing ahead of Thanksgiving holiday. Florida bar shut down after hundreds pack in without masks. Federal prisons to prioritize staff to receive virus vaccine. Miami hospital preparing for COVID-19 vaccine distribution. Growth of COVID cases in Ohio "exponential". Watch Live: Cuomo makes announcement at COVID briefing. From Around The World: How To Have A Happy(ish) Pandemic Thanksgiving. Azar says vaccine distribution could begin within weeks. Dow crests 30,000 points on vaccine hopes, Biden transition. British parents not too keen on school charging their kids for face masks: Report. Live Updates: China says it found COVID-19 on packaging of frozen imports. Need a Covid-19 nurse? That'll be $8,000 a week.

Native Americans feel vulnerable as South Dakota takes hands-off approach to Covid-19. Operation Warp Speed vaccine development adviser discusses distribution plans. Cuomo gives COVID-19 update before Thanksgiving. CEO of a major health system left the company after he said he wouldn't wear a mask. What can states do to save jobs Order people to mask up. 'Hang on': Biden Thanksgiving address calls for hope amid steep rise in Covid-19 cases.

Colorado Gov. Polis is in quarantine after coronavirus exposure. Divorce rates skyrocket during normally quiet Thanksgiving week, lawyers blame pandemic. Concerns over Thanksgiving gatherings continue as U.S. marks deadliest day in pandemic in months. **Government Model Suggests U.S. COVID-19 Cases Could Be Approaching 100 Million [11/26/2020]**. Fire in Indian hospital kills 5 coronavirus patients. Nearly 60,000 Americans could die of Covid-19 in the next three weeks. COVID-19 in custody: Alabama ranks 9th for inmate deaths.

Brazil's president rejects COVID-19 shot, calls masks taboo. Cohen on Trump's vaccine timeline: Let's take a look at reality. Mobile labs target "testing deserts" where virus spreads undetected. NYC couple has given 10,000 backpacks, 200 gallons of sanitizer to homeless during pandemic. U.S. tops 13 million COVID-19 cases as holiday season begins. Amid pandemic, NBA gives teams health protocols for season.

Hospitals anticipate surge of coronavirus patients after Thanksgiving weekend. Americans increasingly turning to fresh Christmas trees during pandemic: 'It really is a memory maker'. The country had seen a decline in suicides but the pandemic appears to have reversed that trend and has disproportionately affected women. Fauci warns Thanksgiving travel could make current Covid surge worse. Singapore mother had COVID-19, gave birth to boy with antibodies. The US has surpassed 100,000 new daily Covid cases for the 27th consecutive day as those who traveled for the holiday risk spreading the virus. 'Pandemic' is named as 2020's Word of the Year by Merriam-Webster. Nurse placed on leave for bragging on TikTok she doesnt wear a mask. Peter King on the week Covid truly wreaked havoc on the NFL.

British singer Rita Ora apologizes for breach of Covid-19 lockdown with birthday party. Hunted and trafficked, pangolins may hold key to COVID-19. Airlines and shipping companies prepare for COVID-19 vaccine distribution. U.S. reports record 93,000 coronavirus hospitalizations. Coronavirus Was In U.S. Weeks Earlier Than Previously Known, Study Says. CDC holding emergency meeting over who should get coronavirus vaccine first. Coronavirus risks of swearing in means House has a lot to figure out. Pandemic causing problems for NFL in Week 12. Will coronavirus vaccine be distributed to prisoners first? Coronavirus vaccine should go to health care workers, long term care facilities first, CDC panel recommends.

First Covid vaccines to be offered to health workers, nursing homes, CDC panel says. Elected officials criticized for not following own COVID-19 advice. CDC will decrease coronavirus quarantine time to 7-10 days. **UK becomes first country to approve Pfizer's Covid-19 vaccine [12/2/2020]**. NYC bar owner who defied coronavirus restrictions arrested.

U.K. regulators approve Pfizer vaccine for distribution ahead of European Union. Biden DHS pick had 'inappropriate' involvement in drug trafficker's commutation: Investigation. Daily Beast ripped for tying Gov. Kristi Noem to grandmother's death over COVID response despite negative test. **Vaccine Cards And Second-Dose Reminders Are Part Of Warp Speed's Immunization Plan [12/3/2020]**. Initial vaccine distribution will cover fraction of health care workers. The US reports 3,100 coronavirus deaths in one day -- 20% more than last record. Phishing ploy targets COVID-19 vaccine distribution effort.

US tops record for daily coronavirus deaths. Watch Live: Pennsylvania's health secretary discusses COVID hospital surge. Ex-Presidents step in to fill the leadership vacuum as Trump ignores a worsening pandemic. **Supreme Court gives temporary win to California churches over coronavirus restrictions [12/3/2020]**. UK approved a vaccine before the US. Here's why..

Coronavirus likely to bring on 'dark winter' for Americans, experts say. Governor addresses Illinois COVID-19 response after record deaths. UN leaders meet with WH officials about coronavirus response following de Blasio snub. Romney: Trump's leadership on Covid 'a great human tragedy'. Biden says he will ask Americans to wear masks for the first 100 days he's in office. Racial disparities create obstacles for Covid-19 vaccine rollout. States face unique challenges with vaccine distribution. Job growth slowed sharply in November as COVID-19 flared. Speaker Pelosi says there is 'momentum' to reach Covid relief deal. Are Covid-19 vaccines safe Dr. Sanjay Gupta has answers.

CNBC's Rick Santelli blasts anchor Andrew Ross Sorkin over lockdowns. Biden confident Congress will pass COVID relief bills. Health care workers ask for help to slow COVID-19 spread. MLB sues insurance providers, cites billions in virus losses. Covid-19 is raging through overcrowded California prisons. Woman describes her experience during a Covid vaccine trial. As Covid surges, so does homelessness. Shelters foresee an 'absolute disaster.'. 1 million new coronavirus cases have been added in the US -- in only 5 days. U.S. vaccine chief sees "light at the end of the tunnel". Rudy Giuliani Tests Positive For Coronavirus, Trump Says. Trump announces Rudy Giuliani has Covid.

Colorado governor's husband taken to the hospital over worsening COVID-19 symptoms. Citing low coronavirus infection rates in schools, NYC reopens for in-person learning for some students. 2021 Ford Bronco launch delayed due to coronavirus -- here's what reservation holders need to know. Dr. Jerome Adams detailed how health care capacity is the biggest problem caused by the current spike and how a vaccine could be most effective in helping. Your Spotify 2020 Wrapped is an archive of your pandemic playlist. Does anyone need that? Coronavirus exposure leads hundreds of Detroit health care workers to quarantine amid staffing concerns. A PhD student tells Anderson Cooper how adopting a positive winter mindset can help during the pandemic.

Biden names health team to lead COVID-19 response. Live Updates: Georgia Senate runoff candidates differ on coronavirus restrictions for religious gatherings. **Florida authorities raid home of ex-official who said she was ousted over coronavirus data [12/8/2020]**. U.S. regulators post positive review of Pfizer vaccine data. FDA confirms safety data and efficacy of Pfizer's Covid-19 vaccine ahead of Thursday meeting. 7-year-old raises money for hospital's pandemic gear. Brazilian state of So Paulo makes coronavirus vaccine mandatory for its 46 million residents. 'Quite frankly shocking': US virus deaths hit record levels. Biden vows to distribute 100 million vaccine doses within first 100 days.

Rudy Giuliani taking remdesivir, says 'you can overdo the masks'. Nearly A Week After Giuliani Hearing, Michigan House Is Accused Of COVID-19 Violations. Ravens' Dez Bryant scratched for Cowboys game after positive COVID-19 test, launches Twitter rant. Iran says US sanctions hinder access to COVID-19 vaccines. Biden lays out his three-point plan to combat coronavirus. Coach K says playing during pandemic doesn't "feel right". Ravens' Dez Bryant quits season, backtracks after COVID-19 positive case: 'I'm being smart'.

Cuomo outlines who will be prioritized for COVID-19 vaccine. House fails to reach deal on coronavirus but is debating ceiling fan bill. Popular travel destination Lake Tahoe closing to tourists amid COVID-19 surge. An advisory panel will take a vote that may clear the way for the FDA to greenlight a Covid vaccine in days. What Joe Biden Can (And Can't) Do To Stimulate This Pandemic Economy On His Own. 'The Perfect Storm': How Vaccine Misinformation Spread To The Mainstream. FDA advisory panel to meet over Pfizer COVID-19 vaccine today. Pope's Midnight Mass to start early to respect COVID curfew. You get the vaccine when it's available. How do you prove it? The deaths of Daisy and Melinda Coleman show how public attention can mask ongoing trauma. Citizen journalist detained for reporting on China COVID outbreak, "may not survive". Pennsylvania announces new COVID-19 restrictions. Pfizer's Covid-19 vaccine receives key FDA panel recommendation. FDA panel recommends emergency use authorization of Pfizer vaccine.

'Help is on the way': How the U.S. will turn the tide of the pandemic in 2021. Communities of color skeptical of COVID-19 vaccine. WH coronavirus testing czar says end of pandemic 'in sight' with 'rapid' vaccination rollout set to start. Former Covid-19 success story is now one of hardest-hit countries in region. Americans hopes for Biden admin outweigh pandemic worries. COVID driving record homelessness figures in NYC, advocates say. Analysis: More Black people need to be part of Covid-19 vaccine trials. Here's why I participated. Biden urges Americans to have confidence in new COVID vaccine. **FDA Authorizes COVID-19 Vaccine For Emergency Use In U.S [12/11/2020]**.

After a vaccine was authorized, two more things will happen, beginning today. CDC advisory board is meeting to discuss vaccine. Pfizer will begin shipping vaccines Sunday. Why a Covid-19 vaccine won't be a magic bullet. Trucks with first COVID-19 vaccine in US get ready to roll. Ben Shapiro: COVID lockdowns -- businesses pay price as politicians eye permanent power grab. FDA commissioner's advice on taking the vaccine if you have allergies. Some Covid patients may need heart damage tests before exercising again. White House staffers to receive Covid-19 vaccine ahead of general public.

Gates says coronavirus could still be risk through early 2022. In Reversal, Trump Says White House Staff Won't Be 1st To Receive COVID-19 Vaccine. New variant of Covid-19 identified in UK, minister says, as London heads back into strict lockdown. Cuomo says another NY total shutdown is 'something to worry about' amid coronavirus spike. First person to receive COVID-19 vaccine in North Carolina calls experience a moment of hope. How hospitals will start distributing the coronavirus vaccine. **U.S. administers first doses of Pfizer coronavirus vaccine [12/14/2020].** An overwhelming toll: What America's children have lost during the pandemic. FDA Analysis Of Moderna COVID-19 Vaccine Finds It Effective And Safe. WWII veteran, 96, receives COVID-19 vaccine, becomes first VA patient nationwide to get shot. Live Updates: First nurse to get COVID-19 vaccine urges US 'not to be afraid'. McConnell says Senate will not leave until Covid aid is passed.

MSNBC medical analyst: Don't travel or stop wearing masks until summer, even after getting vaccine. Health Workers 'Feeling Good As Hell' As Hospitals Begin COVID Vaccine Injections. MacKenzie Scott gives away $4.1 billion in pandemic charity spree. Pelosi says members must wear a mask to speak on the House floor. China Has A Theory About Its New COVID-19 Cases. Many Scientists Are Skeptical. Pompeo quarantining after coronavirus exposure. White House staffer has part of leg amputated after COVID-19 illness, fundraiser says. Mayor resigns after threats over mask mandate: "I do not feel safe". Pence to publicly receive Covid vaccine on Friday, Biden as soon as next week. Tom Cruise scolds film crew for breaking COVID-19 safety protocols.

Some Vials Of COVID-19 Vaccine Contain Extra Doses, Expanding Supply, FDA Says. France's Macron tests positive for coronavirus. Analysis: Why hasn't Biden or Trump gotten vaccinated for Covid? WorldView: U.K. accused of "VIP" pandemic funding; verdicts in 2015 Paris terror attacks. George Clooney defends Tom Cruise's COVID-19 rant. FDA is meeting to review Moderna's Covid vaccine for emergency use authorization. Here's what we know about the vaccine and how it compares to Pfizer's. Oxford COVID-19 vaccine's 2-dose regimen elicits broad immune response. US tops 17 million Covid cases as FDA advisory panel recommends a second vaccine for emergency use. McConnell says he will get vaccine 'in the coming days'. A look inside hospitals battling coronavirus. FDA prepares to OK a second vaccine as Covid-19 deaths top 40,000 this month. Berlin's biggest restaurant, shuttered by coronavirus pandemic, opens to feed city's homeless.

Analysis: Trump's baffling disappearance as coronavirus rages. Advocates say Black and Latino families consistently report low confidence in their ability to pay rent during the pandemic. NY, CA restaurants crushed by government's impulsive COVID-19 decisions, owners say. Newly Released COVID-19 Data Show Most U.S. Cities Are 'Sustained Hotspots'. Both chambers have passed a stop-gap bill that will keep things running through the weekend as leaders continue to negotiate on a Covid relief package. Stanford Apologizes After Vaccine Allocation Leaves Out Nearly All Medical Residents. Alec Baldwin, Leah Remini and more stars react to Tom Cruise's coronavirus outbursts. What's behind the spike in California Covid cases.

Congress under pressure to lock down pandemic relief deal. UK poised for 'Tier 4' lockdown as new coronavirus strain linked to surge in cases emerges. What is the risk of allergic reaction to COVID-19 vaccines? Congress passes temporary government funding to extend coronavirus relief talks. In California, the wealthy are offering top dollar to cut in line for a Covid-19 vaccine. Israel PM Netanyahu gets coronavirus vaccination: 'I believe in this vaccine'. Mossimo Giannulli being held in protective custody due to coronavirus concerns at his prison: report. Maren Morris cancels RSVP tour dates for 2021 over coronavirus pandemic: I truly appreciate your patience'. Congress faces shutdown deadline as it races to secure a Covid relief deal.

Older People, Some Essential Workers Should Get Vaccines Next, CDC Panel Says. New strain of COVID-19 identified in the U.K. Holiday shoppers shift spending habits during pandemic. Lawmakers reach Covid relief deal in major breakthrough. Here's what we know about the new Covid variation. EU Regulator Authorizes Use Of Pfizer Vaccine. Studies show heart disease a risk in COVID-19 survivors. UK's new coronavirus strain leads these countries to close their borders. Cuomo asks airlines to add New York to list of 120 countries with testing mandate for UK flights. How the coronavirus is changing scientific research.

What we know, and don't know, about the coronavirus variant. Heinz Lockdown Lovebaby swag for infants conceived at start of quarantine goes out of stock, again. What we know, and don't know, about the UK coronavirus variant. Dr. Marty Makary: US could reach herd immunity if 20% of US population gets COVID vaccine. Rand Paul's Senate floor speech against COVID-19 relief bill goes viral. US public school enrollment dips as virus disrupts education. **Azar, Fauci receive Moderna's COVID-19 vaccine [12/22/2020]**. Congress And COVID-19: Members' Cases And Quarantines.

Chapter 10

Fears Grow After a New Strain of Coronavirus is Detected in U.K.

December 22nd, 2020 – February 21st, 2021

Biden says 'our darkest days' in battling Covid-19 'are ahead of us'. What does this new coronavirus strain mean for you? Trump Slams COVID Relief Bill, Asks For Changes After Bitter Negotiations. Negative COVID-19 test doesn't make holiday gathering safe: LA top doc. Man who died after collapsing on United flight had COVID-19, coroner confirms.

Judge pulled from cases over coronavirus concerns. Fauci says he's feeling "quite good" after getting COVID vaccine. California nurse defeats coronavirus after 8-month battle: This is my second life. Coronavirus forces NBA to postpone Rockets-Thunder season-opener. Still waiting for a package High volume and employees out with Covid-19 are causing major USPS backlogs. The 'relief' in Washington's paltry Covid relief bill will be short-lived. Here's why.

They live in pharmacy deserts. Some fear these areas will be left scrambling to provide vaccine access. Harris giving Biden 'spotlight' on coronavirus relief talks: Deroy Murdock. **Fauci shifts herd immunity goalposts, now says as much as 90% may be needed to halt coronavirus [12/24/2020]**. U.S. to require COVID-19 tests for airline passengers from U.K.. Black doctor died of Covid-19 weeks after accusing hospital staff of racist treatment. In very different Christmas messages, Biden discusses Covid and Trump barely makes reference.

NBA forbidding teams from getting early COVID-19 vaccinations. The unforgivable thing about the Covid-19 response. Live Updates: Doctor reportedly has severe reaction to Moderna COVID-19 vaccine. **Global coronavirus cases surpass 80 million [12/26/2020]**. Stephen Moore: Dems claim to champion poor and minorities, but hurt them with job-killing COVID lockdowns. The President has not signed Congress' latest Covid relief bill, leaving aid in limbo for many jobless Americans. Loeffler, Perdue back leniency for US teen jailed in Cayman Islands for breaching coronavirus regs. Gottlieb sees "grim month ahead" as virus surges along coasts.

Supermarket chain gives $200K in gift cards to struggling restaurants amid coronavirus pandemic. Fauci predicts when general public will receive vaccine. Citizen journalist in China who reported on COVID-19 sentenced to 4 years. House to vote on $2,000 stimulus checks after Trump signs coronavirus, spending package. Trump finally signs COVID relief bill and funding measure to avert government shutdown. NYC vaccine scandal under criminal investigation, leaves hundreds in limbo for second dose. How will the COVID relief bill impact small businesses? Court whittles Gov. Andrew Cuomo's coronavirus restrictions away.

Republican tax cuts are a lie. And our research proves it -- just in time for Covid. 'Stuck in time': How the pandemic robbed many of their dreams as they put life on hold. 'Like a bathtub filling up': Alabama is slammed by the virus. Restaurants and small businesses hope for help from COVID relief bill. 'Out of control': Fauci on Covid-19 surge. Colorado identifies first known case of UK virus variant in US. Nurse uses social media to warn public about Covid-19. Louisiana Congressman-Elect Dies After Battling COVID-19. U.K. Approves AstraZeneca-Oxford Coronavirus Vaccine.

Coronavirus cases in children surpass 2 million mark. What many Covid survivors have in common with chronic illness survivors like me. Vaccine delivered to prison where feds carry out executions. Coronavirus Is Canceling New Year's Celebrations. California reports case of highly infectious COVID-19 strain. Bernie Sanders agrees with Trump's push for more coronavirus stimulus. Analysis: Trump absent as vaccine distribution lags and thousands continue to die.

As 2020 nears its end, the US reached another chilling Covid milestone and the outlook is grim for January too. **World bidding farewell to pandemic-ridden 2020 [12/31/2020]**. Surgeon general blames COVID-19 vaccination delays on state, local funding shortages. Why coronavirus vaccine distribution is slower than expected. Perdue to quarantine after contact with someone with COVID-19. Kate Beckinsale recalls drinking tequila from ice luge in New Year's Eve throwback before COVID was 'invented'.

Covid variant found in Florida; more cases identified in California. Coronavirus outbreak at Belgian retirement home after Santa visit kills more than two dozen: report. Despite Covid-19 and stay-at-home orders, 2020 saw an increase in homicides across the US. New coronavirus variant case reported in Florida. California bar owner could get 1 year behind bars for repeated openings during pandemic: report. Japanese governors demand state of emergency over COVID. Pandemic's revolution in transportation and commerce rivals 19th-century railroad construction. New York becomes fourth state to record 1 million Covid-19 cases. **US coronavirus death toll surpasses 350,000 as experts anticipate post-holiday surge [1/2/2021]**. COVID-19 Cases Surge In U.S. As Vaccinations Fall Below Government Predictions.

China Reports Tens Of Thousands Inoculated In First Days Of COVID-19 Vaccine Campaign. St. Nick party now linked to 27 virus deaths at retirement home. Coronavirus restrictions could force Formula One to postpone Australia season opener, report says. Public Health Official On Challenges Minnesota Is

Facing In COVID-19 Vaccination. Pharmacist sabotaged vaccines because he thought they were 'unsafe,' police say. England's third national lockdown expected to last 6 weeks. FDA warns of "risk" in U.K. strategy to delay 2nd Pfzier vaccine shot.

EXPLAINER: How do I know when to get my 2nd vaccine shot? TENNIS '21: COVID questions key; Djokovic, Nadal eye records. Pandemic kills Family Video; chain to close last 250 stores. Cuomo's book touting 'leadership' during pandemic released just before huge spike in COVID cases, pundit notes. Some Orthodox Christians ignore COVID warnings on Epiphany. NFL encourages teams to offer stadiums for COVID-19 vaccinations. Japan Issues COVID-19 State Of Emergency For Tokyo As Infections Rise. Japan would have world's 'most powerful passport' if not for travel restrictions, report finds. U.S. tops 4,000 COVID deaths in one day for the first time. New York Governor Cuomo holds COVID-19 briefing.

A person dies of COVID-19 every 8 minutes in Los Angeles County. California hospitals struggle to keep up with surging COVID cases. Capitol attending physician warns lawmakers and staffers of potential Covid-19 exposure following riot. Most Japanese say postpone or cancel the Olympics as COVID surges. Chaplain provides prayers to sick and dying COVID patients. New round of loans to help small businesses struggling in pandemic.

Cuomo's nursing home coronavirus policy: Admin refuses record requests for study absolving him on deaths. 2 congresswomen test positive for COVID-19 after Capitol attack. Man dies after judge forces clinic to use unproven COVID treatment. Illinois Democrat the third lawmaker to test positive for coronavirus since sheltering at Capitol. Schumer says first priority for new Senate will be COVID relief bill. Kirstie Alley calls out NY Gov. Cuomo for sudden change on lockdown days before Biden inauguration.

Three Congressional Democrats test positive for COVID-19 after Capitol riot. Tech hiccups behind COVID-19 vaccine rollout see line-hopping: reports. California To Vaccinate Residents 65 Or Older Against COVID-19. Two members of WHO group on mission to China blocked from travel by Covid symptoms: WSJ. US unemployment claims jump to 965,000 as virus takes toll. Coronavirus could soon become leading cause of death in Arizona, researcher warns. CDC projects up to 90,000 U.S. COVID deaths in next 3 weeks. North Carolina nurse who works in COVID-19 unit wins $1 million prize. Biden's $1.9T stimulus plan is a 'bailout' for blue states' bad lockdown policies: Waltz.

Left-wing activist seen at Capitol wore gas mask, said he had knife during riot: feds. How much do people around the world trust the COVID vaccines? Coronavirus FAQ: Do Airplane Passengers Not Know There's A Pandemic Going On? **Coronavirus lockdowns may have no clear benefit vs. voluntary measures, international study says [1/15/2021]**. OPINION: Moral Tragedy Looms In Early Chaos Of U.S. COVID-19 Vaccine Distribution. Some states are easing Covid-19 restrictions, while others are reaching tragic records. Gottlieb expects new virus variant to dominate U.S. infections in 5 weeks. Covid-19 variant find prompts quarantines in luxury Swiss ski resort. 3 Questions And The Emerging Answers About COVID-19 Vaccine Protection. Liam Neeson tops box office for second time amid the coronavirus pandemic. Cuomo wants New York to buy Covid vaccine directly from Pfizer.

Trump to issue up to 100 pardons and commutations in final days in office. Dr. Marc Siegel: COVID and Biden -- top 7 things new president and his team must do. California driver arrested after 'fully loaded AR-15,' 'It' clown mask found in car, police say. Georgia teen jailed in Cayman Islands for violating COVID restrictions says 'I deserved it'. Biden and Harris honor COVID-19 victims on eve of inauguration. U.S. races to distribute vaccine as new COVID-19 strains spread. Trump issues 143 last-minute pardons and commutations. Biden Adviser Sees Local Answers To Boosting Mask Use, Speeding Up Vaccinations. New York City postpones vaccine appointments as new shipments are delayed. Can COVID-19 vaccines be mixed and matched?

Lilly: Drug can prevent COVID-19 illness in nursing homes. Spanish tennis player says she tested positive for COVID-19. **Biden calls Covid-19 plan a 'wartime undertaking' [1/21/2021]**. Biden has bigger issues to worry about than following own mask mandate: Psaki. Vaccine shortages as U.S. sees 2nd deadliest day of pandemic. Biden signs executive orders on Covid vaccinations, pandemic response. A Covid-19 peak Variants muddy forecasts for coming months.

Cities struggle to keep mass COVID-19 vaccination sites stocked to meet demand. Some health care workers hesitant to get COVID-19 vaccine, complicating public health efforts. Dem govs Whitmer, Murphy flout own coronavirus restrictions for Biden inauguration. New concerns raised over South African variant of COVID-19. More than 100 National Guard members in DC test positive for coronavirus. Biden signs to sign two executive orders on Covid economic relief, worker protections. FDA gives approval for syringes to extract an extra dose from vials of the Covid-19 vaccine. How 'vaccine nationalism' could prolong the Covid-19 pandemic.

Opinion: A year into the pandemic, health care workers have a new source of hope. Year after lockdown, Wuhan dissident more isolated than ever. Birx on the Trump White House, the politics of the pandemic and more. As US passes another Covid milestone, new variants could pose further challenges. 38 Capitol Police officers test positive for Covid-19 after riot. White House begins talks with lawmakers on COVID-19 relief. CDC reviewing new data that suggests UK Covid variant could be more deadly. Mexican president tests positive for COVID-19, symptoms mild. Some patients report long-term effects of COVID-19.

Cactus League asks MLB to delay spring training due to COVID. Like So Much This Year In The NFL, The Pandemic Is Taking A Toll - On Super Bowl Ads. Gorilla Gets Monoclonal Antibody Therapy For COVID-19. White House addresses confusion over coronavirus vaccine supply. Biden: Any American who wants vaccine can get one "this spring". Colombia's defense minister dies from Covid.

Couple allegedly flew to rural area to skip vaccine line. GOP senators balk at $1.9 trillion price tag for Biden's COVID-19 bill. 8 myths about the Covid vaccine -- Dr. Wen explains. Pfizer is 'laying the groundwork' for vaccine booster against variants. Biden shifts on vaccine under pressure from the media. January has been deadliest month for Covid deaths in US. Supply of COVID-19 vaccines causes feud with drugmakers and European Union.

Venezuela's Nicol's Maduro touts 'miracle' cure for Covid, provides no evidence. Tech problems kick off Biden administration's first Covid briefing. Opinion: Humanity is facing a situation even more dangerous than the pandemic. Fauci: 'Not productive' to rehash Trump handling of pandemic: 'Let's look forward'. COVID-19 Vaccine Distribution: How High-Tech California Is Now Trying To Fix It. Only half of Covid-19 vaccines delivered to states have been used, CDC data shows. Here's one reason why. **Dr. Fauci says vaccines prevent illness, not infection, so getting one doesn't give you a free pass to travel [1/27/2021]**. U.S. Economy Slows Sharply As Pandemic Resurges. Florida fire captain accused of stealing COVID-19 vaccine doses. First US cases of South African coronavirus variant identified in South Carolina.

US detects first cases of a more contagious coronavirus strain first seen in South Africa. FEMA requests help from Pentagon to administer COVID vaccine: DoD. White House chief of staff on COVID relief, vaccine rollout. Probe of NY nursing homes says COVID-19 deaths underreported by up to 50%. How delayed doses, unfulfilled requests and last-minute allocations slowed vaccine rollout. State lawmakers are pushing to curb governors' virus powers.

US consumer spending fell 0.2% in December in face of virus. CVS and Walgreens blamed for COVID-19 vaccine issues with nation's oldest and most vulnerable population. Variants are spreading across the U.S. Here's where they are, state by state. Getting the COVID-19 vaccine Don't take over-the-counter pain relievers beforehand, experts say. COVID-19 variant cases will outnumber original strain, Fauci says. See what Dr. Fauci thinks about new vaccine data. From late Monday, all Americans will have to wear masks on public transport. All riders will be required to wear masks on buses, trains, taxis, planes, boats, subways and rideshares. GOP reps slam Pentagon move to give COVID-19 vaccines to Gitmo detainees. "I do feel exhausted": Kate Middleton on parenting in pandemic.

Maryland reports case of Covid variant first detected in South Africa. Anti-vaccine protest briefly shuts down Dodger Stadium vaccination site. Richmond says Biden willing to meet with GOP senators over COVID bill. Even as governments fixate on the glimmer of hope provided by vaccines, there are many people whose situations are unlikely to change in the long-term. Connecticut Governor Ned Lamont urges Biden to "give us some transparency" on COVID vaccine rollout. 100-year-old Captain Tom Moore hospitalized with COVID-19.

Biden to meet with GOP senators who pitched slimmed-down Covid relief bill. Maryland confirms South African coronavirus variant. U.S. Cuts $231 Million Deal To Provide 15-Minute COVID-19 At-Home Tests. 'The Little Things' tops the U.S. box office despite also releasing on HBO Max in the time of the coronavirus. **Yes, your boss has the right to make you get a Covid vaccine [2/1/2021]**. House subcommittee investigates

COVID-19 outbreaks at meatpacking plants. U.S. races to vaccinate Americans amid growing threat of coronavirus variants. Dominant variants could cause reinfections, Fauci says. Visby Medical CEO on developing a portable PCR test for coronavirus. Sir Thomas Moore, WWII veteran who raised COVID-19 funds, dies at 100. Dems push forward with COVID bill after Biden's meeting with GOP senators. The NFL's Covid-19 Finding That Saved the Season.

U.S. vaccination efforts pick up speed as experts warn of variant threat. They risked Covid, cartels -- now U.S. asylum-seekers in Mexico place hope on Biden. 5 Hacks To Make Your Face Mask More Protective. China's Vaccine Campaign Hits A Few Bumps. Sean Penn rips coronavirus vaccine site staffers in fiery letter for complaining of long hours, poor food. **Disneyland still requires guests to wear masks in Downtown Disney after they get vaccine [2/3/2021]**. NWHL cancels rest of season after additional virus positives.

States retrieve hundreds of thousands of vaccine doses held in federal program. Biden administration weighs plan to directly send masks to all Americans. Australian Open Players Quarantining After Tournament Worker Tests Positive For Virus. Florida police search for car stolen while carrying COVID-19 vaccine. One Emergency After Another: Wisconsin Governor And Legislators Battle Over COVID-19. NHL revises virus protocols; Colorado is 5th team shut down.

Senate passes key procedural step to allow Democrats to pass Covid-19 relief without threat of GOP filibuster. Chief: Officer hugged, taunted coworker despite COVID fears. The sneaky way the coronavirus mutates to escape the immune system. Biden vows to 'act fast' on another round of Covid relief, $1,400 checks. States may need to pester thousands of people about a second Covid-19 vaccine dose. These families have suffered the shock and devastation of losing a loved one to

Covid. Tampa Bay police union says officers risk contracting COVID-19 as NFL, mayor, go forth with Super Bowl events.

Opinion: What it takes to get a Covid vaccine in America. About 275,000 women left workforce in January in 'critical' pandemic trend, experts say. Covid reinfections may be 'much more common' than realized. Gottlieb says vaccines should offer "reasonable protection" from variants. How the NFL is holding the Super Bowl during a pandemic. Super Bowl LV post-game celebrations spur COVID concerns. Virginia confirms South African coronavirus variant case in adult resident. Media pundits scold Tampa 'superspreader' Super Bowl celebration, Dolly Parton knocked for ad. COVID-19 variant in South Africa halts rollout of one vaccine. COVID-19 vaccines and the concern about new variants.

White House COVID-19 Adviser Andy Slavitt Says There Are No Vaccine 'Silver Bullets'. **Facebook widens ban on vaccine misinformation [2/8/2021]**. Texas confirms South Africa coronavirus variant case in Houston resident. Delta CEO against mandating COVID-19 testing for domestic travel after Buttigieg says CDC is floating idea. Physician slams YouTube's 'extremely misguided' decision to pull Senate testimony about COVID treatment. Ingraham: 'Sanctimonious snitches' turning Americans against each other in age of COVID, Biden.

Biological anthropologist on COVID-19's impact on love, relationships, safety on Valentine's Day. **CDC updates coronavirus face mask guidance, endorses 'double masking' [2/10/2021]**. Most people are getting their second COVID shots on time, CDC says. Taxing time: How the pandemic will affect filing your taxes. Dr. Ashish Jha discusses new CDC double face mask guidance, COVID-19 variant concerns. Robert Kennedy Jr. banned from Instagram over false COVID vaccine claims. Biden Administration Recruits Community Clinics To Help Solve Vaccine Inequities. Biden Announces Deal For 200 Million More

COVID-19 Vaccines. People With Intellectual Disabilities Are Often Overlooked In Pandemic Response.

Test that detects coronavirus, flu gets FDA emergency use authorization, company says. Pandemic keeps couple, separated by river and border closures, apart. Massachusetts shifts COVID vaccine supply from hospitals to state-run sites. CDC director says U.K. variant could be "dominant strain" in U.S. by March. Gottlieb calls for "bespoke" vaccine strategy for underserved communities. 12-year-old vaccine trial participant shares his experience. WHO Wuhan mission finds possible signs of wider original outbreak. Coronavirus patient believed to be world's first reinfected by South African variant is in critical condition.

Many Hospitals Are Still Overwhelmed By COVID-19 Patients. Is Yours? [2/15/2021] Democratic leaders discuss repealing Cuomo's expanded powers in backlash to Covid nursing home deaths. DeSantis: Florida took 'exact opposite' approach to New York in handling COVID-positive patients. North Korea attempted to hack Pfizer for coronavirus vaccine information: report. Analysis: Biden faces questions as Covid reaches a new stage. Washington state expands COVID-19 vaccine accessibility in minority communities. McCarthy, California Republicans call out Newsom over vaccine rollout: 'We fear more Californians may die'. He hopes the US will be back to normal by Christmas, reassured a child she's not at risk for Covid and condemned hate groups. UK aims to infect healthy volunteers with COVID-19 for medical research.

Chapter 11

New York Sues Amazon Over COVID-19 Workplace Safety

Februrary 21st, 2021 – May 5th, 2021

Biden mocked for claim that 'we didn't have' COVID-19 vaccine when he took office. Players return to COVID protocols as spring training opens. How New York Governor Andrew Cuomo has handled the pandemic. Pfizer, Moderna COVID-19 vaccines protection against South African variant unclear, studies find.

Psychologist details historic ties between pandemics and extremism. Experts warn of another possible coronavirus surge as winter storms delay vaccination efforts. Pfizer files to ease COVID-19 vaccine temperature storage requirements. Pfizer launches first COVID-19 vaccine trial for pregnant women. House Democrats unveil full $1.9 trillion Covid relief bill. 'The Essence Of Truth': A Doctor's Photos Document The COVID-19 Crisis In The ER.

Florida Governor faces criticism over COVID vaccine distribution. Ex-deputy national security adviser Matt Pottinger faults China for trying to cover up coronavirus. How the Miami transplant institute stood up to COVID-19. Biden to mark upcoming 500,000 US Covid-19 deaths with candle lighting ceremony. **Eye Opener: U.S. nears 500,000 coronavirus deaths [2/22/2021]**. Zambia among Sub-Saharan African countries that have not yet received any vaccines. Watch live: Biden marks lives lost as U.S. nears grim COVID-19 milestone. Psaki pressed on COVID bill setting aside most school funds for after 2021. U.S. coronavirus death toll surpasses 500,000. 'Try to honor the loss:' Why CNN aired a national memorial service for 500,000 lives lost from Covid-19. Coronavirus forces Biden to forgo pomp for US-Canada meeting. **Fauci's mixed messages, inconsistencies about COVID-19 masks, vaccines and reopenings come under scrutiny [2/23/2021]**.

105-year-old woman beats COVID-19. Do 'Tight' Cultures Fare Better In The Pandemic Than 'Loose' Cultures? Experts worry variant-fueled surge of Covid-19 could be weeks away. Couple shares warning sign linked to Covid-19 after daughter's death. States pass their own virus aid, not waiting on Washington. House Oversight GOP wants to subpoena Cuomo to testify on COVID nursing home crisis, launch investigation.

Moderna set to test new booster shot that targets South African variant. Fired Texas doctor defends giving away expiring COVID-19 vaccine doses. Analysis: The two Americas of the Covid economy. Booster shots could be needed for people vaccinated against COVID-19. Pfizer studying third COVID-19 vaccine dose to fight new strains. After weeks of sharp declines, new Covid-19 cases are beginning to flatten. Data on pregnancy and the Covid vaccine is sparse. These women are changing that. Italian mafia employs new strategies during COVID-19 lockdown: report. Parliamentarian: COVID-19 bill must lose minimum wage hike.

FCC OKs $50 monthly internet subsidies during pandemic. Don't turn your nose up at the Johnson & Johnson vaccine. Tennessee: Vaccines stolen, given to children in 1 county. Ingraham: Dems justify Capitol lockdown with vague warnings about terrible people? Analysis: A third vaccine will bring us one step closer to normal. Oxford-AstraZeneca researchers attempt to battle variants. Jeremy Lin says he's been called 'coronavirus' on the court. Q&A: How Flint's water crisis shook faith in the Covid-19 vaccine. They shared what was happening at the start of the pandemic. A year on, many have paid a heavy price..

Opinion: Without a global vaccine plan, coronavirus variants could lead to untold number of deaths.

CDC advisory panel recommends Johnson & Johnson one-shot vaccine [2/27/2021]. Johnson & Johnson vaccine gets CDC panel backing, could start shipping within 24 hours. 4 million J&J Covid vaccines ship out, Americans expected to receive shots within 2 days. Johnson & Johnson executive discusses company's COVID-19 vaccine. Two doses of vaccine offer better protection from coronavirus variants, CDC says. As Covid-19 cases start to plateau and more Americans gain access to the vaccine, attention is shifting to people who are not willing to be dosed. US needs to hold on for 2 or 3 more months without easing up on Covid measures, expert says. Here's what's at stake. Hydroxychloroquine shouldn't be used to stop COVID, WHO says.

Novavax COVID-19 vaccine could see approval by May, CEO says. Texas governor lifts mask mandate despite warnings. The President now says there will be enough vaccines for all US adults by the end of May, and is directing states to vaccinate school staff. Biden ramps up COVID-19 vaccine production as states start lifting restrictions. "A dose of her own medicine": Dolly Parton gets COVID vaccine. Fauci Donates Personal Coronavirus Model To Smithsonian. Mississippi lifting mask mandates will 'sabotage' fight against Covid-19, Jackson mayor says. Celebrities react to Gov. Greg Abbott's decision to reopen Texas, end statewide mask mandate. Explosion Outside Dutch Coronavirus Testing Site, Police Say. Ohio GOP Senate candidates call for their Republican governor to reopen state after COVID lockdowns. Senate prepares to take up $1.9 trillion COVID relief bill. Church Leaders Say Johnson & Johnson Vaccine Should Be Avoided, If Possible.

Some US bishops discourage Catholics from getting Johnson & Johnson vaccine if others are available. New U.S. Malaria Czar: Why We Should Care About The Disease, Even In A

Pandemic. Alabama governor extends mask order but says mandate will end in April. Democrats Tweak COVID-19 Relief Package In Hopes of Speedy Senate Approval. How effective is the Johnson & Johnson vaccine What to know. COVID-19 vaccination efforts pick up speed as states begin easing restrictions.

Cuomo advisers altered report on coronavirus nursing-home deaths: WSJ. CNN slammed for 'dishonest' report claiming Texas governor has no evidence of migrants spreading coronavirus. Motor vehicle deaths increased during pandemic despite traffic drop. Detroit mayor turned down J&J vaccine in favor of others. Austin Mayor Steve Adler on Texas ending its statewide mask mandate. 94-year-olds find love in the time of coronavirus. These states are rolling back Covid restrictions, including mask mandates, indoor capacity caps. The Dalai Lama Gets A COVID-19 Shot, Urges Others To Get Vaccinated. Homeless Americans fear vaccine conspiracies. Here's how cities are intervening. Johnson & Johnson vaccines come with uplifting messages. COVID-19 after one year: What will the future bring? 1 year in: "Face the Nation" viewers on coronavirus challenges. COVID-19 research points to repurposed drugs.

Ouch! Fear of needles may keep many people away from Covid vaccines. President Biden on verge of signing COVID-19 relief package. Twitter silent as Louis Farrakhan's misleading COVID-19 vaccine claims go unchecked. COVID-19 bill includes billions of dollars for 'critical' restaurant relief program. Why Scientists Are Infecting Healthy Volunteers With The Coronavirus. White House works to finalize support with Democrats ahead of House vote on COVID relief bill. LeBron James says decision on if he will get vaccine is "private".

Ohio man recovering after COVID-19 vaccine mix-up saw him get 2 doses hours apart, daughter claims. Cuomo announces expanded COVID-19 vaccination eligibility. **Scalise**

demands Biden rescind praise of Cuomo as 'gold standard' of COVID-19 leadership [3/9/2021]. Biden plans to use the $1.9 trillion Covid-19 relief bill expected to pass Congress Wednesday as a platform for a generational transformation of the economy. As pandemic lockdowns swept the US, here's how some found the silver linings. Mental health expert discusses impact of the COVID-19 pandemic. West Virginia governor announces 168 unreported COVID deaths.

House approves Biden's $1.9 trillion COVID-19 relief bill, with no Republican votes. Schumer calls Covid aid bill a 'turning point' in politics that'll stop future Trumps. Susan Sarandon says she's open to dating 'someone who's been vaccinated' for coronavirus. Los Angeles mayor says everyone in county should have vaccine access by early summer. ESPN's Stephen A. Smith urges LeBron James to be more transparent with COVID vaccine decision. Coronavirus declared global pandemic one year ago: 'Together, we will endure'. Farmers react to billions in COVID-19 relief bill for Black farmers: 'Where did common sense go'. 60 Minutes+ on the mental health crisis facing medical workers in COVID pandemic. Reflecting on one year since COVID-19 shutdowns began in New York. JetBlue rolls back coronavirus boarding policy as airline returns to 'new normal'. More European nations pause AstraZeneca vaccine use.

How worried should we be about a more deadly variant of Covid-19? The President directs states to make vaccines available to all adults by May 1, which could allow small July 4 gatherings. Economics of Biden's $1.9 trillion COVID relief bill. Here's why experts think the US may be fooled by improving Covid numbers and what that means for the summer. Republicans scratch heads at Biden's goals for May COVID vaccine eligibility, July Fourth family gatherings. AP-NORC poll: People of color bear COVID-19's economic brunt. Vaccines and stimulus boost US consumer sentiment. Minnesota Governor Tim Walz eases COVID restrictions.

Biden And 'Quad' Leaders Launch Vaccine Push, Deepen Coordination Against China. Coronavirus FAQs: Can I Drink Between Vaccine Doses? What Is 'Vaccine Efficacy'? Woman describes getting empty shot of Covid-19 vaccine. Most of California to reopen as vaccine eligibility expands. Italy headed back to lockdown amid COVID spike. Americans wait for hours hoping to score leftover vaccine doses. 'Vaccine passports': Will they be available in the U.S. in time for summer?

Americans see changed lives, disparate impact of COVID -- CBS News poll. Irish prime minister stresses need for more vaccine doses to meet global demand. Marvin Hagler health update before death sparks anti-vaccine messages, Thomas Hearns tries to quiet noise. How Biden, Republicans and public health leaders are trying to persuade GOP skeptics to get their Covid vaccinations. **US Covid-19 cases have flattened. Here's why that may predict a surge, expert says [3/15/2021].** One year after COVID-19 lockdowns, many small businesses are still being squeezed. 'Partial' Pfizer COVID-19 vaccination cuts infection risk by 63% among nursing home residents: CDC. COVID-19 Data Misses A Lot Of People - Raising Questions. WHO Points to Wildlife Farms in Southwest China As Likely Source Of Pandemic. Test, trace and trust: How Iceland became a Covid-19 success story. The number of unruly passengers on US flights is too high, FAA says, so it's extending a get-tough policy on masking. Opinion: Not everyone sees light at the end of the Covid tunnel.

Stephanie Elam is live at a Los Angeles restaurant as Covid restrictions ease. Coronavirus: Nurse allegedly caught stealing vaccines in Michigan. DeSantis stands tall among US governors on the front lines of Covid fight. Covid cases rising significantly in 14 US states over past week. Political analysis of Biden's $1.9 trillion COVID relief plan.

US could be on the cusp of Covid-19 infection surge officials have been dreading, expert warns. As teachers return to classrooms, COVID-19 vaccines not always included. Seriously, stop sharing your vaccine cards on social media. **See Rand Paul spar with Dr. Fauci over masks [3/18/2021]**. Biden says US will hit his 100-day vaccine goal early. Gavin Newsom admits coronavirus 'communicating' errors as recall battle looms. Experts say two barriers stand in the way of reaching herd immunity in the US.

Groceries And Rent Money: Why Support For COVID Isolation Is More Important Than Ever. COVID-19 Outbreak Forces Idaho Legislature To Close Its Doors For Weeks. **U.S. surpasses Biden's goal of 100 million coronavirus vaccines administered in his first 100 days [3/20/2021]**. More Black And Latinx Americans Are Embracing COVID-19 Vaccination. University of Florida suspends conservative groups on campus for allegedly violating mask policy. Too little, too late Pamela Brown calls out Trump's vaccine endorsement. The Covid pandemic almost didn't happen, a new study shows. Operation Warp Speed Doc: 90% of Biden vaccine rollout plan was same as Trump's.

Germany looks set to extend lockdown measures again. Air travel reaches a pandemic-era record despite concerns over a coronavirus variant. U.S. study finds AstraZeneca COVID vaccine 79% effective. Feds "concerned" about AstraZeneca info on its COVID vaccine trial. Regeneron, Roche's antibody cocktail cuts COVID-19 hospitalizations, deaths by 70%, company says. More states open COVID-19 vaccine eligibility to pregnant women. Brazil Is Looking Like The Worst Place On Earth For COVID-19. India Sees Spike In Confirmed Coronavirus Cases -- And Variants. How the vaccine roll-out overcame doubts to be a point of pride. AstraZeneca updates report, insists COVID vaccine highly effective. How AstraZeneca went from pandemic hero to villain. US jobless claims fall to 684,000, fewest since pandemic. The President is expected to address several pressing issues, including gun control, immigration and his administration's Covid response.

The President announces a new Covid vaccine goal and gets a grilling on immigration and the filibuster. **Top tech CEOs testify on role of social media misinformation regarding Capitol riot and COVID [3/25/2021]**. Dangerous Covid-19 variants could mean all bets are off on the road to normalcy, expert warns. Redfield says, citing no clear evidence, he thinks the likely origin of the pandemic is a lab in China. Trump's Covid team spoke with Dr. Sanjay Gupta. Fauci says large trial on asymptomatic COVID spread is underway.

Harris acknowledges major new social welfare spending in $1.9T COVID relief bill was intentional? 'A huge, huge toll': For households reliant on two incomes, Covid job loss changed everything. Coronavirus infections rising nationwide as states face pressure to reopen. Libraries Are Key Tools For People Getting Out of Prison, Even During A Pandemic. U.S. surgeons perform successful "COVID to COVID" double-lung transplant. Six leading US health officials now reveal to CNN the real challenges they faced during the nation's fight against the pandemic. Mask allows athletes to simulate high altitude training.

Amish community may have reached coronavirus herd immunity, health official says. Dr. Rochelle Walensky said the US has come 'such a long way' with three vaccines and pleaded with the nation to keep following mitigation measures. Biden says 90% of adults will be vaccine eligible in three weeks. Trump accuses Fauci, Birx of 'trying to reinvent history' of coronavirus pandemic response. Laura Ingraham slams CDC's doom and gloom outlook on coronavirus: Medical left is holding onto power? NPR/Marist Poll: Biden Gets High Marks On COVID-19. It's Not The Case On Immigration. WHO report on COVID-19 origin inconclusive, calls for further studies. New

Biden says most adults should be eligible for COVID-19 vaccine by April 19. Rachel Campos-Duffy: The pandemic power grab.

The B.1.1.7 variant is more contagious and may cause more severe disease, an epidemiologist says. Recent research suggests it may also be more deadly. Pfizer to test freeze-dried COVID-19 vaccine that doesn't need ultra-cold storage. COVID-19 pushed total US deaths beyond 3.3 million last year. Cotton boosts COVID 'lab leak' theory, slams WHO as 'obsequious sycophants' to Chinese Communists. Republicans trumpet elements of Covid-19 relief bill they voted against. Take an exclusive look inside a busy Covid-19 vaccine facility. Pfizer says trials suggest vaccine works against South African variant, is effective after 6 months. Stillbirths, maternal deaths up by one-third amid pandemic: study.

Don't freak out if you get these side effects from a Covid vaccine. They can actually be a good sign. MLB's opening day marked by a COVID-19 postponement, weather impacts and limited fans. Dr. Anthony Fauci Does Not Expect A 4th Coronavirus Wave To Hit The U.S. Brazil is breaking Covid-19 records. Here's what's happening. Puerto Rico fining tourists $100 for violating mask mandate. Pandemic Has Strengthened Faith For Some. **Florida governor bans Covid-19 'vaccine passports' [4/3/2021]**. Officials across several states have reported alarming Covid-19 data. These types of people 'won' the Covid quarantine. After COVID outbreak, Nats wait to hear about facing Braves. DNC launches billboard blitz to sell Biden's $1.9T coronavirus relief law. Fauci weighs in on COVID-19 vaccine safety in pregnant women. Coronavirus vaccine passports wont be mandated by federal government, Fauci says.

Robots in California test wastewater to predict COVID outbreaks. In Michigan's latest Covid-19 surge, there's a new kind of patient. Bar reopening linked to 46 COVID-19 cases, school closure: CDC. WHO against coronavirus vaccine passports for the time being, spokesperson says. Biden to call for all to be eligible for vaccine by April 19 amid COVID 'concern'. Montana Gov. Greg Gianforte tests positive for Covid-19. Couple married for 55 years reunites for first hug since start of pandemic. Opinion: Three vaccines to stop voter suppression.

Biden expands vaccine eligibility to all adults by April 19. Many Republican men are hesitant to get COVID vaccine. California research center tests COVID vaccine pills. French Open postponed by a week because of pandemic. Brazil's Bolsonaro says 'no national lockdown' despite record Covid deaths. Coronavirus survivors might experience more intense COVID-19 vaccine side effects, experts say. 'Only hot people get the Pfizer': Vaccine rivalries descend on TikTok. Is India Running Out of Vaccine Doses?

American Airlines cancels flight after crew member tests positive for COVID. As America's youth faces mental health 'crisis,' Biden admin sets focus on pandemic's impact on children. Prince Philip's funeral plans being revised due to coronavirus pandemic: report. Several states report adverse reactions to Johnson & Johnson COVID vaccine; states report increase in cases in kids. How to stay safe at church in the Covid era. Analysis: Michigan's Covid surge is a reality check. Covid-19 hospitalizations rising among those who aren't vaccinated. Protests break out in Montreal after the city's latest Covid curfew. Woman loses 118 pounds with online rock dance class during pandemic. UN chief urges wealth tax of those who profited during COVID. Greg Gutfeld: Vaccine virtue signaling and peer pressure -- this is CNN.

Australia has 2nd likely AstraZeneca COVID-19 vaccine clot case. 'Don't freak out' over Johnson & Johnson vaccine pause, infectious diseases professor says. Selena Gomez, Jennifer Lopez headline concert to get coronavirus vaccines to poor nations. China to use 'vaccine diplomacy' to increase influence, US intel community warns. Tucker Carlson: Two COVID vaccine questions that no one will answer.

A key component of J&J vaccine could explain link to extremely rare blood clots. Tucker responds to Fauci's calling his vaccine questions a 'conspiracy theory': What are you telling us? Signs Of Economic Boom Emerge As Retail Sales Surge, Jobless Claims Hit Pandemic Low. Canucks' JT Miller questions quick return after massive COVID outbreak: 'This isn't about hockey for our team'. U.S. officials: Zika virus scarier than we thought. US setting up $1.7B national network to track virus variants. **Doctors close in on cause of blood clots potentially linked with Covid vaccines [4/17/2021].**

Post Vaccine Happy Dance: Not Just Showing Off. U.S. COVID-19 cases rise despite vaccine efforts. Vaccine supplies have dried up on the ground, with at least five states in India reporting severe shortages and urging federal action. **Israel drops outdoor mask mandate with 80% of adults vaccinated [4/18/2021].** Teenage girl gets head stuck in Barney mask. Poll finds almost half of GOP doesn't want vaccine. Fauci reacts. Half of US adults have received at least one Covid-19 vaccine shot.

Eco-Activist Greta Thunberg Has A New Issue: The Moral Threat of Vaccine Inequality. EU regulator to issue advice on Johnson & Johnson COVID-19 vaccine. The trouble with maskless tourists. Scalise accuses Biden administration of 'exempting' illegal immigrants from COVID-19 restrictions. US may soon reach a tipping point on Covid vaccine demand. That's concerning. Pfizer confirms fake COVID vaccines found in Mexico, Poland black markets. FDA report details flaws at Emergent facility making Johnson & Johnson vaccine. Iowa governor urges residents to get vaccines as demand falls in 43 of 99 counties. US jobless claims fall to 547,000, another pandemic low. Vaccine Passports: Israel, Bahrain Reach Landmark Agreement.

People With Severe COVID-19 Have Higher Risk Of Long-Term Effects, Study Finds. Biden Administration Looks For Help With Next Phase Of Pitching COVID Vaccines. FDA: N95 masks, now plentiful, should no longer be reused. **CDC 'looking' into whether masks are necessary outside [4/23/2021]**. Where Dr. Gupta says most Covid-19 transmissions happen may surprise you. FDA, CDC lift pause on J&J Covid vaccinations. Muslim Americans Reflect On Another Ramadan During The Pandemic. Navajo Nation nears herd immunity thanks to vaccination efforts. COMIC: How I Cope With Pandemic Numbness.

NASCAR president Steve Phelps says requiring COVID-19 vaccinations not under consideration. U.S. to provide Covid vaccine components, medical supplies to India. Indians rely on "COVID warriors" as new cases set another record. How A U.K. Imam Countered Vaccine Hesitancy And Helped Thousands Get The 'Jab'. Airline bans state lawmaker for violating mask mandate. Anxiety over post-pandemic socialization on the rise.

How you and your kids can avoid Covid-19 at playgrounds. Deadline for Real ID for air travel pushed back due to Covid pandemic. Experts fear India has more than half a billion Covid cases. US to begin sharing AstraZeneca coronavirus vaccine doses soon. Burning Man canceled for second year in a row over coronavirus concerns. Janice Dean reacts to Cuomo leading COVID conference call with governors: I'm not surprised anymore. Top NFL Draft prospect tests positive for COVID-19, will skip in-person event. The President has moved fast since his inauguration, signing a Covid relief bill into law and issuing executive orders. Here are some charts showing just how he did. Atlantic writer slams CDC's new mask guidelines: Too timid, too complicated, and too late.

After year of coronavirus restrictions, oldest woman in US wants to eat with friend again. Study identifies coronavirus mental health impact on New York City nurses during pandemic's first wave. Biden Takes The Stage In His Dream Role, But The Pandemic Still Sets The Scene. India's Covid crisis has global repercussions. Weekly average of Covid deaths in US hits lowest point since October. **Covid-19 cases surpass 150 million globally [4/30/2021]**. Covid vaccination centers in India's largest city close as crisis spirals. Mumbai closes vaccination centers as India's Covid cases surpass world record. Biden bans travel from India amid COVID surge. WHO lists Moderna vaccine for emergency use. No breaks: Huge auto lender didn't give borrowers deferrals during Covid. How Opioids Could Treat COVID Long Haul Symptoms. Smerconish: We need a better vaccine 'carrot'.

John Avlon on vaccine refusal: There's no cure for stupid. Here's why so many people are skipping their second Covid shot -- and why they shouldn't. Witness describes being on lockdown during hospital shooting. Why India's coronavirus data is vastly undercounted. CVS, Walgreens have wasted more vaccine doses than most states combined. **Sports stadiums asking fans for their "vaccine passports" [5/3/2021]**. How to avoid parental burnout as pandemic lingers. Here's what is really happening in India's Covid outbreak.

Vaccines are helping bring down US Covid numbers. But the virus is now hitting one group harder. Biden's new COVID-19 vaccine goal aims for 160M fully inoculated by July 4. FDA preparing to authorize Pfizer Covid vaccine for 12- to 15-year-olds as early as next week. Biden sets goal of giving at least one Covid vaccine to 70% of US adults by July 4. Hotels And Restaurants That Survived Pandemic Face New Challenge: Staffing Shortages. Canada OK's Pfizer COVID-19 vaccine for kids ages 12 and over. 'COVID Bandit' leaves $4,600 tip for Colorado restaurant staff.

They Desperately Need COVID Vaccines. So Why Are Some Countries Throwing Out Doses?

Chapter 12

U.S. Coronavirus Infections Continue to Decline Despite a Slowing Pace of Vaccinations

May 5th, 2021 – July 19th, 2021

Analysis: The big lie. The Covid misinformation. It all comes back to Russia. India reports highest-ever 24-hour surge in Covid cases and a record-high daily death toll. US rolls out carrots and expands access in push to get holdouts vaccinated against Covid. South Carolina and Montana to end all pandemic unemployment benefits for jobless residents. China opens Everest's north side to 38 virus-tested climbers. Wuhan 'lab leak' coronavirus theory in focus as House Republicans demand answers. Is The Variant From India The Most Contagious Coronavirus Mutant On The Planet? EU calls on US to push exports to counter vaccine shortage. Elementary school lockdown training saved lives. More nations are being ravaged by Covid waves. As the pandemic impacts the global supply chain, here's what CNN Business writers say will be hard to get, why and for how long.

Andrew Cuomo investigation expands over politicization of vaccine distribution. Gottlieb calls for easing restrictions on indoor gatherings as COVID-19 cases drop. Why do we still need to wear masks? Dr. Sanjay Gupta explains. **Fauci: It may be time to rethink indoor mask mandates [5/10/2021]**. David McKenzie is live in South Africa as the region grapples with vaccine scarcity. When we could see Covid-19 cases and deaths plummet in the US. Nearly 80% of people in the US live within 5 miles of all three Covid-19 vaccines. Bloomberg columnist deletes tweet saying 'so what' if COVID came from Wuhan lab leak in China. Tucker Carlson: Anthony Fauci let the coronavirus pandemic happen, why isn't there a criminal investigation? Families, Communities Divided Over COVID Vaccination In Rural Montana. Podcast: Gupta explores how neuroscience can help us prepare for the 'new normal'. Renewable Energy Capacity Jumped 45% Worldwide In 2020; IEA Sees 'New Normal'.

Biden administration combats slowing coronavirus vaccination pace. WHO should have more power to stop pandemics. Disney World reducing coronavirus social distancing protocols. CVS will begin administering Pfizer's Covid-19 vaccine in 12-15-year-olds on Thursday. CDC recommends use of Pfizer vaccine in 12-15-year-olds. A pediatrician answers safety questions on kids and the vaccine. JetBlue passenger fined $10,500 for blowing nose in blanket, not wearing mask.

New guidelines say those fully vaccinated against Covid-19 can take part in indoor or outdoor activities without a mask [5/13/2021]. Losing pandemic unemployment benefits early Share your story. Yankees' Gleyber Torres tests positive for COVID as team deals with 'breakthrough' cases. CDC says fully vaccinated people can go maskless in most places. CDC mask guidance opens doors for the vaccinated, but a long road is ahead for those who are not, experts say. Mask Or No Mask That Depends Where You Live. The CDC changed its guidance on masks for fully vaccinated people, but the new recommendations raise a lot of questions. Here's what we know.. Bill Maher tests positive for COVID-19. Laura Ingraham on CDC updating mask guidance for vaccinated Americans. What the new CDC mask guidance means for dining out. New mask guidance sends states and businesses scrambling. McCarthy dings Biden: Notice mask orders ended 'Gasoline went to $7, and they wanted change in news'. Where vaccinated customers can shop without a mask.

'Race for the Vaccine'. Vaccinated Gupta explains what you can do without a mask. Some Americans are questioning the CDC guidance and whether they should trust that people would wear a mask if they were unvaccinated. CDC chief on masks: People should be honest with themselves. The US ushered in a quick return to normalcy this weekend, responding to the CDC's latest mask guidance, but some experts say the move came too fast.

Larry Madowo is live in Nairobi, Kenya, as a global vaccine-sharing initiative falls short. Passenger snorts white powder, refuses to wear mask and forces flight to divert to Minneapolis airport. Kentucky nonprofit delivering groceries, essential items to people in need during pandemic. For small businesses, a conundrum over change in mask guidance. Several days since the CDC said fully vaccinated Americans can ditch their masks, experts are worried about the rapid changes. It's reasonable for US businesses to keep mask mandates in some cases, Fauci says. About 60% of Americans 18 and older have had at least one dose of Covid-19 vaccine. No Masks Are Required At Most Texas State Facilities Anymore.

House GOP lawmakers fined after defying mask mandate. Mask comes off: Indoor mandates for vaccinated people ending in at least 25 states. Hong Kong's vaccine drive is slowing. Covid booster shot will likely be needed 'within a year or so' of vaccination, Fauci says. New York City reopens after being pandemic's epicenter. 'The Ingraham Angle' on climate lockdowns. As COVID-19 restrictions ease, gym franchise owner says crowds are certainly coming back?

UN urges Biden to end Title 42 restrictions that allow for migrant removals due to COVID-19 risk. Dan Gainor: On COVID, forget 'follow the science' now it's follow the liberal media as they attack the CDC. UVA to mandate COVID-19 vaccination for in-person students this fall. New York Yankees' breakthrough infections demonstrate the Covid-19 vaccine works. Here's why. These states slow to vaccinate against Covid may struggle this summer, expert warns. The states where a vaccine is also a lottery ticket. A vaccinated person might need a booster to stay protected against the original Covid strain and variants. U.S. coronavirus infections steadily declining.

Texas Gov. Abbott says declining COVID numbers, day with zero deaths prove opening economy was 'right move'. Their lives haven't changed since getting vaccinated. This is their new normal. Wuhan lab director says US intelligence report is 'a complete lie'. The US economy is operating at 90% of where it was before the pandemic. White House insists COVID-19 origins requires 'transparent' international investigation.

2-time Olympic medalist weighs in on Olympics amid pandemic. 'Ignorance': Doctor reacts to Rand Paul going maskless on Senate floor. About 39% of US population is fully vaccinated against Covid, CDC says. Moderna says COVID-19 vaccine 100% effective in kids ages 12 to 18. Japan faces pre-Olympics COVID surge, prompting CDC to warn Americans against traveling there. **Half of US adults now fully vaccinated against COVID-19: CDC [5/25/2021]**. After mocking and dismissing Wuhan lab theory, media now taking it seriously. Experts say those who are not inoculated against Covid shouldn't rely on protection from those who are. Rep. Marjorie Taylor Greene facing criticism for comparing mask mandates, vaccines to the Holocaust.

Biden asks intelligence community to 'redouble' efforts to determine the origins of Covid-19. Biden Asks U.S. Intel To Push For Stronger Conclusions On The Coronavirus' Origins. **Facebook lifts ban on posts claiming COVID-19 was man-made [5/27/2021]**. The mystery over Covid-19's origin has political implications for the world, as well as dueling legacies of two presidents that will be defined by the pandemic. Every

Possible Explanation For COVID-19 Should Be Investigated, Expert Says. Sanofi, GlaxoSmithKline COVID-19 vaccine production to begin in weeks. Watch Live: Minnesota governor to announce vaccine incentives.

First-time unemployment claims hit a new pandemic low. NHL pandemic playoffs outside bubble off to thrilling start. "So-called" election to hand Assad new mandate in Syria. **Employers Can (Mostly) Require Vaccines For Workers Returning To The Office [5/28/2021].** Coronavirus FAQ: Kids In India Ask Heartbreaking Questions. How Do You Answer Them? Idaho governor repeals mask mandate ban issued while he was away.

With all the progress that's been made in containing Covid-19, you can begin to make plans for an almost-normal summer. Travel surge expected this weekend as COVID vaccination rate climbs. Florida man accused of stealing ventilators intended for Covid-19 patients. Life in Europe was halted by Covid. Domestic terror efforts weren't. TSA sees record pandemic air travel to start Memorial Day weekend. ABC's chief White House reporter: A lot of reporters have 'egg on their face' over Wuhan lab-leak theory. Callista and Newt Gingrich: Memorial Day heroes -- nation honors those who stood on front lines for freedom. Jason Chaffetz: COVID funeral payments -- Biden program an invitation to commit fraud. Here's how.

Accidental drownings a concern as pandemic postponed swimming lessons for some. **No Covid deaths recorded in UK for first time since pandemic began [6/1/2021].** Pandemic worsens pre-existing mental illness. West Virginia offering guns as prizes in COVID vaccine lottery. Scientists push for full investigation into COVID-19 lab leak theory. Sackler Family Empire Poised To Win Immunity From Opioid Lawsuits. The White House's partnership with Anheuser-Busch offering free beers if the country reaches its Covid vaccine goal by July 4 is more than a gimmick. "Month of action": Free beer among the incentives as Biden urges COVID-19 vaccinations. Fauci: Don't be 'accusatory' with China on coronavirus investigation. Scalise, Comer say Fauci must testify about published emails, COVID-19 origin.

Surge In Traffic Deaths In 2020 Linked To Drivers' Risky Behavior During The Pandemic. Kevin McCarthy: Democrats ignored truth about COVID origins putting politics before American lives. Giving kids COVID-19 vaccine 'not a high priority' amid shortage, WHO says. Unemployment rate falls to 5.8%, a pandemic-era low. COVID Is Crushing Nepal, From Remote Villages To Kathmandu To Mt. Everest. Wall Street Journal editorial: 'Reasonable to ask' why Fauci was slow to accept coronavirus lab-leak theory. CDC: Rise in teen hospitalizations shows importance of vaccine. CDC urges parents to vaccinate their teens after spike in COVID hospitalizations. The slippage in new adults getting the vaccine isn't shocking. And on the current trajectory, we'll miss Biden's targeted date.

US begins reopening as Covid cases decline. Wrongfully convicted man was released after 27 years, but then the world went on lockdown. Much of the information on the card is straightforward, but other parts, such as the vaccine lot number, point to key details that are less widely understood. Glenn Greenwald rips media who 'pretended' to have scientific knowledge on coronavirus origins. Analyzing the slowdown of U.S. COVID vaccinations. CNN's Cuomo enlists Sanjay Gupta to bash U.S. response to coronavirus while ignoring brother's mishaps. Expert says some vaccine hesitancy is due to misunderstanding over natural immunity. Joint Base Pearl Harbor-Hickam goes on lockdown over 'security incident. Lindsey Graham says lab leak theory coverup 'stinks to high heavens'. Suddenly a presidency built on multitrillion-dollar Covid relief and a vast federal jobs and families plan is looking a little shaky. New Covid variant and rising cases spark fears over U.K.'s grand reopening.

Biden to announce plan to give 500M vaccines to countries in need. Post-pandemic recovery is in full swing and the global economy is struggling to keep up. Why do some people get side effects after COVID-19 vaccines? Experts are concerned the risk of variants could bring an end to the nationwide reopening. President Biden announces U.S. new global vaccine efforts. Sanjay Gupta reacts to Ohio doctor's unhinged vaccine claim.

Some Bitcoin conference attendees report testing positive for Covid after event. G7 leaders expected to pledge 1 billion COVID vaccine doses for countries in need. Doctor on rare cases of heart inflammation following COVID-19 vaccines. **CDC to discuss reports of heart inflammation in young people after COVID vaccines [6/11/2021]**. YouTube suspends GOP senator's account over Covid-19 post. The woman who spent lockdown alone in the Arctic. Noel Gallagher discusses his music career and what he's been up to throughout the pandemic. Less than half the adults in five US states have received their first Covid-19 vaccine dose. Blinken says China "has to cooperate" with COVID origin probe. California to remove mask mandates as it prepares to fully reopen. As COVID-19 cases wane, vaccine-lagging areas still see risk.

UK to face 'substantial third wave of coronavirus as Delta variant spreads, expert says. The company says the pandemic created 'significant' financial challenges. Retail analysts say more malls could soon follow suit as online shopping surges. Workers push back against hospitals requiring COVID vaccines. California readies for its grand Covid-19 reopening. Former CDC director Redfield explains why he believes COVID-19 emerged from lab, WHO 'compromised'. California is still requiring masks in these places. **Newly deemed 'variant of concern' delta accounts for 10 percent of U.S. cases [6/15/2021]**, CDC says. California reopening signals U.S. recovery from COVID-19 pandemic. Royal Caribbean delays cruise ship after 8 crew members test positive for Covid-19. NFL loosening many COVID restrictions for vaccinated players.

Delta variant fuels fears of new COVID-19 surge in U.S. Dentists are busier than ever as focus shifts to hidden Covid loss: smiles. These communities are at high risk for dangerous Covid-19 variants, expert says. Some unvaccinated Americans waiting on full FDA approval before getting COVID shot. South battles COVID-19 vaccine hesitancy as Delta variant spreads. Ohio ends COVID-19 state of emergency after 15 months. Couple waiting two years to finalize adoption from China as pandemic leaves families in limbo. Delta variant will likely become dominant Covid-19 strain in US, CDC chief says. Legendary sprinter dies of COVID-19 dies days after his wife. Sen. Rand Paul: 'In all likelihood' COVID escaped from a Wuhan lab.

Brad Paisley says it's 'patriotic' to get the coronavirus vaccine, blames 'Hollywood elite' for hesitancy. They lost their loved ones to Covid. Then they heard from them again. India struggles with COVID-19 as a new infection targets survivors. Tokyo Olympics will allow some domestic spectators to attend despite Covid fears. Biden administration announces plan to share 55 million Covid-19 doses abroad. **CDC advisers will discuss Wednesday whether heart ailment is linked to Covid-19 vaccines [6/21/2021].** Newsom says California will pay off unpaid rent accrued during coronavirus pandemic. Nursing home deaths up 32% in 2020 amid pandemic, watchdog says.

WorldView: Spain to pardon 9 Catalan leaders; WHO reports COVID vaccines running low in poor nations. Jill Biden touts vaccine in poorly inoculated Mississippi. Secret Service saw nearly 900 employees infected by coronavirus, documents say. **Data suggests 'likely' link between COVID-19 mRNA vaccines, rare heart issues in teens, CDC panel says**

[6/23/2021]. Fox News Poll: Majority believes COVID-19 leaked from lab in China. CDC panel confirms "likely" association between mRNA COVID-19 vaccines and rare cases of heart inflammation. **Scientist says early Covid samples were deleted from NIH database [6/23/2021]**. Delta Plus: India raises alarm over a new COVID mutant. WHO flags concerns at Sputnik V COVID-19 vaccine production plant.

First coronavirus case likely appeared in China weeks before documented, UK study says. Biden criticized for using woke term 'Latinx' in comments about 'equity' in COVID-19 vaccinations. UK virus cases hit highest since Feb 5 amid 'grab a jab'. Arkansas governor says final FDA approval of COVID-19 vaccine would help fight hesitancy. Nearly every passenger vaccinated on first U.S. cruise ship to set sail since pandemic began. Disney delays test cruise over 'inconsistent' virus results. How the lumber industry misread Covid and ended up with a global shortage and sky-high prices. **Pfizer, Moderna COVID vaccines likely produce lasting immunity against coronavirus [6/29/2021]**. Problem: Keeping Vaccines Cold With Limited Electricity. Solution: Solar Fridges.

Should you wear a mask amid Delta variant surge Watch doctor's answer. Kim Jong Un warns of 'grave consequences' and fires top officials after Covid incident. **Myocarditis after COVID-19 vaccination higher in military population than expected, study finds [6/30/2021]**. The U.S. Will Add A Third Gender Option On Passports. Japan says Olympics with no fans still possible as COVID spreads. CDC isn't changing mask guidelines despite risk of COVID-19 Delta variant. House Republicans who opposed Covid aid still see funds flow to local police departments. The delta variant is forcing outbreaks around the world. Do vaccines work against it? Washington lawmaker apologizes for wearing yellow Star of David to protest Covid mandates.

VA congressman introduces amendment asking Biden to declassify intel linking Wuhan lab to COVID-19 origins. Vaccine hesitancy continues for some younger Americans. Here's one reason why. They didn't want to get Covid-19 shots. This is what convinced them. White House looking to next pandemic challenge as July 4th signals a reopened nation. Independence Day traditions return as pandemic restrictions are eased. Duchess of Cambridge forced to self-isolate after Covid-19 contact. Open-air museum of rebuilt historic buildings in UK becomes TikTok hit during lockdown.

Watch Live: Biden delivers remarks on COVID-19 vaccines. Dozens of Covid cases tied to Texas church camp, pastor says. Biden launches new plan to ramp up COVID vaccinations. WaPo urges US to 'get serious' on COVID origins after calling Wuhan lab-leak theory 'debunked' 'conspiracy'. Delta variant gains ground among unvaccinated.

Watch Live: NYC ticker-tape parade honors pandemic's essential workers. US to send millions of Covid-19 vaccines to Latin America. With Delta variant spreading, experts split on whether to test vaccinated people for Covid-19. When should vaccinated people wear masks now? An expert weighs in. US jobless claims tick up to 373,000 from a pandemic low. 'Virtually all' COVID-19 hospitalizations, deaths in US among unvaccinated, White House says. **Pfizer to seek OK for 3rd Covid vaccine dose [7/8/2021]**. Delta variant threatens U.S. communities with low vaccinations. **Americans 'do not need' COVID-19 booster shot, FDA, CDC say [7/9/2021]**. Updated CDC schools guidance prioritizes in-person learning, even if all Covid-19 safety measures aren't in place.

This couple was among the rising number of hospitalizations in Southwest Missouri. Other areas of the US are vulnerable to surges in Covid-19 cases. With an uptick in Covid-19 cases, there is growing alarm. 'We've seen almost an entire takeover in the Delta variant,' one state official says. Nixa, Missouri mayor discusses pandemic's impact and calls for his removal. Lt. Gov. Dan Patrick touts Texas COVID approach, says CPAC should stay in Lone Star State. Gottlieb says "prudent" to get started now on COVID vaccine booster approval. The ex-President showed that defeat, the disgrace of his insurrection and the deaths of 400,000 Americans in a pandemic he downplayed don't hurt his appeal. Marsha Blackburn renews criticism of media, Big Tech, Fauci for suppressing coronavirus lab-leak theory.

New coronavirus variants seen as too contagious for hotel quarantines. CDC, FDA investigating possible J&J vaccine link to rare neurological disorder. Iraqi Health Officials Say 50 People Died In Coronavirus Ward Fire. Americans need to make a choice in order to avoid a Covid surge, expert says. Pandemic saw worsening mental health among teens, young adults, study finds. No Fast Music Or Fast Running: COVID Rules In Seoul Force Gym-Goers To Slow Down. These 2 maps tell the story of Covid-19 in America. Norwegian Cruise Lines sues state of Florida over vaccine passport ban

Death toll rises to 92 in blaze at coronavirus ward in Iraq. Bach meets Suga as Tokyo virus cases approach 6-month high.

Remarkable overlap: 2 maps that tell the story of Covid-19 in America. Superspreader 'explosions' plague efforts to curb pandemic. Hear the anti-vaccine rhetoric from Fox News amidst Covid deaths. More than 90% of new Covid-19 cases in Mississippi are of unvaccinated people, governor says. Millions of children worldwide missed routine vaccinations during the pandemic, study suggests. Can vaccinated people get long Covid Doctors say risk is 'very, very small'. COVID-19 saw millions miss childhood vaccinations, WHO warns. Pandemic made pregnant women's hunt for drug rehab harder. Olympic athlete, staffer test positive for virus in Tokyo.

Olympic athlete and five other personnel test positive for COVID-19. NFL Network's Rich Eisen tests positive for COVID-

19 despite being vaccinated. WHO chief says it was 'premature' to rule out Covid lab leak. House Republicans introduce bill to ban 'tyrannical' federal mask mandates. U.S. Sports Teams Are Back In Action. But Coronavirus Infections Are Still A Threat. Las Vegas officials recommend masks indoors, regardless of vaccination status.

Biden blasted for accusing Facebook of 'killing people' over COVID misinformation as WH partners with Big Tech [7/17/2021]. First Covid case reported in Olympic village days before games kick off. Los Angeles County sheriff will not enforce mask mandate. 'A pandemic of the unvaccinated': COVID-19 infections rising among those without vaccines. Las Vegas cafe owner says he and his employees are 'shocked' by renewed mask mandate.

Do fully vaccinated people need to wear masks because of this Delta strain? Five things that are cheaper now than before the pandemic. Conservative hostility to Biden vaccine push surges with Covid cases on the rise. The teenage alternate has no symptoms and is quarantined in her hotel room days before the Olympics.

Chapter 13

Unvaccinated People Risk the Most Serious Virus of Their Lives

July 19th, 2021 – September 8th, 2021

Analysis: Trump is the opposite of leadership on vaccines. COVID patient: Rejecting the vaccine is "playing Russian roulette". Dow sinks more than 800 points as delta variant stokes new fears for recovery. Fox has quietly implemented its own version of a vaccine passport while its top personalities attack them. Indiana University's Vaccine Requirement Should Stand, Federal Judge Rules. Hear Dr. Fauci's warning about about Covid-19.

The Life Cycle Of A COVID-19 Vaccine Lie. COVID vaccination delays let killer 3rd wave slam South Africa. Vaccinated Pelosi aide tests positive for COVID after contact with Texas Dems. Fauci blasts Rand Paul's Wuhan lab funding claim: 'You do not know what you're taking about'. Dutch court convicts men of torching virus testing center during protests. Viruses are landing kids in the ICU this summer, but it's not all Covid. 3 GOP House members lose appeals over $500 mask fines. US life expectancy falls by more than a year due to pandemic. A growing number of Republicans urge people to get vaccinated as COVID-19 cases climb. Tokyo Olympics chief not ruling out COVID canceling the Games. New study suggests Johnson & Johnson coronavirus vaccine less effective against Delta variant.

'I'm sorry, but it's too late': Doctor says unvaccinated Covid patients beg for vaccine. Sixth-generation company reinvents itself during pandemic: Made in America. As GOP supporters die of Covid, the party remains split in its vaccination message. **US virus cases nearly triple in 2 weeks amid misinformation [7/22/2021]**. Man with COVID disguises himself as wife to board flight. Former Miami Beach mayor criticizes Florida Governor Ron DeSantis' COVID-19 response.

Not all Republicans are embracing McConnell's vaccine push. NFL says COVID outbreaks among unvaccinated players may result in forfeiting games, loss of pay in new policy. Runaway Texas Democrat slammed for call to let schools impose mask mandates. NFL says COVID outbreaks may force teams to forfeit games. LA sheriff explains why he won't enforce mask mandate. 'Special Report' on the resurgence of COVID. Low vaccination rates and Delta variant fuel COVID-19 surge in U.S. Texas Democrat: I'm sure colleagues who got Covid wished they'd worn masks on private flight. Biden administration not mandating COVID vaccines for White House staff, Psaki says. Unvaccinated former nurse Christy Henry felt because of her rural location and lifestyle, her Covid-19 risk was low. Then she got sick. State Department suspends online passport appointment system. A Missouri hospital just hit its all-time high for Covid cases. But the county fair that attracts thousands won't be canceled.

I'm vaccinated but just tested positive. What should I do? And other Covid questions, answered [7/24/2021]. Snow leopard at San Diego Zoo tests positive for COVID-19. French protesters reject virus passes, vaccine mandate. LA County Covid hospitalizations more than doubled in 2 weeks. Covid-19 cases surge nationwide as vaccination rates plummet from spring highs. **Demonstrators protest against vaccine passports in France, Italy and Australia [7/25/2021].** Global protests against COVID-19 restrictions.

How A U.S. Olympic Pair Keeps Going After One Tests Positive For Coronavirus In Tokyo. COVID-19 infections up across the U.S.. NYC to require vaccines or weekly testing for city workers. Analysis: Call vaccine hesitancy this instead. Wildfire smoke exposure linked to COVID-19 case increase: study. Protests erupt across Europe against coronavirus mandates. California, NYC to workers: Get vaccine or face weekly tests. Moderna may expand pediatric COVID-19 vaccine trial.

Mayor of Florida county home to Disney World sounds alarm on surging Covid cases. 'Ingraham Angle' on mask mandates, Biden's failure in his role. Biden administration to recommend the vaccinated wear masks in some areas. White House calls masks 'extra' protection for vaccinated while reiterating 'the vaccines work'. CDC Urges Vaccinated People To Mask Up Indoors In Places With High Virus Transmission. Tokyo COVID cases reach record-high amid Summer Games.

Rivera opens Washington camp frustrated by vaccine hesitancy. Tucker Carlson: New mask guidelines are about politics and control. The science didn't change, the virus did, Fauci says as CDC updates mask guidance. Eye Opener: CDC recommends masks again. Masks are back, as Delta variant forces dramatic reversal in US. Pelosi calls McCarthy 'a moron' for his mask mandate criticism. **Mask mandates pour in nationwide after CDC revises guidance for vaccinated people [7/28/2021]**. Texas police department warns public after COVID-positive migrants released by Border Patrol into town.

Democratic congressman calls on Biden to put a 'pause' on border crisis, as COVID spikes in Texas. MLB game postponed due to positive coronavirus tests on Washington Nationals team. Coronavirus Knocks U.S. Pole Vaulter Sam Kendricks Out Of Tokyo Olympics. Doctor: The heartbreaking Covid cases I'm seeing. Biden Hopes To Jolt COVID Vaccination Rates By Focusing On Federal Workers. FDA OK's Emergent BioSolutions plant to resume manufacturing J&J's Covid vaccine. Randi

Weingarten ripped after telling MSNBC 'we're going to try' to reopen schools after CDC mask guidance. If you aren't vaccinated and haven't had COVID, you will get Delta variant: Adm. Giroir. Israel Is Offering Its Older Citizens A 3rd COVID-19 Shot As Infections Rise.

She's living in ICU as her daughter battles Covid. Biden defends previously saying vaccinated don't need masks: 'That was true at the time'. **Biden announces measures to incentivize Covid-19 vaccinations, including a requirement for federal employees [7/29/2021]**. A CDC Internal Report Says The Delta Variant Is More Transmissible Than A Cold. Analysis: Biden opens up new front in Covid-19 vaccination war as concerns over variant deepen. Nikki Haley: Global COVID vaccine campaign -- US can be generous without being stupid. Tucker: Democrats rode virus panic all the way to the White House. CNN accused of hypocrisy, pro-regime propaganda for sounding alarm on Cuba COVID surge amid protests. Atlanta students in quarantine after two staffers and a student test positive for Covid-19.

Six cruise ship passengers test positive for Covid. 'The View' co-host Meghan McCain: I have a better chance of getting shot in DC than contracting COVID. **Walmart mandates vaccines for all corporate employees [7/30/2021]**. Louisiana governor considering mask mandate amid COVID surge. CDC finds Delta variant more contagious than common cold. As Covid-19 cases surge in Florida, governor says parents should decide whether their children wear masks to school. As COVID Concern Grows In Kansas, So Does Confusion Over Who Is In Charge. Shot in the arm: CBS News Medical Contributor Dr. David Agus Breaks down Delta variant.

US fencer accused of sexual misconduct confronts teammates after pink mask protest on Olympic stage. Florida has more new Covid cases than ever before. Sharon Stone says she's been 'threatened' with losing work over coronavirus vaccine insistence on set. Her family was scared to get vaccinated. Then her dad and brother died of Covid. Local Matters: Ranking last in the U.S. for vaccinations, Alabama faces its 2nd-largest COVID wave. U.S. passes 35 million Covid cases as California tops 4 million. Florida's largest school district is worried about funding after governor bans school mask mandates. Avlon: GOP trying to profit off of vaccine polarization. Doctor explains what we know about the Delta variant and kids. NFL Alumni, CDC fight COVID-19 vaccination hesitancy. Breyer rejects Maine church's attempt to block Delta variant restrictions that don't exist. Is it legal to mandate Covid vaccines? In many circumstances, yes.

CDC adds 16 places to 'very high' Covid travel risk list. Largest hospital in Louisiana sees 'darkest days of the pandemic'. CDC extends order restricting border crossing amid claims of regular release of COVID-positive migrants. Firefighter battling western wildfires shares his story on front lines. McDonald's again requiring masks as Delta variant spreads. A Bright Spot Amid Haiti's Woes: Its First Mass Rollout Of COVID Vaccines. Biden administration to announce new efforts to limit evictions during pandemic. Officer killed in stabbing attack at Pentagon transit station that led to lockdown.

Texas firefighter lied about having COVID-19 to get $12K in paid time off. A teacher is suing an Arizona school district for implementing a mask mandate despite governor's ban. The 2021 Met Gala will require guests be vaccinated, masked indoors. Global number of Covid-19 cases will exceed 200 million next week, WHO says. WNBA star Katie Lou Samuelson on missing Olympics over COVID: 'Devastated'.

Biden's top health officials sending mixed messages on Covid-19 response. What is the new delta plus variant? Why WHO Is Calling For A Moratorium On COVID Vaccine Boosters. New Mexico Education Dept. suspends school board that refused to comply with mask guidance. 'Hannity' on Gov.

Cuomo's sexual harassment allegations, COVID vaccinations. Chad Wolf: Border apprehensions at 'astronomical' level as COVID-positive migrants released into Texas towns. COVID-19 surge and looming end of rescue programs raise economic worries. DeSantis clashes with Biden as Florida faces mounting COVID surge. Schools sue and mayor defies Arkansas mask mandate ban.

Gulf Coast Businesses Struggle To Stay Open As COVID-19 Outbreaks Surge Among Staff. United Airlines to require COVID vaccinations for all US based employees. Arkansas judge blocks state from enforcing mask mandate ban. Summer smoke might be the new normal in Colorado. Coronavirus FAQ: Is It Ethical To Lie To Get A Booster Or A Shot For An Under-12 Kid? Italy mandates vaccine pass for restaurants and museums. Unvaccinated dad hospitalized for Covid makes heartbreaking request for daughter's wedding in case he dies.

Opinion: Dear Mum, Your Son The Doctor Thinks You Should Get A COVID Vaccine. 'We've never seen numbers like this before,' health expert says as Gov. DeSantis doubles down on banning mask mandates in schools. San Francisco sheriffs' union warns officers will quit or retire if forced to receive COVID vaccine. Motorcyclists gather for Sturgis Rally as Delta variant cases surge. Mixed bag: Erratic Pandemic Olympics come to a nuanced end. GOP senator breaks with DeSantis on school mask mandates: 'The local official should have control'. New Orleans Jazz Fest canceled again due to COVID-19. UK health chief sees 'unfair' pricing for COVID travel tests. CNN's Jim Acosta ripped for renaming Delta variant the 'DeSantis variant': 'Performance art'. 'Bleak to say the least': John King shares startling Covid numbers.

Pentagon to require mandatory COVID vaccines by mid-September [8/9/2021]. The Pfizer vaccine may receive full approval soon, and the ramifications could alter the course of the pandemic. Florida grapples with record Covid surge as school looms. DeSantis escalates war on masks in schools. 'Can we talk about common sense': Lemon on politicians and mask mandates. What happens to migrants with COVID at the border. 'Gutfeld!' on vaccine mandates, Cuomo brothers. Ravens' Lamar Jackson noncommittal on vaccine after second COVID bout: 'I can't dwell on that right now'.

Texas struggles to contain latest COVID-19 surge. Pediatric COVID infections rise as some school districts impose mask mandates. Cuomo's fall serves as a warning for other governors whose flaws are magnified in the Covid spotlight. A psychiatrist's advice on how to approach talking to your vaccine-hesitant loved ones. GOP seizes on backlash to new mandates. Being Unvaccinated For COVID Will Cost Students At A Small College An Extra $750.

Florida investigating school districts that defied ban on mask mandates. Florida county ask residents to use 911 sparingly amid COVID surge. FDA expected to allow third vaccine dose for some immunocompromised Americans. Debate grows over mask mandates in schools as Delta variant poses risk to children. Pandemic deja vu: Limits on indoor gatherings, lines at test sites are back. HHS the latest agency to mandate COVID vaccinations for health care workers. HHS to mandate vaccinations for more than 25,000 employees. San Francisco mandates proof of vaccination when indoors. Sony delays "Venom" sequel release amid Delta variant surge.

DeSantis says the units will administer monoclonal antibody treatments to infected residents. The state's Covid cases have exploded in the last month. The US has seen a 1,200% increase in orders for monoclonal antibodies to treat Covid-19, HHS says. Extra vaccine dose OK'd for some with weakened immune systems, FDA'says. Rep. Lauren Boebert: COVID vaccine mandates vs. personal freedom -- here's how to decide what's right for you. COVID Cases Are Rising In ICE Facilities, Putting Detainees And The Public At Risk. Young mom dies of COVID days after giving birth. Vaccine mandates for workers are just getting started.

Hundreds of Palm Beach students forced into COVID quarantine. Supreme Court allows Indiana University's COVID vaccine mandate, blocks part of NY eviction freeze. CDC director OKs COVID-19 booster shot for some Americans with weak immune systems. Federal health officials greenlight coronavirus booster shot for some vulnerable Americans. DeSantis and the GOP claim Covid is 'pouring through' the border. Experts are debunking them. School districts battle over mask mandates as COVID-19 Delta variant spreads.

Covid-19 vaccination is increasingly becoming a ticket of entry into public spaces. Here's how to prove your status on your phone [8/15/2021]. Mask mandates aren't allowed in Florida schools. One school found a loophole. Colorado deputies will be at schools due to 'tensions' over mask mandate. Cardinal hospitalized with COVID, breathing with ventilator. Atlanta Falcons become the first NFL team to be 100% vaccinated against COVID. Korn singer Jonathan Davis tests positive for coronavirus, forces band to change summer 2021 tour schedule. Catholic cardinal, a vaccine skeptic, on ventilator with COVID-19. Texas Gov. Greg Abbott tests positive for COVID-19.

US destroyed some Afghans' passports as they prepared to evacuate embassy in Kabul -- but it's unclear why. COVID-19 vaccine boosters: Here's what to know. As Covid-19 cases rise among teens, so do vaccinations, CNN analysis finds. Colleges Begin The Fall Semester In Person With COVID Worries Abound. Staff member for Queen Elizabeth II tests positive for the coronavirus: report. Special Report: Biden speaks on COVID-19 vaccines, boosters and nursing homes. Texas superintendent speaks out after parents accosted 2 teachers over masks. Bills' Dion Dawkins on COVID battle: 'I just wish that I could have been fully vaccinated'.

Mississippi doctor on surge in COVID-19 cases, strain on hospitals. Garth Brooks cancels tour dates because of COVID Delta surge. The shipping supply chain is stressed from Covid. That makes it ripe for hackers. 3 senators test positive for COVID-19 as U.S. prepares for booster shots. Do I need a booster if I got the Johnson & Johnson vaccine? Dr. Sanjay Gupta: Simple steps for coexisting with the coronavirus.

Montana only state to ban vaccine requirements for employees [8/20/2021]. More than 3,000 fake COVID vaccine cards seized at Anchorage airport. A Biden administration official said approval of the two-dose vaccine 'could be as early as Monday'. Full FDA approval of Pfizer/BioNTech Covid-19 vaccine is 'imminent', senior federal official says. University of Virginia disenrolls 238 students over vaccine mandate. **'Stop it': FDA warns people not to take veterinary drugs [ivermectin] to treat Covid-19 [8/21/2021]**. Jesse Jackson and his wife, Jacqueline, hospitalized with COVID. Large events canceled due to delta variant, wallop states' economies.

A Texas school district changed its dress code to get around a mask mandate ban. New Evidence Points To Antibodies As A Reliable Indicator Of Vaccine Protection. WHO head calls for two-month vaccine booster moratorium. **FDA grants full approval to Pfizer's Covid vaccine [8/23/2021]**. Rev. Jesse Jackson and wife hospitalized with COVID-19 breakthrough infections. Special Report: Biden speaks on COVID-19 vaccines after FDA grants Pfizer full approval. So many people in this Texas town got Covid that schools shut down and the city essentially closed. Opinion: I voted to defy Ron DeSantis on masks for schools.

It's Pronounced Koe-mir'-na-tee. How The Pfizer-BioNTech Vaccine's Name Came To Be. Use These 6 Expert Tips To Find The Best Masks For Your Kids. Missouri AG files class action lawsuit against schools enforcing mask mandates on children. A Woman Who Coughed On Store Food, Claiming She Had

Coronavirus, Gets A Jail Sentence. Two Florida counties double down on school mask mandates, defying governor's order. Texas man strips down to underwear over masks at heated school board meeting. Johnson & Johnson says booster shot provides 'rapid and robust' Covid antibody increase. Covid vaccinations in Afghanistan plummet. N.Y. Gov. Hochul adds 12k deaths to total coronavirus tally in show of 'transparency'. Janice Dean calls for federal probe into all COVID-19 nursing home deaths after NY adds 12K to previous total. Johnson & Johnson says its booster shot strengthens immunity. Washington school district halts program requiring athletes wear COVID tracking monitors.

Oregon National Guard deployed to aid hospitals overwhelmed with COVID-19 patients. More Than 100,000 People Are Hospitalized With COVID-19, The Most Since January. Why COVID Takes A Harsher Toll On Children With Cancer. 1 in 3 Americans had COVID-19 by end of 2020, study says. Two siblings banned from high school for not wearing masks.

Florida Judge Throws Out Gov. Ron DeSantis' Order Prohibiting School Mask Mandates. HHS diverting millions in funding marked for vaccine efforts to housing migrant children. Unvaccinated, unmasked teacher infected students in class with Covid, CDC reports. **There is no room to put these bodies.' Covid deaths climb [8/28/2021]**. Facui says COVID vaccination mandates for school children good idea? How COVID is creating a challenge during Hurricane Ida. Insider Q&A: What's next for student loans in the COVID era. Delta variant may double risk of hospitalization for the unvaccinated, study finds. Louisiana hospitals brace for victims of Ida amid regional Covid surge. In Ida's wake, experts worry Covid cases will surge. COVID-19 live updates: Vaccine effectiveness against hospitalization drops slightly.

More Americans getting vaccinated following full FDA approval of Pfizer vaccine. Texas school system closes after 2 teachers die of COVID-19. Texas school district shuts for week after 2 teachers die of COVID. A School System Closes After 2 Teachers Die Of COVID-19. Joe Rogan Says He Has COVID-19 And That He's Been Taking Ivermectin. Reported texts claim Americans stranded at Kabul airport waved passports; weren't let in: Solomon. Colts activate QB Wentz, WR Pascal and C Kelly from COVID list. Doctors sound alarm over surge in pediatric COVID cases. Video posted by Oregon trooper on vaccines may leave him out of a job. U.S. Hiring Slows Sharply As Latest Coronavirus Surge Slams The Brakes On The Economy. CDC research shows where more kids are being hospitalized with Covid.

Florida teen who got Covid has message for the unvaccinated. **Already vaccinated against Covid-19 Experts say you're protected, even without a booster shot [9/4/2021]**. 15-year-old Paulina Velasquez has a message for others: 'If you're eligible to get the vaccine, please do'. Mystery woman struts through airport wearing only a bikini and mask. Oregon police, firefighters sue Gov. Kate Brown over vaccination mandate. Across The COVID-Ravaged South, High-Level Life Support Is Difficult To Find. After 781 students must quarantine, Texas school district requires masks. Employment won't soar now that pandemic benefits have expired. 'Completely incorrect': Dr. Fauci pushes back on DeSantis' vaccine claim. Idaho enacts crisis hospital care standards amid COVID surge.

Idaho hospitals begin rationing health care amid COVID surge. Biden to lay out new strategy against delta variant of COVID-19. Schools don't need to see a big uptick in Covid-19 cases if they follow these measures, Fauci says. Pediatric weekly COVID-19 cases hit pandemic high. World Health Organization forecasts 25% fewer Covid vaccines for the world this year than earlier hoped.

Chapter 14

Child Covid Hospitalizations Hit Record High

September 8th, 2021 – December 7th, 2021

Mandates, testing among Biden's plans to fight Delta surge. "Appalled" WHO chief slams rich nations over COVID booster plans. Where things stand in the Biden administration's Covid-19 response. United orders workers vaccine-exempt workers to take unpaid leave. No major religious denomination opposes vaccination, but religious exemptions may still complicate mandates.

Biden Dangles New Federal Funds For Schools That Defy Mask Mandate Bans. **White House announces COVID-19 vaccine mandates [9/9/2021]**. Dr. Marc Siegel: Top takeaways from Biden's COVID battle plan. Kentucky Lawmakers Scrap Statewide Mask Mandate In Schools. COVID vaccine creator says mass boosters may be unnecessary. Rep. Tenney blasts Biden's vaccine mandate, says pregnant women lost jobs for waiting to take vaccine. Kentucky: Hospital pushed to its limits as lawmakers extend state of emergency due to Covid-19 surge. Analysis: Biden's six-step Covid strategy, explained. TSA Is Doubling Fines For Those Who Refuse To Wear A Mask While Flying. More kids shot in Chicago than have died from COVID-19 across US this year. 'World is on fire': Exhausted Kentucky hospital staff lament dire COVID surge. Gorillas at Zoo Atlanta test positive for COVID-19.

Vaccine mandates for companies will be messy but effective, experts predict. How kids can help dodge the Delta variant before, during and after school. Harris started politicization of COVID-19 vaccines, Christie says. NYC schools reopen without vaccine mandate for students. US will give aircraft companies $482 million for pandemic. California parents of 5 children die of COVID weeks apart. Overwhelmed Kentucky hospitals fear the worst during Covid surge. Elder has helped galvanize many Democrats, who have recoiled most virulently from his views on Covid and his opposition to mask and vaccine mandates. Census: Relief payments staved off hardship in COVID crash. Arizona sues Biden administration over COVID-19 vaccine mandate.

MSNBC's Joy Reid addresses Nicki Minaj dustup, admits her own vaccine hesitancy under Trump. The Democratic governor's stringent Covid measures got a boost on Tuesday, proving that strict pandemic policy can also be good politics. Nicki Minaj said Covid vaccine could make you impotent. Fauci shut her down.. 1 in every 500 US residents have died of Covid-19. Winston praises Payton as Saints assistants deal with COVID. There is no question about the effectiveness of vaccines, expert says, as FDA weighs possible booster shot. MSNBC's Joy Reid slammed for bizarre rant on Republican 'love' for the coronavirus: 'COVID-loving death cult'.

Jobless claims edge up as latest COVID-19 wave takes toll. Broadway stars find friendship during pandemic with unique project. White House offers to call Nicki Minaj on COVID vaccine. Scientists split on COVID vaccine booster shots. FDA vaccine adviser says Covid-19 booster decision is being rushed by Biden administration's Sept. 20 target. Opinion: What vaccine advocates need to understand about religious exemptions. Doctor on COVID-19 vaccine mandates and vaccine hesitancy in U.S. Moderna Leads The Authorized COVID Vaccines In Lasting Effectiveness. Gottlieb condemns CDC's handling of the COVID pandemic: "A failure of vision". Rand Paul: Coronavirus antibody distribution may be stalled by socialism, other political reasons? Times Square swarmed by hundreds protesting COVID vaccine mandate, chanting 'F--- Joe Biden'. Saints see 2 more coaches test positive for COVID-19, total reaches 8 ahead of Panthers game. Unvaccinated dad survived Covid thanks to a doctor who stumbled upon his story. California reports lowest COVID-19 case rate in the country.

4 steps that have to happen before Covid-19 vaccine is available for younger children. Pfizer says its lower dose COVID-19 vaccine is safe for kids ages 5 to11. **US death toll from Covid surpasses that of the 1918 flu pandemic [9/21/2021]**. Two dose version of Johnson & Johnson shot 94% effective against Covid-19, study finds. New parents landed themselves a rare night out. But it was cut short when the restaurant kicked them out for wearing face masks, they say..

Rep. Bob Latta becomes Congress' second breakthrough COVID case this week. Brazilian health minister tests positive for COVID-19 during U.N. summit. "This virus is an evil, evil thing": Kentucky health care workers overwhelmed by surge of COVID patients. Why Liquor Shortages Caused By The COVID-19 Pandemic Persist In Some States. **US again at a point where more than 2,000 people die of Covid daily [9/22/2021]**. Florida Students Are No Longer Required To Quarantine After Being Exposed To COVID. DeSantis says parents can send asymptomatic kids exposed to Covid back to school. Clay Travis: When will it ever be appropriate to stop wearing masks? Arizona AG hits Biden admin's 'laissez-faire' approach to migrant COVID risk. **New Wuhan COVID docs 'completely contradict Fauci' on gain-of-function claims, ex-State Dept official says [9/24/2021]**.

CDC director endorses Pfizer Covid vaccine booster shots. Moments before Kamala Harris interview, 'The View' announces two hosts tested positive for Covid. Harris interview with 'The View' delayed after co-hosts test positive for COVID-19. Tucker Carlson: This is proof Biden and his lackeys in the media are lying about COVID. NBA denies Wiggins' religious exemption for Covid-19 vaccine. What could be motivating the wild Covid recklessness in states like Florida. New York City anti-vaccine mandate protesters storm mall food court: 'My body, my choice'. Teen drivers giving parents cause for concern over hitting the road during COVID-19 pandemic, survey shows. **Biden to receive Covid booster shot on-camera Monday [9/27/2021]**.

COVID-19 reduced life expectancy for U.S. men by 2.2 years. Biden gets COVID-19 booster shot before cameras, pushes vaccinations. New York state vaccine mandate for medical workers goes into effect. NFL urges players, team staff to report COVID-19 symptoms. Atlanta hospital makes tough choices amid Covid patient influx. Newsom says statewide vaccine mandate in schools in 'on the table'.

Sen. Marshall, Doctors Caucus send letter to CDC urging recognition of COVID-19 natural immunity [9/29/2021]. China kills 3 housecats that tested positive for COVID-19. Federal judge suspends ban on mask mandates in South Carolina schools. CDC issues urgent alert: Pregnant women need the Covid-19 vaccine. Are You Pregnant The CDC Really Wants You To Get Vaccinated Against COVID-19. Woman who survived 1918 flu, world war succumbs to COVID. Prisons, border wall: How GOP is looking to use COVID money.

NY PPE manufacturer says pandemic highlights importance of domestic manufacturing amid increased outsourcing. Justice Brett Kavanaugh tests positive for Covid. Gov. Newsom announces California first state to require COVID vaccinations for K-12 students. Opinion: This group has a lot to lose when Covid ends. Sotomayor denies NYC teachers' plea to block vaccine mandate. Alabama GOP governor signs bills to use Covid-19 relief funds to build prisons into law.

Sotomayor refuses to block NYC school mandate. Expert weighs in on when you should get a Covid booster. Republicans' actions in intel briefing show unwillingness to accept findings of

90-day investigation into Covid origins. US is turning a corner in fight against Covid-19, Fauci says. But it can't let its guard down. Thousands protest Washington state's vaccine mandate, sing national anthem. The fight over vaccine and mask mandates across the U.S.. Rural Alaska at risk as COVID surge swamps faraway hospitals.

Warriors' Andrew Wiggins says he felt forced to get COVID-19 vaccine or not play. Mother blames school 'nurse' role for 10-year-old daughter's Covid death. Sen. John Barrasso: Biden's COVID messaging is muddy and mandates make things worse. Charlize Theron takes on new role of fighting vaccine hesitancy. ESPN sidelines Sage Steele after comments on network's vaccine mandate, Barack Obama. Black Americans are being priced out of pandemic housing boom. Booster shots outpace the rate of Covid vaccinations, but the millions still unvaccinated could trigger 'future waves,' expert says. Covid supply chain's latest victims: Halloween shoppers. Many people are vaccinated, so why are COVID tests flying off shelves? GOP demands Biden stop 'bullying' airlines with vaccine mandate, says taxpayers 'saved' industry.

Baltimore schools work to refine classroom coronavirus testing program. Pandemic has exacerbated "diaper need" in the U.S. **Psaki grilled on Biden's 'really terrible polls,' blames Delta variant and unvaccinated Americans [10/8/2021]**. Blood clot symptoms to look out for. Thousands pack streets in Rome to COVID vaccine work rule. Allen West, Texas GOP gubernatorial hopeful, has COVID-19.

One of Newsom's kids lacks vaccine despite mandate, report says. Protests in Rome against COVID-19 Green Pass turn violent. Italy's strict COVID-19 vaccine mandate sparks violent protests. Former Labor Secretary Chao warns worker shortages could be 'tomorrow's new normal'. Texas Gov. Greg Abbott bans 'any entity' from enforcing a COVID-19 vaccine mandate. America's Civil War: The real virus in our media and political culture. Moderna and J&J say their data supports COVID vaccine boosters. Braves' Soler sidelined after testing positive for COVID-19. CNN Exclusive: China to test thousands of Wuhan blood samples in Covid-19 probe. Texan charged in Baltimore with threatening vaccine advocate. Study of COVID vaccine boosters suggests Moderna or Pfizer works best.

Vaccine mandates could lead to police and firefighter exoduses in urban areas. **With hospitals crowded from COVID, 1 in 5 American families delays health care [10/14/2021].** FDA vaccine advisers are meeting to consider Moderna Covid-19 vaccine boosters. The group recommends authorizing a half-sized dose of the Covid-19 vaccine for certain groups, including those at high risk of disease. Job Creators Network CEO: Biden vaccine mandate 'ridiculous' and will impact everything. New Mexico judge denies lab workers' claim in vaccine fight. Biden blamed Trump 'leadership' for shortages during COVID, won't accept blame now as leader: 'The Five'. Vaccine mix-ups are rare and there are systems in place to keep it that way. Robert Durst, convicted murderer, has Covid-19. Police officers face grim reality of Covid deaths. Supply chain issues and inflationary pressures spurred by the pandemic are already raising the price of pork. And now comes another potential wildcard. The rates of cases, hospitalizations and deaths are improving. It's an optimistic sign for the future of the pandemic. Colin Powell dies of COVID-19 complications despite vaccine: Medical experts weigh in. Woman denied organ transplant over refusal to get COVID-19 vaccine.

How Colin Powell's cancer may have limited COVID vaccine's effectiveness. Washington State University fires football coach for refusing Covid-19 vaccine. After a family member died of Covid-19, a man took aim at Florida's top health official in sarcastic letter. Russia hits another record of daily coronavirus deaths. California school district tells parents their children must eat lunch in the rain due to COVID. Hawaii's governor welcomes travelers as COVID counts drop. Putin orders nonwork week as COVID numbers rise in Russia. Harvard professor urges schools to scrap mask mandates by end of year in Washington Post column. USS Theodore Roosevelt returning to sea after being sidelined by the coronavirus. What Colin Powell's death can and can't tell us about COVID breakthrough cases. From Neil Cavuto to John King to Colin Powell, the personalizing of the vaccine debate.

Can new COVID-19 variants continue to emerge? Chicago police union boss on vaccine mandate fight: 'Welcome to day three of 'The Hunger Games''. Elise Stefanik slams Biden for mocking pushback on vaccine mandates at CNN town hall: 'Un-American'. Pfizer says Covid vaccine more than 90 percent effective in kids. People wonder if they should keep calm and carry on in the face of delta plus variant.

White House further postpones disclosure of JFK assassination documents, citing Covid. Vaccine mandates create conflict with defiant workers. Ed Sheeran has COVID, will do performances from home. Biden administration to speed up authorization of at-home Covid tests. Biden coughs into hand, proceeds to shake hands with public while maskless. Marjorie Taylor Greene fined third time for not wearing mask on House floor.

John Oliver says 'f---ing let' policer officers who resist vaccine mandates quit. Chicago vaccine mandate: Police union boss no longer banned from speaking out against policy, judge rules. 'We may have vaccines for children 5 to 11, possibly as soon as next week,' Chicago health official says. Why are cops fighting vaccine mandates? United States issues its 1st passport with 'X' gender marker. How parents can help students struggling because of COVID. Georgia police seeking eighth suspect in home invasion where masked men held mother, daughter at gunpoint.

Judge denies NYPD union's bid to halt COVID vaccine mandate. Media pressure on Wuhan lab-linked scientist grows after he was once oft-cited voice decrying lab leak theory. Doctor on vaccine mandate opposition and COVID-19 cases. Opinion: How to talk to your kids about the Covid-19 vaccines. FDA authorizes Pfizer's COVID vaccine for kids as young as 5. NYC vaccine mandate: FDNY 'sickout' forces closure of several firehouses. Bears coach Matt Nagy to miss 49ers game because of COVID-19. City workers battle COVID-19 vaccine mandates.

FDNY rescue paramedic rips de Blasio over COVID vaccine mandate: Mayor is not allowing us to work? From Covid vaccine and mask mandates to teaching critical race theory, adults are making angry speeches at school board meetings. These students are tired of it. U.S. releases declassified COVID-19 origins report. Judge pauses Chicago police vaccine requirement. The new faces of Covid deaths. Doctor discusses Pfizer's COVID-19 vaccine for kids ages 5 to 11. CDC advisory group votes to recommend Pfizer kids vaccine. Children 5 to 11 can now receive Pfizer vaccine after CDC director signs off.

Where LA County's employee vaccine mandate stands a month after initial deadline. Colorado hospitals allowed to turn away patients amid Covid-19 surge. Experts believe Russia's COVID death toll is almost four times higher than government reports. As constituents clamor for ivermectin, Republican politicians embrace their cause. COVID-19 vaccination and young children: What to know. Vaccine mandate could cost border patrol more than half of its agents, internal report says. Hours after the White House issues its new vaccine mandate, GOP-led states sue. Mother goes from QAnon believer to vaccine advocate.

COVID's impact on immunocompromised adults. Health care company cuts ties with Aaron Rodgers after COVID-19 vaccine comments. Antiviral pills for Covid-19 -- not a cure, but a great tool. International travelers set for emotional reunions as U.S.

lifts Covid travel ban. Big Bird got 'vaccinated' against COVID-19, drawing outrage from Republicans. US reopening borders to the global Covid epicenter. Filipino American health workers reflect on trauma and healing on COVID's frontlines.

Pfizer seeks FDA authorization for Covid vaccine booster for all adults. Germany reports daily high number of new coronavirus cases. **What's causing another coronavirus surge in Europe? [11/10/2021]** Texas school mask ban violates Americans with Disabilities Act, judge rules.

10 states sue Biden administration over COVID vaccine mandate for health care workers. Doctor on COVID-19 booster shots and potential winter surge. LAPD chief on vaccine mandates: "I believe the mandates are lawful". Boosters for all A look at some of the latest COVID-19 developments. Steelers' Roethlisberger on Covid-19 reserve list, out of Sunday's game. 20 states report rise in COVID-19 cases and hospitalizations. Little kids can likely read your emotions even when you wear a face mask, study finds. Florida woman dies after suing hospital to get ivermectin. States that have opened COVID boosters to all adults.

Eye Opener: FDA expected to authorize Pfizer booster for all adults amid rising COVID cases. Biden shakes hands maskless but decides to put mask on before photo. Jobless claims have dropped for a 7th straight week, hitting a pandemic low. Rising COVID cases strain Minnesota hospitals. U.S. scientist touts "strong evidence" COVID came from Wuhan market.

Doctor on FDA authorizing Moderna and Pfizer COVID booster shots for all adults. Pandemic causing Great Resignation of doctors and nurses. The Covid booster question just got a lot simpler. FDA clears confusion by signing off on Covid boosters, but some experts say it's 'too late'. For the unvaccinated, Biden bets billions on Covid treatments as another surge threatens. Gottlieb says that COVID-19 vaccines could be considered a "three-dose vaccine".

Austria enters nationwide lockdown to fight soaring cases. Dr. Fauci on potential winter surge as COVID cases in U.S. rise nearly 30% over past two weeks. WHO Europe warns of possible surge in COVID deaths ahead. Steve Burton fired from 'General Hospital' for refusal to get Covid vaccine. Hit hard by COVID, Native Americans come together to protect families and elders. Health officials urge COVID caution for holiday. **New Covid-19 variant in South Africa raises concern [11/25/2021]**. WHO holds emergency meeting to discuss 'heavily mutated' COVID-19 variant, UK takes action. FDA: Merck COVID pill effective, experts will review safety. A new coronavirus variant leads to global concern, travel bans and market jitters. Reinfection from Covid-19 is rare, severe disease is even rarer, a study of people in Qatar finds. Omicron COVID-19 variant: US to limit travel from 8 southern Africa countries.

New York Gov. Kathy Hochul issues state of emergency in response to omicron variant. As the Omicron variant sparks concern, experts say it's time for unvaccinated Americans to get their shots. Omicron concerns should spur millions of unvaccinated Americans to get their Covid shots, experts say. Smerconish: No matter the US vaccination rate, this virus knows no boundaries. Pandemic worries reach Biden in Nantucket. Expert says this is the most important thing we need to know about the Omicron variant. A small-town mom was the chair of her local school-board. When Covid put pressure on the public, cracks began to appear. **World is put on high alert over the Omicron coronavirus variant [11/27/2021]**.

ABC's 'Good Morning America' guest worries omicron variant could hurt Biden's economic 'progress'. Two cases of Omicron variant detected in Canada, govt says. Omicron variant slams travel doors shut. WHO says overall global risk related to the new variant is assessed as 'very high' and urges member states to accelerate vaccination efforts. World takes decisive action against Omicron as new variant prompts fears of another COVID wave.

A growing number of countries have reported confirmed cases of coronavirus variant as travel restrictions are imposed around the globe to try to contain it. Travelers are stranded over restrictions tied to the Omicron variant. COVID-19 Omicron variant poses risk for worldwide infection. Dr. Ashish Jha on new Omicron variant. US urges vaccination over Omicron variant concerns. Covid vaccine rules in France, Italy and now Austria provide a window into what to expect. What if the Omicron variant turns out to be good for markets? Omicron doesn't carry some of the mutations seen with Delta. Federal judge blocks Biden vaccine mandate for health care workers nationwide. Courts block two Biden administration Covid vaccine mandates. Hear what Dr. Fauci thinks about vaccine boosters for kids. MSNBC contributor can't believe Biden coronavirus policy under consideration: 'This is nuts'.

First U.S. case of omicron variant is found in California [12/1/2021]. Trump tested positive for Covid three days before debating Biden, subsequently tested negative. White House set to announce new COVID-19 measures today after the first case of the Omicron variant reported in the U.S.. UN headquarters on lockdown on report of man outside with gun. Armed man in custody after standoff forces lockdown at UN headquarters. Biden launches plan to combat Omicron variant. Biden unveils new strategy to tackle COVID-19 and the Omicron variant. Judge expresses skepticism of 3 House Republicans' challenge of mask fines. Father of autistic boy asks Supreme Court for emergency relief over TSA airline mask requirement. Do vaccines work against omicron Lab studies are coming, but won't tell whole story. U.S. prepares to fight Omicron COVID variant as new travel restrictions set to take effect. Scientists studying whether Omicron is more resistant to vaccines.

Illumina CEO explains what scientists are studying to determine if Omicron variant is more transmissible. Study shows men spread COVID particles more than women and children. COVID-19 omicron variant: Steps you can take to protect yourself. Next pandemic could be 'more contagious, or more lethal, or both,' vaccine co-creator warns. U.S.-bound travelers scramble as new COVID test rules take effect. The world could end Covid quicker. Here's how. Early reports on the quick spread of the Omicron variant in South Africa were at first frightening, but then began to offer some hope. White House to tout vaccine milestone amid rising cases.

Chapter 15

Pfizer Shot Offers Partial Protection Against Omicron Variant, Study Finds

December 7th, 2021 – March 6th, 2022

Some teens may get a vaccine booster soon. Tenn medical board takes virus misinformation policy offline. FDA clears first Covid antibody treatment for immunocompromised before exposure. Three states are using the troops to staff facilities with dangerously low capacity due to a spike in Covid-19 patients. Eye Opener: FDA considering whether to authorize COVID boosters for some teenagers. **U.K. reimposes COVID rules amid claims government itself ignored them [12/9/2021]**. FDA authorizes Pfizer's COVID-19 booster for teens age 16 and up. 'When crazy comes knocking at the door, slam it shut': Gov. on Johnson's Covid claim. New York orders mask mandate for indoor public spaces statewide. British PM Johnson facing crisis as nation reacts to government parties held during COVID lockdowns.

NY gov. orders temporary indoor mask mandate. Vermont's Middlebury College reverts to remote learning due to COVID-19 with 99% of students vaccinated. New Hampshire governor says state is prepared for winter COVID-19 surge. South African president tests positive for COVID, mildly ill. British Prime Minister Boris Johnson warns of Omicron tidal wave, announces new COVID restrictions. Ex-NFL player Bellamy gets 3 years for COVID relief fraud. Supreme Court declines religious challenge to N.Y. vaccine mandate for health care workers.

Supreme Court again leaves state vaccine mandate in place for health care workers. The latest COVID-linked shortage? Salvation Army bell ringers. Atlantic readers erupt over article declaring pandemic doesn't matter where they live. **U.S. COVID-19 death toll approaches 800,000 [12/14/2021]**. Biden's vaccine mandate will decimate our military. Omicron COVID-19 variant: Cornell, Princeton shift to remote format. Flames, Boston, Nashville latest NHL teams hit by virus woes.

Montana woman beats COVID after weeks on ventilator. As omicron spreads, health experts push for mask mandates. But few states have one. Dr. Makary on 'Kilmeade Show': Omicron fear fueling a 'second pandemic of lunacy'. CDC advisers vote to narrow use of J&J vaccine due to concerns about rare blood clots. Marine Corps discharges 103 active duty personnel for defying Pentagon's COVID-19 vaccine mandate. CDC narrows use of J&J vaccine due to concerns about rare blood clots. The NFL and NBA are changing their Covid protocols. Biden's COVID-19 vaccine mandates: What are employers required to do?

The rapid spread of Omicron has broken pandemic records. Pfizer is testing a third Covid vaccine dose in young kids. COVID Impact: Los Angeles students lost over 90,000 days of in-person school due to coronavirus restrictions. Arizona mayor defies governor's COVID vaccine mandate ban: 'No authority'. DC area school district shifts to remote learning through mid-January due to 'stark rise' in COVID cases. A poorly matched flu shot could mean a bad flu season on top of a Covid surge. Test prep: What you need to know about at-home Covid tests. Ohio governor mobilizes 1,050 National Guard troops to ease hospital staff shortages amid COVID-19 surge. NFL reduces testing for asymptomatic vaccinated players. State senator who called for Governor's resignation over Covid rules dies after saying he was sick with Covid.

California school system is sending every student and staff member home with a Covid-19 antigen test for the holidays. Pfizer COVID-19 pill may not see approval for 'months' despite 'impressive' data. Elizabeth Warren tests positive for COVID-19. 3 Democratic lawmakers announce positive Covid tests. Analysis: 7 Covid lessons for 2022. Surgeon General Vivek Murthy discusses Omicron variant and how to combat its rapid spread.

The riddle of Japan's dramatic drop in COVID numbers. Omicron strains COVID-19 testing capacity. New COVID restrictions in Europe as cases soar. Trump met with boos after revealing he received Covid-19 booster. The NHL pauses season until after Christmas due to COVID-19 risks. **Eye Opener: Omicron variant is now the dominant strain in the U.S. [12/21/2021]**

CDC: Daily Covid-19 case numbers 'could exceed previous peaks'. W.H.O. chief warns against holiday gatherings amid COVID surge. Prisoners sent to home confinement because of the pandemic might remain free. Hospitals in New York region say they've run out of antibody treatment for omicron variant. President Biden unveils Omicron plan as variant surges across U.S. With rising Covid-19 cases ahead of holiday plans, the availability of testing is becoming severely strained. Omicron symptoms: What we know about illness caused by the new variant. Possible COVID treatment sees renewed promise after new study. As cases surge, there are questions around the number of days to isolate if you test positive for Covid but don't have symptoms and are vaccinated.

EXPLAINER: What to do if you test positive for COVID-19. Army develops COVID-19 vaccine that may provide protection against all variants. US passports fees are about to pop way up. FDA authorizes Pfizer pill to treat COVID-19 as Omicron hits all 50 sates. US denies man held in Turkey for fake passport is diplomat. Police chief placed on unpaid leave for telling officers about 'clinic' to obtain Covid vaccination cards without getting the shots.

FDA authorizes second antiviral pill [molnupiravir, paxlovid was first] to treat Covid-19 [12/23/2021]. For a 2nd Christmas in a row, the Holy Land will be closed to visitors due to COVID. Truckers frustrated by looming Biden vaccine mandate for cross-border Canada shipments. Newly authorized Covid pills won't change course of pandemic right away. Doctor describes getting death threats by families of Covid patients. There's a new drug to prevent Covid-19, but there won't be nearly enough for Americans who are eligible. COVID-19: Ways you can protect your young child who can't get a vaccine. CDC cuts isolation time for health care workers with Covid-19.

Antiviral pills to fight COVID are 'game changers' for the high risk: Adm. Giroir. Trump speaks out about vaccines to right-wing media host. Omicron variant drives holiday COVID surge and flight cancellations. I already had Covid. Can I get Omicron? Your pandemic questions, answered. Supreme Court to review vaccine rules as Biden administration requires some healthcare workers, business employees to be vaccinated. Five bowl games called off due to Covid. COVID delays holiday travel for thousands: "Omicron is the Grinch".

Doctor on spike in COVID-19 cases, increase in children hospitalized, and best masks to wear. Stay home and shut your windows: Chinese city of 13 million goes into lockdown. CDC shortens recommended Covid-19 isolation and quarantine time. Impact of Omicron COVID-19 variant on Americans' mental health. Food recalls have dropped off during the pandemic, but no one is entirely sure why. Eye Opener: CDC changes COVID isolation guidance. Column: Virus finds its way into the NFL playoff picture. FDA: At-home Covid-19 antigen tests may be less sensitive to picking up Omicron. People reinfected with omicron variant had fewer symptoms, small CDC study finds. A Supreme Court that's declined to block several vaccine mandates is now considering Biden's Covid vaccine requirement.

Here's a look at how Covid-19 is spreading in communities across the US. What are we watching COVID puts fairness, quality in limbo. FDA says Covid-19 antigen tests may be less sensitive to Omicron variant, but they're still an important tool. Douglas Murray: The left never wants to return to pre-COVID world. Westminster Dog Show 2022 postponed due to COVID-19. People should celebrate the New Year, experts say. But the size and kind of party determine Covid-19 safety.

Vaccinated Democratic congressman announces he has tested positive for COVID-19. U.S. daily COVID cases hit record high. A pandemic-scarred year ends in darkness -- but with hope on the horizon. Thousands gather to welcome 2022 in Australia amid surging COVID cases. Liberal journalists shift on coronavirus as omicron variant surges: 'We don't orient our lives around the flu'. New Year's Eve crowd in NYC's Times Square still parties despite coronavirus limits. The Omicron variant is 'extraordinarily contagious,' an expert says. Now, even a quick, transient encounter can lead to an infection. Colts activate Carson Wentz from COVID-19 list.

House GOP committee deletes tweet spreading disinformation on Covid boosters after backlash. 'There will be further clarification' on CDC guidelines to end Covid-19 isolation, Fauci says. Further clarification 'coming very soon' to CDC Covid guidelines. Florida Covid cases up 948% in last two weeks. FDA authorizes COVID booster shots for Americans as young as 12. DeSantis urges hospitals to distinguish those hospitalized due to COVID and those who just happen to have it. Japan companion robots help the lonely smile and patients in recovery during COVID's isolating times. Biden will make 'brief remarks' Tuesday on rapid spread of the Omicron variant. Teachers at culture war front lines with Jan. 6 education. Navy blocked from acting against 35 COVID vaccine refusers. **Why vaccinated people are getting COVID-19 [1/4/2022]**.

Liverpool wants Arsenal cup match postponed over COVID. Biden calls COVID-19 testing situation 'frustrating,' says unvaccinated should be 'alarmed' by omicron. China COVID lockdown causes some food shortages. Biden again insists COVID a pandemic of the unvaccinated even as fast-moving omicron spreads widely. Chicago teachers vote to switch to remote learning amid COVID surge. **In 'zero-Covid' Hong Kong, this is what happens when you test positive [1/5/2022]**.

The CDC says a test to get out of COVID isolation is not needed, resisting pushback. Tucker: COVID lunacy will end in 2022. Immune system T-cells can fight omicron COVID-19 variant, study suggests. US advisers endorse Pfizer COVID boosters for younger teens. COVID concerns close Chicago public schools. NFL drawing up Super Bowl contingency plans in case COVID forces move from Los Angeles area. COVID testing FAQ: When to test, what kind of test to use and what your results mean. Short-staffed and COVID-battered, U.S. hospitals are hiring more foreign nurses. U.S. hospitals facing worst staff shortages due to COVID-19. North Korea says it will miss Beijing Olympics, blaming pandemic and 'hostile forces'.

Listen Live: Supreme Court to consider Biden's vaccine requirements. Up to a million COVID tests expired in a Florida warehouse. Supreme Court appears poised to block Biden's vaccine and testing rules for businesses. Amazon shortens Covid paid leave time for US employees. Biden admin trying to 'work around Congress,' Ohio AG claims after Supreme Court session on vaccine mandates. California governor activates National Guard to boost COVID testing capacity.

Nearly twice as many military members died from suicide July-Sept than from coronavirus since pandemic's start. Children grapple with emotional toll from Covid lockdowns.

Gavin Newsom proposes $2.7B in new anti-COVID spending as more Californians learn to adapt. Chicago's COVID-19 fight with teachers hangs over a 2nd week. **Worldwide COVID cases rise 71% in one week [1/10/2022]**. COVID mandates keep Americans from getting back in the game. COVID home tests: Americans to be reimbursed starting Saturday. Democrat mayors and governors embrace remain-open approach to COVID after lecturing Republicans. Tucker Carlson: It's terrifying that Americans are being denied COVID treatment based on race.

The idea of intentionally trying to get infected with Covid is spreading, an expert says, but it's like 'playing with dynamite'. Covid-19 hospitalizations reach record high, HHS data shows. **U.S. sets new record for COVID-19 hospitalizations [1/11/2022]**. 'Zero-Covid' China fights to contain Omicron. Ted Cruz slams podium over reporter's mask questions: 'Just once' I'd like you to ask Biden, Psaki about that. It might be time to upgrade your mask. Guidance will not change on face masks, COVID-19 cases predicted to peak in US: CDC Director Walensky. Study finds COVID-19 may increase risk of diabetes in kids: What parents should know. Biden to send medical teams to six states in response to COVID-19 case surge: report. Biden to announce new federal medical team deployments to help hospitals grappling with Covid surge. UK government cuts COVID isolation period to 5 days, from 7. The President says his administration will buy an additional 500 million Covid tests and will soon detail plans to make high-quality masks available for free.

Americans can get reimbursed for at-home COVID-19 tests starting January 15. SCOTUS blocks vaccine mandate for big businesses. New York restaurant owner has message for governor over vaccine mandate. Judge finds no reason to charge Texas mother who allegedly put her son in the trunk to avoid Covid-19 exposure. Opinion: SCOTUS vaccine opinions reveal a frightening prospect. Average daily new cases nationwide are now more than three times the pandemic's peak last winter.

Thousands take holy dip in India's Ganges River amid Covid surge. How to get your at-home Covid-19 test for free. Snail noodles go viral in China during the pandemic. But the dish is a bit... funky. Fauci, COVID-19 origins to be investigated if House flips back to GOP control in 2022: Jim Jordan. 'The Five' on Supreme Court rejecting Biden's vaccine mandate. WaPo laments SCOTUS decision to block Biden vaccine mandate, advocates business and state mandates instead. Mom with 1-year-old battling Covid has a powerful message. **Omicron probably won't be prevented by fourth vaccine jab, Israeli researcher says [1/18/2022]**. Boris Johnson denies lying about lockdown parties amid COVID pandemic. More than three-quarters of Covid-19 deaths in the US have been among seniors. 'Kids very rarely do better than their parents are doing:' How to help kids deal with changes due to the pandemic. Biden administration to give out 400 million free N95 masks. Biden administration offers free at-home COVID tests as Omicron surges.

The Biden administration will give out 400 million free N95 masks. Pelosi says Democrats are considering adding Covid-19 relief to larger bill. Vaccinated and boosted Democratic congressman tests positive for COVID-19. Placebo effect the true cause of many reported COVID-19 vaccine side effects: Study. Caitlyn Jenner says NCAA transgender participation policy a symptom of a 'woke world gone wild'. China mandates 3-day Olympic torch relay amid virus concerns. Why some people are having problems ordering free Covid tests. Trump appointee blocks Biden federal worker vaccine mandate. Judge in Texas blocks enforcement of federal employee vaccine mandate nationwide. Wall Street has worst week since the start of the pandemic. For all of Biden's successes or failures, it's really about 'COVID, stupid'. Remote nation in the Pacific goes into lockdown for the first time. Kiribati and Samoa implement rare lockdowns after travelers test positive. Gottlieb doesn't expect COVID-19 vaccine for kids under 5 before late March.

Washington DC 'Defeat the Mandates' march calls for end to 'draconian' COVID-19 vaccine requirements. Seniors are at high risk of COVID, but Medicare doesn't pay for rapid tests. CNN's Acosta, liberal media melt down over Bari Weiss COVID remarks: 'Grow up'. Here's how to request free at-home COVID tests. Marine denied of religious exemption says DoD enforcing vax mandate 'to the detriment of national defense'.

Police investigating 'number of events' at UK Prime Minister's office while country was under Covid restrictions. Photojournalist-turned-nurse captures COVID patients' intimate moments. Rep. Comer pushes Biden admin on millions of dollars shifted from vaccine efforts to housing migrant children. This Nigerian doctor has a tough new job: Stopping the next pandemic before it strikes. Education Secretary Miguel Cardona calls on US to 'reset' after COVID-19 and 're-imagine education'. A universal vaccine could be the future of the coronavirus fight. Norway king ill after meeting virus-positive minister. COVID strikes Kiribati: One of the last uninfected places on Earth. Northern masks, Southern indifference: How Covid precautions differ widely by region. Singer Diego Verdaguer, whose hits include 'Volver, dies of COVID complications.

VA AG Jason Miyares: Masks creating mental health crisis among school children. The company responded after several artists left the platform because it continues to host Joe Rogan, whose show has spread Covid-19 misinformation. Virginia mother slams schools for not following governor's order on masks: 'Psychological warfare'. **Moderna announces full US approval for its COVID-19 vaccine [1/31/2022]**. The work-life-Covid juggling act has robbed many Americans of their hope and patience. **Scientists speak out about how they were**

ignored, even silenced, when they suggested a lab leak in 2022 [2/1/2022].

'Gutfeld!' on Canadian truck drivers protesting COVID vaccine mandate. Pfizer asks FDA to authorize Covid vaccine for kids under 5. US daily COVID-19 cases fall below 500K, data shows. Los Angeles Garcetti mocked for response to maskless picture. Giuliani's reveal on 'The Masked Singer' reportedly sparks outrage from judges. CDC to unveil its latest weapon in Covid-19 detection: wastewater. COVID-19 jeopardizes medal hopes for some Olympic athletes in Beijing.

Europe nears 'ceasefire' on Covid as countries do away with restrictions. CDC launches COVID-19 wastewater surveillance dashboard. Biden reflects on 900,000 Americans dead from Covid-19. Olympians face strict COVID-19 rules in Beijing as China steps up surveillance. COVID in the maternity ward. Steve Hilton: The 'lockdown lunatics' did this to America. Marc Thiessen rips Stacey Abrams as 'politically incompetent,' bad at 'virtue signaling' after maskless photo. Connecticut, New Jersey and Delaware set timelines to end mask mandates for schools. 4 states set dates to end school mask mandates. 32 Olympic athletes in isolation after testing positive for COVID. A pub that claims to be England's oldest could close its doors because of COVID.

GOP Rep. Hal Rogers apologizes to Black Caucus chair for telling her to 'kiss my a--' during mask dispute. Stacey Abrams apologizes for maskless photo op at school, says she wouldn't lift mandate for kids. **Fauci says full-blown COVID-19 pandemic is almost over in US [2/9/2022]**. New York to lift indoor mask mandate, but not for kids in schools. Take a look at SARS-CoV-2's family tree. It's full of surprises. Dems' masks coming off? Homeland Security warns that American truck drivers are planning a COVID-19 protest similar to Canada convoy. Connecticut governor says 'you have earned this freedom' as he rolls back school mask mandate.

States lift mask mandates for adults in bars and restaurants but still require kids at school to mask up. After COVID 'nightmare,' Sanderson joins Team USA at Olympics. 3,000 NYC workers could lose their jobs over vaccine rule. John Stockton has Gonzaga tickets suspended over mask refusal. NYC protesters fight vaccine mandate as mayor doubles down on 'the rule'. Democratic state, city leaders split on COVID mandates as country recovers from pandemic. CNN correspondent: Hard to get 'straight answers' from Democrats on mask mandates. As state medical boards try to stamp out COVID misinformation, some in GOP push back. Novak Djokovic says he will skip tournaments rather than get the COVID vaccine.

'Jersey Boys' Still Going Strong All These Years Later, This Time Off-Broadway And Despite COVID-19. US Disney resorts lift mask requirements for vaccinated guests. Germany to chart way out of coronavirus restrictions. Excess deaths in US top 1M since COVID-19 pandemic start: report. Mothers vaccinated against COVID during pregnancy may reduce risk of infants being hospitalized with COVID-19. Trump-backed Arizona candidate called Covid vaccine a 'crime against humanity'. Newark Catholic schools to lift mask mandate next month.

Switzerland announces it will roll back almost all coronavirus restrictions. Texas mom runs for judge seat, says COVID school mandates have 'turned educators into enforcers'. Sen. Lankford demands DOD IG audit after Navy chaplain denied religious exemption to COVID-19 vaccine. Canada police quickly push back COVID protesters. Queen Elizabeth II tests positive for COVID. Atlantic piece ridiculed for arguing mask mandates 'don't need to make sense'.

Connecticut Lawmakers Extend Statewide School Mask Mandate. Can a corporate exec speak as a mom about COVID rules Consider the Levi's saga. Hong Kong orders mandatory COVID-19 tests for all residents. Kentucky mom who resisted school mask mandates says she was 'fighting for' her child.

Long-time NBA official says he lost job for refusing to take vaccine. Queen Elizabeth still has cold-like COVID symptoms, postpones two virtual audiences: palace. Rare multisystem inflammatory syndrome appears in some teenagers after COVID-19 vaccination: study. Warehouse manager wanted in theft of $1 million worth of COVID-19 tests. Biden claims COVID-19 keeps Americans from seeing 'things have gotten so much better for them'.

How long COVID sheds light on other mysterious (and lonely) chronic illnesses. British queen holds virtual audiences after COVID symptoms. State of the Union attendance required a COVID test. 6 legislators tested positive. Sen. Ron Johnson accuses CDC of making false statement on mask mandate study, demands information. Biden wants more COVID relief funds. The GOP wants to know where previous relief went. **More than 90 percent of Americans can go without masks: CDC [3/4/2022]**.

Chapter 16

Boston's Indoor Mask Mandate For Businesses Is Lifted

March 6th, 2022 – February 25th, 2023

The new normal according to the CDC. Puerto Rico to lift mask mandate for 2nd time in pandemic.

'Test to Treat' gets COVID pills to at-risk patients fast but its reach is limited. Ingraham: High gas price-induced self-restrictions are 'Biden's new lockdown'. TSA extends travel mask mandate through April 18. DOJ appoints prosecutor for pandemic relief fund fraud. What comes next in COVID-19 fight two years into pandemic? **Marking two years since the COVID-19 pandemic started [3/12/2022]**. Better air in classrooms matters beyond COVID. Here's why schools aren't there yet. A surge in COVID-19 spurs new lockdowns in China's cities. COVID-19 outbreak in China threatens global supply chains. COVID-19 infections soar in China and Europe. People with 'medium COVID' are caught in a gray area of recovery with little support.

WHO says global rise in COVID cases is 'tip of the iceberg'. Samoa locks down after recording its first community COVID-19 case. U.K. COVID cases are rising. Health officials are watching to see if the U.S. is next. What the latest data suggests about the Johnson & Johnson Covid vaccine. Supreme Court Justice Clarence Thomas hospitalized for "flu-like symptoms". COVID-19 infection increases risk of developing diabetes up to 1 year later: Study. Moderna says its low-dose COVID shots work for kids under 6. How the pandemic killed the five-day office work week.

'The Five' on COVID mandates, Ukraine war and NATO. As highly transmissible Omicron subvariant spreads, what do Americans need to know? Cruise ship in San Francisco docks with multiple passengers testing positive for COVID-19. Israeli PM tests positive for COVID, is working from home. FDA authorizes a 2nd Covid booster shot for people 50 and older. DHS officials brace for a new surge at the border if pandemic restrictions are lifted. WHO: COVID deaths jump by 40%, but cases falling globally. Biden receives second COVID-19 booster shot on camera. Tests and vaccines push Walgreens past expectations in 2Q. COVID-19 infection increases your risk for diabetes, a new study says. Bongino: COVID lab leak, Hunter Biden the exact same story of media malpractice.

Man allegedly got up to 90 COVID vaccine shots to sell the cards. 26 million people in Shanghai are locked down due to a surge in COVID cases. China stops separating families under COVID lockdown amid outcry. Attorney General Garland and Commerce Secretary Raimondo test positive for Covid. Rep. Val Demings backs Biden admin move to end Title 42, says COVID numbers are 'way down' What to do if you test positive for COVID at this point in the pandemic. One of the most powerful tools against Covid-19 is finally gaining traction. California, New York handled COVID-19 lockdowns the worst, Florida among the best, a new study shows. Dr. Saphier: NYC Mayor Eric Adams should be removed from office for 'negligent' toddler mask mandate. Philadelphia to reinstate its mask mandate after a rise in COVID cases. U.K. leader Boris Johnson fined for breaking his own COVID rules.

Joe Rogan, Bill Maher bash politicization of Wuhan lab-leak theory: Why was that 'the conservative view'. London Calling: Boris Johnson fined for COVID lockdown breaches. Title 42 decision reveals Biden admin's 'total hypocrisy' on COVID, says

Heritage Foundation president. Pfizer to request COVID booster approval for kids ages 5-11. House subcommittee attacking Trump admin's COVID response 'acting like' 'political vigilantes': Dr. Giroir. How to tell the difference between seasonal allergies and COVID-19. Hip hop pioneer DJ Kay Slay dies of COVID-19 at age 55. California high school on lockdown after trespasser allegedly stabs a student. **Masks no longer required on planes, trains after judge rules CDC mandate 'unlawful' [4/19/2022].** Reporter details challenge leaving largest Covid-19 lockdown.

What to know about Judge Kathryn Mizelle, who struck down the travel mask mandate. Candace Owens: The CDC, OSHA should face consequences for unconstitutional mask mandates. NYC parents slam Mayor Adams as toddler mask mandate remains: 'Cruel and unusual punishment'. **DOJ to charge nearly two dozen for allegedly defrauding $150 million in COVID-19 aid [4/20/2022].** The DOJ will appeal the recent mask ruling by a federal judge. Maine resident dies from rare tick virus. Battle over CDC's powers goes far beyond travel mask mandate. Los Angeles County once again requiring masks on all public transit. Americans criticize Biden admin's push to reinstate mask mandate.

Gottlieb expects FDA to start considering child vaccines in early June. China starts mass-testing, local lockdowns in Beijing as COVID spreads. Authorities to test 20 million people for COVID-19 amid outbreak in Beijing. Life expectancy in Chicago declined during 1st year of COVID pandemic. Pfizer seeks emergency authorization for COVID-19 booster in children ages 5 to 11. Doctors warn against universal lifting of mask mandates.

Moderna asks FDA to approve COVID vaccine for children under 6. Moderna seeks COVID vaccine authorization for young kids. China manufacturing weakens further as lockdowns continue. Alabama police seeking masked woman caught on camera stealing lawnmower with Crimson Tide yard sign. Research suggests some people who now live with long Covid may have showed little or no Covid-19 symptoms at all when they were first infected. NYC COVID-19 cases, alert level rise. Blinken tests positive for COVID, latest Biden Cabinet official to contract virus. Beijing relaxes COVID quarantine restrictions, Hong Kong reopens beaches. What we can learn from the WHO Covid mortality numbers.

Dr. Agus weighs in on Johnson & Johnson COVID vaccine, risks of Omicron variant. Twins born during pandemic thriving after 2 years. Travel nurses raced to Covid hot spots. Now they're facing canceled contracts. The number of Americans who say they won't get a COVID shot hasn't budged in a year. Bill Gates tests positive for COVID-19, says he's experiencing mild symptoms. **Biden economic adviser claims inflation is part of the 'effective strategy against the pandemic' [5/11/2022].** North Korea identifies its first case of Covid-19, state media reports. China rejects World Health Organization's criticism of "zero-COVID" strategy. South Korea plans to send vaccines to coronavirus-stricken North Korea. North Korea's Kim remains fixed on military might amid COVID outbreak.

Former Biden Covid advisor dismisses White House warning on case numbers: 'Based on pixie dust'. North Korea reports another jump in suspected COVID-19 cases. Growing concerns about how North Korea is handling its COVID-19 outbreak. Man gambles away $358,000 in mistakenly deposited COVID relief in 11 days. Judge blocks Biden from ending Trump-era Covid restrictions for migrants at border. Opinion: Why North Korea's Covid surge could shock the world.

Monkeypox sounds a lot like Covid. Here's one big reason it's different. Health and Human Services chief on baby formula shortage, monkeypox, COVID aid. COVID fight in Chinese capital leads to curbs, punishments for violations. Jeff Bridges says he was 'close to dying' battling COVID while in chemo for cancer: 'I was ready to go'. Physician explains why heterodox views on COVID led to his Republican conversion. COVID-19 cases rising in the U.S. heading into summer.

DOJ asks federal appeals court to reverse order lifting travel mask mandate. Dogs can detect Covid with high accuracy, even asymptomatic cases. Melatonin poisoning in kids sharply increased during coronavirus pandemic, study says. The U.S. has discarded over 82 million Covid vaccine doses, led by CVS and Walmart. Study: Ineffective blood oxygen readers have endangered Black and Latino Covid-19 patients. US has 'very serious' problem with Covid-19 vaccine uptake. White House lays out its plan for Covid vaccinations for children under 5.

Pfizer Covid-19 vaccine appears effective for kids under 5, health officials say. Young children may soon be eligible for COVID-19 vaccines. Canada to no longer require vaccines for domestic travelers and government employees. FDA vaccine panel supports COVID shots for young children. DeSantis spokesperson Christina Pushaw blasts CNN anchor for his hit on Florida COVID-19 policy. COVID cases are upending cycling, and the Tour de France starts in 2 weeks. CDC advisers vote to recommend Covid-19 vaccines for children as young as 6 months. Jessica Barrios lost her young father to Covid-19. Here's what she and others like her want kids -- and adults -- to know. Doctor encourages parents to get their young children vaccinated against COVID-19. Educators respond to NPR report on COVID-19 impact on student development: 'Told ya so'. SC nurse admits to COVID vaccine card fraud. **New Hampshire governor blocks pharmacists from dispensing ivermectin to treat COVID-19 without prescription [6/25/2022]**. FDA advisers recommend updating COVID booster shots for the fall.

Actress Shay Mitchell catches funny moment from "pandemic baby". Delays expected as July 4 travel nears pre-pandemic levels. Omicron subvariants fuel a new wave of COVID-19 infections across the U.S. Long COVID symptoms cost woman her job. Medicines agency says EU is seeing 'new wave' of COVID-19. Chuck Schumer tests positive for Covid-19, spokesman says. Faced with COVID and monkeypox, new USAID leader draws strength from African proverb. Agencies weigh 2nd COVID booster for more people; admin urges shots for those over 50.

Americans over 50 urged to get COVID-19 vaccine amid surge of Omicron variants. Many try to return to normal from COVID, but disabled people face a different reality. The omicron subvariant dominating U.S. COVID-19 cases is more vaccine-resistant. Toys 'R' Us coming back amid a surge in toy sales during the pandemic. Bennie Thompson tests positive for COVID-19; Jan. 6 hearing to proceed. **The CDC endorses Novavax, a more traditional COVID vaccine, for adults [7/13/2022]**.

Biden tests positive for COVID-19, White House announces [7/21/2022]. Biden tests positive for Covid, experiencing mild symptoms. Biden's age puts him at risk for severe Covid, but experts predict a quick recovery. Omicron subvariant BA.5 driving U.S. COVID cases. Coronavirus FAQ: I got it on a family vacay! Can my relatives stay (relatively) safe? Biden's Covid symptoms 'continue to improve,' doctor says. Sen. Joe Manchin tests positive for COVID-19.

Kentucky parents stand up to school mask mandates: 'We just need normal'. Biden tests negative for COVID-19 twice, ending isolation at the White House. Biden admin plans to roll out updated Covid booster shots in September. Biden shares video after testing positive for COVID-19 again: 'I'm feeling fine'. Dems, union leaders responsible for school lockdowns face few repercussions, despite evidence that kids harmed. Judge dismisses Trump's 'immunity' claim in Jan. 6 lawsuits.

Mall of America lockdown lifted after shots fired: Police. Precautions to take against COVID-19 and monkeypox, and the possible spread of polio. Elizabeth Warren blasts GOP's 'political gamesmanship' after Dems reportedly ditch COVID tests for key vote. CDC draft report points to possible easing of COVID restrictions in schools. Coronavirus lockdowns had 'significant' effect on childhood obesity, especially in poor communities: Study. COVID vaccine production from South Africa's Aspen Pharmacare to end this week due to low demand. CDC updates its COVID-19 guidelines in sweeping overhaul.

Georgia to use $240 million in COVID-19 relief funds to construct broadband internet for rural locations. COVID-19 gain-of-function research too dangerous for Fauci to work with China. Jill Biden tests positive for COVID-19. California appeals court rejects COVID-19 fines for church. Updated Covid boosters are coming in weeks. Should you wait to get yours? Cardona says states should use COVID-19 funds to stem teacher shortages. Pfizer and BioNTech seek FDA authorization for updated Covid-19 booster. CDC Director Walensky admits agency 'didn't reliably deliver' during pandemic, outlines change: 'Learned a lot.

First Lady Jill Biden tests positive for COVID-19 once again in rebound case. Novak Djokovic, unvaccinated against COVID-19, out of U.S. Open. First lady Jill Biden recovers from rebound COVID-19 case, will return to Washington. Florida man pleads guilty to stealing more than $2.6 million in COVID-19 relief funds. Ron Johnson torches COVID response as 'miserable failure': 'They've done great harm to our children'. Should you get one of the new COVID boosters that targets Omicron?

Restoring what the pandemic took: Social and emotional learning for kids. **COVID vaccine likely to become annual like the flu shot, Fauci says [9/7/2022]**. New York's subway now has a 'you do you' mask policy. It's getting a Bronx cheer. Pandemic, labor shortage keep hurricane victims in limbo. WHO director says COVID "end is in sight". **Joe Biden says the COVID-19 pandemic is over [9/19/2022]**. This is what the data tells us.

White House ridiculed after walking back Biden's statement that pandemic is over: 'He is not in charge'. LAURA INGRAHAM: Dems don't ever want COVID to end because more emergencies equal more government dependency. CDC now tracking rise of BF.7 and BA.2.75 COVID variants nationwide. States spend federal COVID aid on roads, buildings, seawalls.

Pandemic stress may have had a lasting impact on our personalities. New Covid wave may be brewing in Europe. Japan welcomes solo travelers after 2 years of COVID-19 restrictions. In drawn-out recovery, NYC inches out from COVID's shadow. Surge in cases of RSV, a virus that can severely sicken infants, is filling hospital beds. College dropout becomes sleeper candidate, COVID policies devastate public safety, and more top headlines.

COVID-19 linked to increase in US pregnancy-related deaths. China deletes reports of teen girl's death in COVID quarantine center. District: Nearly half the students at a Virginia high school are absent with flu-like symptoms. Biden to receive updated Covid booster shot Tuesday. **State AGs say Fauci, Zuckerberg 'colluded' to kill COVID lab leak theory [10/25/2022]**. Biden gets updated COVID booster.

'Scrabble variants' now cause the majority of new Covid-19 infections in the US. China's strict COVID-19 policies 'indirectly killed' son, father says. Reports say China aiming for less disruptive COVID policies. People and businesses suffer, but China won't budge from "zero-COVID". Hochul ripped for being maskless while joyfully dancing around masked children in viral clip. Doctors fear a triple threat of viruses this winter: COVID-19, RSV and flu. Biden admin backs Saudi crown prince immunity claims in Khashoggi killing lawsuit. Dear Life Kit: How do I get out of my pandemic rut Michelle Obama weighs in.

Vaccinated Americans a majority of COVID deaths for first time in August: analysis [11/24/2022]. Things have been relatively quiet on the Covid front. That may come to an end soon. CDC says it's now tracking a new COVID variant known as XBB. Protests of China's strict "zero-COVID" policies hit Shanghai, other cities. At the heart of China's protests against zero-Covid, young people cry for freedom.

Connecticut struggling to fund program that offered 'hero pay' to essential workers during the pandemic. Covid protests escalate in Guangzhou as China lockdown anger boils. China signals possible shift from "zero-COVID" policy after protests. Daily border crossings have stayed near record highs, and the end of a Covid ban this month could mean a new surge. Their preemie was already a fighter. Then at 3 weeks old, she caught the virus that's packing hospitals across the US. Ashton Kutcher describes vasculitis symptoms in emotional sit-down interview. Study: Teens' brains aged faster during the pandemic.

Investigation finds Connecticut prison employees misused COVID-19 hotel program. Biden admin fumes as end of military vaccine mandate appears imminent. The Biden administration wants more than $3 billion to prep for a possible migrant surge at the border after Covid ban ends. COVID-related hospitalizations increasing among US seniors. Less than 20% of Minnesota residents current on COVID-19 shots. A lagging economy prompted China's leaders to ease pandemic restrictions, paving the way for a reopening economists say will be painful. COVID-19 cases are continuing to rise in the nation's largest county.

Florida pastor accused of Covid fraud a no-show in court due to 'grave medical concerns'. Rep. Mike Turner says intel community will be subpoenaed over COVID origins. 'Utter betrayal': Florida pastor accused of Covid scam slammed by ex-associate's son. New study estimates COVID deaths could reach 322,000 in China by April. Gym owner arrested for defying lockdowns blasts WaPo's delayed admission on exercise and COVID: 'Infuriating'. Omnibus bill defunds risky research involving 'pathogens of pandemic potential' in any 'country of concern'. China's COVID-19 surge raises odds of new coronavirus mutant. China says it will resume issuing passports and visas as virus curbs ease. Major health findings of 2022: Latest COVID-19 vaccines, treatment to fight obesity and more. New COVID rules for travelers from China helps with variant response, doctor says. Canada and Australia impose COVID testing requirements on travelers from China.

Hamlin's collapse spurs new wave of vaccine misinformation. China suspends social media accounts of its COVID policy critics. Canadian reporter speaks out after scary on-air health incident: 'No way related to the COVID-19 vaccine'. Challenges faced by striking nurses predate the pandemic, union official says. Appeals court affirmed ban against vaccine mandate in 3 states.

NY department of health 'exploring options' after judge strikes down COVID vaccine mandate for health workers. **CDC identifies possible safety issue with Pfizer's updated vaccine [1/16/2023]**. Republicans introduce 'Pandemic Is Over' act after Biden's 'unacceptable' extension of COVID emergency. Fed's Powell tests positive for COVID, has 'mild' symptoms. $163 billion of COVID relief was stolen. Republicans must get to the bottom of it. Biden to tap former COVID czar Jeff Zients as new chief of staff. Aaron Rodgers blasts 'woke culture,' says stance on COVID made him a 'villain'. Arkansas Supreme Court overrules judge on mask mandate ban. WHO: COVID still an emergency but nearing 'inflection' point. Rand Paul leads investigation into 'disturbing' $5.4B in pandemic fraud as Biden moves to end COVID emergency.

House ignores White House objections, votes to end COVID health emergency [2/1/2023]. SNAP recipients will lose their pandemic boost and may face other reductions by March. Offices are more than 50% filled for the first time since the pandemic started. Biden set to discuss COVID-19 and mental health at the State of the Union. **As the pandemic ebbs,**

an influential COVID tracker [Johns Hopkins Coronavirus Resource Center] shuts down [2/12/2023].

Dick Van Dyke and Sara Evans unmasked on 'The Masked Singer' leaving one judge in tears. The art of Venetian masks. Illinois is expected to mandate paid leave for nearly all employees. Lori Lightfoot accused of ignoring 'social contract' with police by lowballing COVID disability benefits. CDC advisory group finds insufficient evidence to recommend more than one COVID-19 booster a year. Republicans erupt after Energy Dept reportedly says COVID-19 likely came from Chinese lab: 'We need answers'. DeSantis slams China's COVID-19 'cover-up' in new book, says US response to CCP a 'major failure'.

What we've learned about the Covid 'lab leak theory'. GOP fires warning shot at Biden over 'deeply flawed' WHO treaty on pandemic response.

Chapter 17

Biden Signs Bill Ending COVID-19 Pandemic National Emergency

February 25ᵗʰ, 2023 – April 26ᵗʰ, 2023

CDC advisory group finds insufficient evidence to recommend more than one COVID-19 booster a year. FDA approves first at-home test to detect both flu and COVID. Some have argued that the hardship the industry faces now is a painful but necessary correction from pre-pandemic trends. Another US agency assesses COVID-19 origin likely a Chinese 'lab leak': report. **This proposal aims to place daily essentials within a 15-minute walk of your home [2/26/2023]**. Dr. Fauci blasted over new revelations about COVID lab leak: 'We need to crack this egg open'. Department of Energy finds COVID Wuhan lab leak theory "plausible" but with "low confidence". Media scolded, lampooned for dismissing now-likely COVID lab leak theory as misinformation.

Food banks brace for end to pandemic-era SNAP benefits boost. Biden admin has reached no consensus on how COVID-19 started. Los Angeles ringleader of $18M COVID fraud scheme extradited. Analysis: US-China relations deteriorate from new disagreements over Ukraine and Covid-19. CCP government 'intentionally released' COVID-19 'all over the world,' Chinese virologist says. GOP fires warning shot at Biden over 'deeply flawed' WHO treaty on pandemic response.

FBI director accuses China of trying to 'thwart and obfuscate' Covid origin probe. Wray publicly comments on the FBI's position on COVID's origins, adding political fire. House

Republicans warn about loss of public trust after COVID lockdowns at tense roundtable. **Republicans call for 'full transparency' after FBI director says COVID 'most likely' originated in Chinese lab [3/1/2023]**. Ron DeSantis calls on Fauci to be held accountable for COVID response: 'He was wrong'.

Pandemic food assistance that held back hunger comes to an end. 16 million households lose Covid-era boosts to food aid. 3 charts show who will hurt the most. Man gets 6 years for $4.2M COVID relief fraud scheme. **NYC police want shoppers to remove masks before entering stores [3/1/2023]**. FDA authorizes first at-home test for both COVID and the flu. White House pushing Congress to pass funding to combat pandemic-related fraud. 3 years since the pandemic wrecked attendance, kids still aren't showing up to school. COVID call centers and testing sites close as US moves past the pandemic.

Flu and COVID combo shots won't be ready this year, FDA official says. What the end of COVID call centers and testing sites means for the US. First responders win major COVID-linked free speech lawsuit against New York City. Media lied about COVID lab leak, and 4 other things the press got wrong. Credibility crisis: NPR insisted COVID originated naturally by dismissing lab leak theory as nonsense. New Mexico to end COVID emergency March 31. Oregon, Washington to end healthcare settings mask mandate. Bill Maher says COVID 'dissenters' are 'looking pretty good' following lab leak theory developments.

Credibility crisis: MSNBC's Nicolle Wallace insisted COVID originating in Wuhan lab was 'conspiracy theory'. You'll probably need a passport to visit the least-visited US national park. Dr. Scott Gottlieb says COVID origins may never be known "with certainty," but focus should be on "taking the steps" to ensure a lab leak never happens. Rep. Brad Wenstrup says House COVID subcommittee hasn't "seen all that we want to see" about intelligence on virus origins. Jim Jordan demands answers on COVID origins: Why was Dr. Fauci 'so consumed' with countering lab leak theory? Census data reveals over half a million left California during the pandemic. The COVID mask controversy could have been answered two and a half years ago: Dr. Marty Makary.

Novak Djokovic withdraws from BNP Paribas Open after being denied entry to US over COVID-vaccine status. COVID deaths deserved better from CDC. Here's how we fix it. Djokovic withdraws from U.S. tournament after his bid for a COVID vaccine waiver fails. **New York City Mayor Eric Adams urges shoppers to remove face masks to deter rising robberies [3/6/2023].** Dr. Fauci got a lot of things wrong, remained silent on COVID censorship: Jonathan Turley. Conservative group wins legal victory in case over teachers union's $12.5M COVID loan. Influencer pleads guilty to $1.5 million COVID relief fraud scheme. Study finds some parents lied about their children's COVID status.

How San Diego is bouncing back from COVID. Post-COVID, chest pains may linger for up to a year, new study finds. U.S. to end COVID testing requirement on travelers from China. Moderna's COVID vaccine gambit: Hike the price, offer free doses for uninsured. Understanding how COVID began will help us prevent future health crises, maligning experts won't. House GOP calls on Marine Corps to fill critical roles with Marines cut due to vax mandate: 'an utter shame'. Former CDC director slams gain-of-function research: 'Probably caused the greatest pandemic' in history. NYC Mayor Adams under fire for asking store owners to confront potential criminals on removing masks.

House panel holds first hearing on COVID-19 origins. 'Band-Aid over a bullet wound': Should schools use Covid aid to fix crumbling facilities? San Francisco police officer 'separated' for refusing COVID vaccine champions free choice: 'I know who I am'. California Governor Gavin Newsom tests positive for

COVID-19 days after return from 'personal trip'. Thousands of unvaccinated service members could still be booted over rescinded COVID-19 policy. Trump made me do it: Liberal media blames its dismissal of lab leak theory on ex-president's 'xenophobia'.

Some long Covid patients face big medical bills and denied insurance claims. China writes furious letter to Hawley on COVID origins bill: 'Political manipulation'. 'Crisis' of 'COVID-era' high school grads 'jaded,' skipping college after remote learning: report. House Dems, GOP vote unanimously to declassify COVID origins intel, send bill to Biden. California landlords furious as COVID eviction bans drag on: 'I'm owed $120K' in rent payments. Michigan mayor charged with fraud related to COVID-19 relief grant. House votes 419-0 to declassify intelligence on COVID-19 origins. Labor force participation is back to pre-pandemic levels.

What's your current risk of getting long Covid? LA County eases COVID vaccine, testing restrictions as emergency declarations end. What people with 'super immunity' can teach us about Covid and other viruses. Biden 'dragging his feet' on COVID origins intel because it will 'open Pandora's box,' Kat Cammack says. Federal telework isn't going away when COVID ends: 'Face time is not a proxy for performance'. CDC, FDA warn Florida surgeon general over his COVID-19 vaccine guidance. US agencies debunk Florida surgeon general's vaccine claims. Critics wonder what will be done with 40,000 empty quarantine units as Covid measures wane.

Saturday marks 3 years since COVID-19 was declared a pandemic [3/11/2023]. Dr. Fauci claims a coronavirus lab leak could still be considered a 'natural occurrence'. Ronny Jackson says Biden may have tried to cut corners on COVID vax approval: 'Real problem'. US Merchant Marine Academy rescinds vaccine mandate days after accusations of 'illegal attack'. Whitmer blasted for 'gaslighting' residents on COVID-19 restrictions, admitting some didn't make sense. Three years into the global COVID-19 pandemic, here's how the battle continues.

What research shows about heart health risks from COVID-19 versus vaccines. How the COVID-19 pandemic has affected businesses nationwide. Law group alleges Stanford fired doctor for criticizing COVID policies: 'Engaged in employment discrimination'. It's been 3 years since COVID lockdowns. But we still haven't learned from these 3 mistakes. Assisted living facility faces felony charges over deadly COVID-19 outbreak. California care home charged in connection with Covid deaths. Massachusetts Gov. Maura Healey announces state's COVID-19 public health emergency ends May 11.

Parents fed up as hundreds of colleges still mandate COVID vaccines: 'Laboratory of guinea pigs'. No clear association between Paxlovid and COVID-19 rebound, FDA says. The Shifting Workplace: What workers want now, after pandemic sparks surge in remote work. California church fights back after $2.8 million fine for defying COVID lockdown order. Canada to remove mandatory COVID testing requirements for travelers from China. COVID and kids' mental health: Financial hardship took a big toll. Over $700 million in COVID aid for US schools never made it to the classroom: study.

WHO calls on China to share data on raccoon dog link to pandemic. Here's what we know. New genetic analysis finds clues to animal origin of COVID outbreak. A crippling impact of long COVID Insomnia.. Long COVID symptoms often include sleep disorders, study shows. Trump calls for 'retribution' against China for role in COVID-19 pandemic. **Latest Twitter Files tackle 'Great Covid-19 Lie Machine' flagging true content as 'disinformation' [3/17/2023]**. Rick Scott demands answers on NIH funding that went to Wuhan Institute of Virology. Older Americans reject more vaccines, opt instead for 'natural healing,' says report.

Scientists parse another clue to possible origins of Covid-19. Raccoon dogs may have been linked to the pandemic. What are they? Novak Djokovic denied COVID-19 vaccine exemption, will not compete at Miami Open. COVID-19 pandemic expected to end this year 'as a public health emergency,' says World Health Organization. WHO blasts China for withholding info on COVID origin after data pulled offline. **Biden signs bills reversing D.C. crime changes, declassifying COVID-19 info [3/21/2023].** Josh Hawley says 'accountability' is next after Biden signs COVID declassification bill.

From addiction treatment to nursing homes, end of COVID rules will bring change. North Carolina House advances ban on COVID-19 vaccine mandates. Former Florida GOP legislator pleads guilty to Covid-relief fraud charges. COVID-19 death rates varied dramatically across US, major analysis finds. White House to disband Covid response team in May: report. Wages surged for lowest-paid Americans after the pandemic. Former Connecticut city employee sentenced to over a year in prison for role in COVID-19 fund theft. COVID left some with damaged immune response, study finds. Wife of Connecticut Democrat involved in COVID fraud scheme gets 6 months.

Federal court rejects Biden vaccine mandate for federal workers. **Biden White House urged Meta to crack down on 'vaccine-skeptical' content on WhatsApp private chat platform [3/25/2023].** WaPo columnist parties with celebrities maskless after months decrying 'horrifying' unmasked crowds. COVID's education crisis: A lost generation? COVID-19 pandemic experiences vary from state to state in U.S. COVID cases and hospitalizations are on the decline but long COVID cases prevail. Here's why. Long COVID remains an uphill battle for many Americans. COVID vaccines are not needed for healthy kids and teens, says World Health Organization. The FDA may soon authorize a spring round of COVID-19 boosters for some people.

Biden 'strongly opposes' resolution ending COVID-19 national emergency, but won't veto it after Senate vote. Biden won't veto Republican-led bill ending COVID emergency. Heart disease, the silent killer: Study shows it can strike without symptoms. Seattle Fire Dept. facing mass staff shortage after vaccine mandate: 'Gambling' with lives. Nebraska Economic Development director resigns over COVID grant concerns. Millions could lose Medicaid as pandemic protections expire. COVID vaccine nasal spray shows strong immune response in study: 'Could be a game changer'. Biden HHS sends warning shot to states on civil rights as COVID emergency expires, I don't recommend FDA's infinity vaccine booster strategy.

China health officials lash out at WHO, defend COVID virus search. China called out by World Health Organization over COVID origin data. Home-based workers became younger, more diverse in pandemic. While remote work is still well above the 7% of people who did it full-time before the pandemic, telework is declining. Americans hold mixed views on getting back to 'normal' after Covid-19, new polling shows. One California city's remedy for poverty and COVID? Free cash. Conspiracy theorists made Tiffany Dover into an anti-vaccine icon. She's finally ready to talk about it.

Biden signs bill ending COVID-19 pandemic national emergency [4/10/2023]. New Hampshire man sentenced to over 2 years in prison for fraud involving 6 million in COVID-19 loans. What the end of the COVID-19 national emergency means for Americans. Alabama bill would let K-12 parents 'opt out' of school mask mandates. China opts out of UN wildlife survey aimed at preventing future pandemics caused by animals. California judge orders church that defied COVID rules to pay $1.2M.

Former head of China's CDC says there is 'no evidence' coronavirus came from animals. Chinese Embassy emails House Republican staff expressing 'grave concern' with COVID-

19 origins hearing. Orthopedic surgeon sounds off on COVID vaccine after developing career-ending condition: I've been 'abandoned'. Chinese Embassy urges House Republican stop 'targeting China,' focus on 'own failure' in COVID origins search. Former Intelligence chief to say a lab leak is the 'only explanation' for COVID. COVID during pregnancy may alter brain development in boys. A bill in this state could have lawmakers making decisions about vaccines in schools. FDA authorizes 2nd dose of updated Covid booster for older adults. Alex Berenson sues Biden, Pfizer honchos over Twitter ban that came as he raised concerns about COVID vaccine.

One-third of US households used free at-home COVID test website, report finds. The world lost faith in childhood vaccines during COVID, UNICEF reports. House Republicans to hold hearing on consequences of Biden admin's forced pandemic school closures. Lockdowns, mandates and scandals: How Gavin Newsom's COVID-19 response brought California to its knees. Weekly COVID deaths hit the lowest point since the start of the pandemic. Young and 'healthy' British doctor died from severe reaction to AstraZeneca COVID vaccine: coroner. Robert F. Kennedy Jr. argues American middle class 'systematically' wiped out under COVID-19 lockdowns. New theories of possible link between Covid vaccines and tinnitus are emerging. Chicago must rehire, pay back wages to workers punished over COVID-19 vaccination mandate: Judge. Rand Paul celebrates Chicago Mayor Lori Lightfoot's COVID vaccine 'comeuppance': 'Petty tyrants'. CDC to stop tracking Covid levels in communities. **What lessons have we learned from the COVID pandemic? [4/26/2023]**

Afterword

As a history, headlines can only provide so much value. They were never designed to accurately reflect detailed information, but rather to entice readers and encapsulate basic facts conveyed in seconds. They weren't meant to work together as I have forced them to do, but even so, I hope you'll agree that they've done a great job given their many constraints.

For my part, it has been fascinating to go back and look at the media messaging from the pandemic time period. When I first experienced this messaging during the course of the pandemic, it was rolling out daily, hourly, or even faster. The stress this caused made it impossible to view things objectively. To revisit all three years again in the process of creating one continuous "story" has been a new and enlightening experience, quite different from the first.

My emotional response to revisiting the headlines from this time period was mixed: on the one hand, I felt a greater measure of patience at the mistakes that were made by those in authority, and the way things unfolded; on the other hand, I felt continued anger and frustration concerning many of the developments these headlines represent.

The story of the pandemic extends well beyond the dates that I selected for my database queries, in both directions. There are and will be volumes written on it. Though incomplete, I hope this small work will stand as a unique monument to the raw experience of the pandemic, from the perspective of the individual looking to the media for information each day. It was a pleasure to compile for me, I hope the experience has been a positive one for you.

About the Author

When it comes to news media, Joseph is very much a product of the events that occurred on 9/11. As he arrived to work that fateful morning, he was met with a barrage of information—and not being too interested in world affairs at the time, he understood almost none of it. He determined on that day that he would never again be in the dark about what was going on in the world.

These many years later, Joseph is much more interested in understanding his fellow human beings and in writing fiction, than he is in the news. And yet, the determination that was born on 9/11 stubbornly persists, primarily in the form of the NotFox.com project.

Joseph founded NotFox.com in 2015 after more than a decade as an average news consumer. The effort was in response to the bias that was so ubiquitous—and so very annoying—in every outlet available. While not perfect, NotFox.com continues to serve its purpose today: to openly demonstrate to users the messages the media outlets are working hard to promote, and to give a small peek behind the curtain in the process.

Apart from writing, Joseph enjoys the gopher protocol, retro computing, making music, friends, the Gospel of Jesus Christ, and time with his family.